Anti-Racist Social Work

A Challenge for White Practitioners and Educators

Lena Dominelli

Foreword by John Small

MACMILLAN

First published 1997 by
MACMILLAN PRESS LTD
Houndmills, Basingstoke, Hampshire RG21 6XS
and London
Companies and representatives
throughout the world

ISBN 0–333–68719–1 paperback

A catalogue record for this book is available
from the British Library.

This book is printed on paper suitable for recycling and made
from fully managed and sustained forest sources.

10 9   8   7   6   5   4   3   2   1
06 05 04 03 02 01 00 99 98 97

Editing and origination by
Aardvark Editorial, Mendham, Suffolk

Printed in Hong Kong

Contents

Foreword to second edition

Within the eight years since this book was published there have been significant changes which have been amplified by the political transformation in Eastern Europe. These changes have resulted in hope and optimism in some quarters. However, behind this hope and optimism lurks fear and anxiety about the reactivation of the far right ideology which is manifesting itself through attacks on 'migrants' or black people. This has brought into focus the forces in society that are supporting attitudes that are adverse to the welfare of the black population. Social work and social services are key players in the process. The free market philosophy and privatisation have resulted in the trimming of the welfare state and a rolling back of the gains of black people which were achieved through hard struggles.

Against this background, *Anti-Racist Social Work* is revised in order to take account of these developments. These developments have caused consequential shifts in the social, political and economic landscape. Social work and social services must therefore be seen and analysed as political phenomena; not in the narrow party sense but within the context of the distribution and the use of power to reward or punish on the basis of race and colour. It is within this context that Lena Dominelli analyses social work and social services, by putting the discipline under the microscope and demonstrating how the 'purchaser', 'provider', 'community care', 'care management' and 'value for money', as the guiding principles of the new social work, have worked against the welfare of the majority of black people in Britain. Out of this process is emerging a new form of specialism in social work. This is being anchored in traditional social work, without any regard to the vital roles of racism within the structure of ideas that underpins the method. This revised edition of *Anti-Racist Social Work* forces us to recognise the political nature of social work and social services.

It shows how social work can influence ideas, structures, values, institutions, behaviour and also determine the types of relationship that exist between individuals within the client–worker relationship. In this regard, the challenges facing black people are not only those to do with separation from the familiar and attachment to the unfamiliar but confronting the multi-dimensional characteristics of racism as they go about their daily lives. It is sad that even after such a long history of black people residing in Britain and the contribution that they have made to the development of the economy and society, nevertheless they are still regarded as aliens and are cut off from the main stream of British society and its institutions.

Anti-Racist Social Work shows that the major obstacle confronting black people in Britain today continues to be institutionalised oppression. As a part of this process, racism is still the fundamental barrier preventing access to opportunity, privilege, power and social justice for the majority of the black population. It is against this background that the book is written. It is designed to bring to the foreground the effect of racism in social work education and training and to demonstrate how the various elements of racist practice are stitched into the fabric of social work.

It has been said that the teacher today is teaching what has been learned at least two generations ago from textbooks that were written several decades before. In the field of social work this is certainly the case and in relation to social work with black people the problem is multiplied in that social work theoreticians have largely ignored the presence of the black population, and so in their theory-building little attention has been paid to the effects of racism on the black population. The immediate and central task of the discipline must therefore be to reorientate the value base of social work in a real way to confront racism in its various forms.

This book recognises the urgent need for transformation in the field of social work. Without work of this nature, stereotyping and the reinforcing of racist practices is likely to continue into the distant future without being challenged. The first task is to acknowledge differences and identify similarities but the danger, of course, is that often differences become generalised into stereotypes, and this we must constantly guard against. Lena Dominelli's work demonstrates that generalisation performs an important function in terms of making sense of new situations. However, as she shows, generalisation should not be a substitute for accurate description of new situations, of observation, analysis and logical deduction based on the level of current knowledge. This book illustrates how the process of generalisation can be transformed into stereotyping and then fed back into the structure of ideas, thereby reinforcing racism.

Dominelli shows that racist ideas have survived the past, exist in the present and will continue into the future, not as a reuslt of the conservative nature of the society but because of the essential function that is served by the phenomenon. In fact, racist ideas are often reactivated from the past to serve the same function in the present.Through a thorough analysis of racism she shows that although certain symbols of racism have changed as a response to the anti-racist onslaught others have taken their place, thereby articulating the old and bringing to the surface the adaptive nature of the phenomenon. With this analysis she shows that a change in symbolic form does not necessarily result in a concomitant change in symbolic function, in that the same function is served by new symbolic forms. It is therefore of critical importance that anti-racist strategies are brought into the social work profession to safeguard its value base.

This work shows that racism is a dynamic force, with the inherent nature to change over time and that it is profoundly influenced by the political, economic and social forces that are in operation at a particular period of time. It can be articulated through the medium of culture – 'cultural racism'. For example, where certain cultural features are seen as British and desirable, or 'black' and undesirable and therefore 'superior' or 'inferior'. It is also used to explain the poverty of black people in Britain or the existence of poverty in former colonial countries. In this way the underdevelopment and poverty in the countries from which the black population descend are not seen as due to imperialism and colonialism but as a result of cultural and genetic inferiority.

Dominelli shows that racism is inherently exclusionary and is embedded within the structure of the society. Consequently, it is vital that the variables be isolated and analysed in order to bring into focus its exclusionary characteristics, the elements within, its articulation, its persistence and the process of its operation through a dialectic of inclusionary and exclusionary representations. In this regard Dominelli conceives it as being of primary importance that individual and institutional racism are to be studied simultaneously in order to discover the interrelationship between them and the impact on individuals and society. To do otherwise would be to operate at a level of description and to leave her work unfinished.

In arriving at this position, Dominelli avoids the usual analytical problem of applying different meanings and different terms to the same phenomenon. In this work, racism is seen not only as discriminatory treatment on the basis of race and colour but also an ideology which fuels institutions by the use of power within a class society with conflicts permeating every level of the social structure. The exclusionary and inclusionary nature of the phenomenon together with its collective representational forms provide her with a convenient tool of anlysis, 'white' and 'black', which are the constituent elements of the phenomenon under study.

Lena Dominelli calls for positive action in the area of anti-racist practice and contextualisation of the black experience and white reaction in order to contribute to current dialogue with those who are becoming increasingly aware and concerned about the extent and effect of racism. She shows that racism does not only exist in the network of our institutions but also in our white students as they pass through the teaching institutions, as actors in society, and in their interaction with their black clients. The book appropriately begins with identifying the nature of racism and need for anti-racist training in which the context of the subject is clarified, and anchored within the real world, thereby suggesting that the white population must take positive action to eradicate racism and then goes on to show the ways in which racism permeates all aspects of society, thereby becoming a common concern for the theoreticians and the professionals alike.

The book shows how important the issue of racism is for the practice of social work with black people. It suggests that if social workers do not understand the dynamics of racism they cannot deliver effective services to black communities, since the experience of black people in Britain is being constantly shaped by racism. Lena Dominelli cautions us against conceiving the experience of black people as one lodged exclusively within the context of class, thereby conveniently avoiding the necessity to define, to analyse and to take action that enables social workers to become much more aware of the nature and effect of racism within the social work profession. Her analysis suggests that contemporary social work has given the impression that it has taken on board issues to do with class, gender, racism and ethnicity. However, this is not the case. In the process of conceptualising, imparting knowledge and in the application of social work principles, racism and the subjective experience of the black population in Britain are largely ignored. Consequently, the profession has maintained a pathological view of black families based on conceptualisations anchored in racism and transmitted through concepts of deprivation and maladaption to the existing social order. This is no doubt true to and consistent with the tradition, framework and elements that govern the relationship between the colonialised and the colonialiser.

In this book, the power relationship between the black client and the white worker is brought out in a way that gives a glimpse into the dynamics of social relationships between the races in an oppressive and racist society and also the intricacies and the part played by bureaucratic structures as they operate within teaching institutions and social work agencies. In this regard, the expertise of the black worker is seen as rooted in the knowledge and experience of the black community and so gives the black worker a special authority which threatens the white bureaucracy, who authority is based not on the knowledge and experience of black people but on the authority of office rather than the authority of expertise.

Lena Dominelli does not fall into the trap of suggesting that social work can transform society or that the sole responsibility for anti-racist practices lies with social workers. Far from it; she recognises that 'there is much that the state can do which is not only consistent with liberty but is essential to it'.

In this book power is conceived within the context of social relationships. Therefore, the central concern must be with the process and phenomenon of institutionalisation which perpetuates certain social patterns causing them to endure over time, outlast the individual, transmitting behaviour and attitudes from one generation to the next. This work indicates very clearly that our lives are affected by our face-to-face interpersonal relationships. Consequently, the eradication of racism should necessarily increase the quality of life for both the black and white population.

Social work practice involves the use of the knowledge from a variety of traditions and disciplines, and so there are conflicting approaches and conflicting evidence. However, it is becoming increasingly clear that because of the nature of racism and ways in which it is embedded in the various traditions there must necessarily be a radical anti-racist approach to social work. Society has accepted the responsibility to educate and train social workers. Therefore society must also acknowledge the existence of racism and accept the responsibility for taking affirmative action to eradicate racism.

The book also describes the experience of the black population in Britain in terms of the entrenchment of racism not only in the national but in the local states. It emphasises the relationship between the development of racism both in its historical and contemporary context, and explains the processes whereby the black population is relegated to the lower strata of society and, at one and the same time, it shows how the colour-blind and pathological view is brought to the understanding of the needs of the black population. For example, Lena Dominelli gives us a view as to how the pathology of the black family has developed among white practitioners and converged with white sexism, which is then played out among professionals and between the white professional and the black client alike. In order to create a profound shift, Lena Dominelli addresses the issue of positive action by tackling racism within the context of the organisation; and so calls for an anti-racist strategy in this area. But by what means can this be brought about? Lena Dominelli's proposal is to bring about the transformation of social work through the development of equal opportunities policy anchored in an anti-racist framework, followed by fair recruitment and selection processes, combined with training which attacks the values and norms of the organisation, together with checks and balances to monitor the process of implementation with appropriate feedback mechanisms to reflect a clear anti-racist path. Lena Dominelli sees a central role for managers both at the senior-management and middle-management levels, since any manager who manages others has a significant and supporting role in terms of implementing policy and ensuring that subordinates do not act in a discriminatory or racist manner. To this end, it is made clear that at the outset key managers must necessarily undergo anti-racism awareness training to become sensitive to how their own attitudes can perpetuate racism. Anti-racism awareness training should be related to the impact of discriminatory practice on day-to-day decision-making processes of higher- and lower-level managers alike, resulting in managers, and indeed practitioners, developing the requisite skills and appropriate attitudes in relation to the black population.

Irrespective of the increasing concern about racism in this society and its impact on black people and white people alike, teaching institutions, social services and voluntary agencies have paid little regard to the issue of racism. The welfare state and services have failed miserably in identifying the needs of black people and providing relevant services. As a result of racism a disproportionate number of black children are in the care of the state. These children are less likely to be re-united with their families. Many black children are placed transracially and, although the negative consequences are recognised and although black families are ready, willing and able to provide substitute care, there is little commitment on the part of the state to cease this destructive practice. In fact, there is now a rolling back of the commitment to place black children in black families. There is a disproportionate number of black youth in custody, a disproportionate number of black people in mental hospitals and more black children than white children are suspended from schools.

Black people face discrimination in housing, employment, health and their life chances are limited. Lena Dominelli is therefore pessimistic, but her pessimism has brought into focus the major challenge for social work, which must be the removal of racism – to constitute the starting point for the reconceptualisation of social work in a multi-racial society. It must be recognised that racism permeates all aspects of society and therefore educational institutions and social welfare agencies are affected similarly. Consequently, for Lena Dominelli, the effect of racism on social work practice should be obvious. The greater part of the problem which is currently being experienced by black people, she suggests, is engendered by the underlying structure of racism and therefore any attempt to alleviate this problem from the traditional casework basis is doomed to fail. It should therefore be clear that what is required is a radical rethinking and recasting of social work programmes based on an anti-racist strategy. The field of social work with black people is composed of contradictory philosophies, muddled thought and racist assumptions. Indeed, social work has been a moving frontier of confusion, particularly when it attempts to move across race and cultures. Lena Dominelli shows that the social work approach has moved from grand concepts of assimilation, integration, adaptation (and colour equals problems), to cultural explanations which currently leave the profession unwilling to change, and uncertain about challenging racism. Lena Dominelli's book goes beyond this method of thinking and practice; it will continue to meet the needs of social work practitioners and educators alike. It will continue to be an invaluable source for teachers, social workers, community workers, and people who are interested in the nature of racism and its effect on the black and white population and the process whereby measures can be taken to remove this destructive phenomenon from the profession in particular and society in general. It will undoubtedly continue to be a source of reference and practical assistance to those who are concerned with the creation of a truly multi-racial society.

JOHN SMALL, 1996
Co-ordinator, Social Work Unit
University of the West Indies, Jamaica

In honour of the struggles of little girls who long for blonde hair and blue eyes, but learn after much hardship and pain to be proud of their own attributes

Preface to second edition

Racism in its myriad forms continues to flourish despite the spread of equal opportunities policies and the formal disavowal of racist actions on the part of politicians. Social work, like the rest of society, reflects this contradictory situation. Although more black people are now employed in welfare settings and within the criminal justice system than when the first edition of this book was written, their progress to the higher echelons of management and mainstream positions has been minimal. Indeed, in some instances movement has been backward. For example, the abolition of the Greater London Council and Metropolitan Counties has forced into retreat many of their anti-racist initiatives. Consequently, instead of the handful of black men as directors of social services departments, today there are none. No black woman has yet reached this level and there have still been no black chief probation officers. Moreover, social work has been at the sharp edge of the backlash against anti-racist initiatives. Yet, black people and white anti-racists have continued to fight for racial justice despite the unpropitious environment in which their work proceeds. The general climate of both hostility and indifference towards programmes seeking to end racial injustice has increased the necessity for more people to commit themselves to anti-racist struggles. Thus, it is timely for this book to be revised in a way that encourages greater numbers of social work practitioners and educators throughout the world to make their contribution to bringing about the demise of racist attitudes, behaviour, legislation, policies and practice.

The various travels and pieces of research I have undertaken since the original publication of this book have revealed the widespread nature of racism and the relevance of much of what I have said about the dynamics of racism in Britain for other countries. In this edition, therefore, I shall attempt to include developments in other countries. However, the extent to which I can do this is limited by the short length of a book that fits into the BASW–Macmillan series. In many respects, it is events in other parts of the world – for example, the ending of the apartheid regime in South Africa – which provide the impetus for great optimism about possibilities here at home. It is in this spirit that I ask all of you who read these words to join those of us who have already embarked on projects that aim to vanquish racial oppression.

LENA DOMINELLI

Acknowledgements

Black people and their struggles to assert their humanity and dignity in a racist world have been crucial in inspiring the reclamation of my own humanity following the experiences of being a non-patrial immigrant in several continents. The lessons I have drawn from these have influenced my thinking as well as my practice and are reflected in my approach to the question of eliminating racism. The insights I have gained from these experiences have led me to feel passionately that racism is more than evil, irrational prejudices held by individuals. It is also a powerful social force which operates coherently and systematically to invade and structure every human interaction. I want to thank my many friends, both black and white, who have helped in the writing of this book by making me think deeply of who I was and what I am. I also wish to express my gratitude to the many generations of Warwick students and practice teachers who have influenced my thinking about the subject and who have taught me a great deal, as did the clients and workers, black and white, who agreed to be interviewed by me in connection with this book. I should add that the material contained in the case studies has been altered to protect the identity of the individuals concerned. Finally, I wish to thank the readers of the text who have provided me with the encouragement and comments which have enabled me to maintain my arguments in an emotionally fraught and complex area. In particular, I would like to thank Paul Stubbs and Martin Willis. I also extend very special thanks to John Small for finding time in his busy schedule to write the Foreword.

LENA DOMINELLI

Introduction: Anti-Racist Social Work – A Critical Issue for White People

The electoral successes of the Far Right in Europe since the late 1980s, including the election of a councillor from the British National Party in a by-election in Tower Hamlets, London in 1994, are overt manifestations of the growing respectability being accorded to right-wing extremists who popularise racist sentiments, aimed specifically at 'immigrants' – a euphemism for black people[1]. Others include the rise in the number of life-threatening racist attacks in Europe (Bjorgo and Witte, 1993); the increasingly vociferous white backlash which is legitimating anew the racist discourses being articulated, for example, in both Britain and America (see Dunant, 1994; Murray, 1990); the advent of 'Fortress Europe' with its overriding preoccupation of keeping people from the Third World out of the European geographical terrain, whether they are seeking admission as labourers or asylum seekers (Gordon, 1992); and the spread of narrow-minded nationalistic fervour (Cheles et al., 1991). Set against these developments are black people's struggles for liberation and the elimination of racial oppression (S. Small, 1994); the promotion of equal opportunities legislation (Dalrymple and Burke, 1995); and anti-racist struggles initiated by both individuals and groups.

This social context provides the backdrop against which anti-racist social work is being elaborated. Contradictions abound, making the task of initiating social change which promotes racial justice hazardous and difficult. Thus, those embarking on this project need to be prepared for the risks they will have to take and the resistance they will encounter.

However, the problems that anti-racists confront are of a different order of magnitude from those black people face every moment of their

1

lives in the course of 'normal' living. Relationships between black and white people have been characterised by notions of white supremacy in which white people refuse to accept the human worth of black people and structure social interaction between them accordingly. Black people have been portrayed as 'naturally inferior and dangerous', making *difference* – whether expressed through physical or social attributes – a basis for and the justification of unequal social relations which privilege white people (see Murray, 1994). This concept underpins racist dynamics and has meant that white people do not accept black people for what they are – equal beings with their own contribution to make to the development of humankind. Instead, black people have been subjected to an onslaught in which they have been expected to emulate the white man (Fanon, 1968) whilst maintaining their distance. The main options which white people have placed before black people, therefore, occupy a continuum encompassing assimilation at one end and repatriation at the other.

Assimilatist ideologies require black people to accept white norms and mores as the standards for measuring social organisation and behaviour without conceding equality, no matter how successful black people are in living up to these expectations. Integration draws heavily on assimilationist dynamics. Segregation allows black people space to develop separately, particularly in the cultural and religious spheres, but their development is characterised as inferior by the dominant white power-holders and is constrained by the lack of access to societal resources. In denying black people the opportunity to establish a holistic independent development, segregation exacts terrible costs from them. Moreover, the casting of black people as 'dangerous' has led to their being subjected to strict and coercive forms of control aimed at keeping them in their place. Repatriation schemes are segregation by displacement to another locale. What white people have not promoted collectively are forms of egalitarian co-existence. Nonetheless, throughout the history of black–white relations, black people have not been cowed by white dominated definitions of their place and role in the world. They have resisted their subordination overtly and covertly, in the routines of everyday life and in liberation struggles (Collins, 1991; Essed, 1991; Fryer, 1984; Gilroy, 1987).

The British population consists of people with diverse national origins, different cultural backgrounds, religions and economic positions. Despite various initiatives, white social workers have not adequately addressed the ethnically pluralistic nature of society and reflected this in their practice by making available services which cater for the specific needs and demands of ethnic minorities (ADSS/CRE, 1978; Ahmad, 1990). Their failure to do so continues to make countering racism a pressing issue in social work education, training and practice. Working out how to respond to this task remains difficult and controversial. The paths whereby the elimination of racism is achieved are covered in minefields. That there are no easy answers lying readily to hand is amply revealed when we examine the history and outcome of our recent struggles against racism. The definitions of what it is 'appropriate' to do have varied significantly as our understanding of the nature of the forces we have been opposing has deepened. What seemed permissible yesterday is being exposed as suspect today and looks like being even more questionable tomorrow. White liberals desperately seeking to do the 'right thing' by black people have found it increasingly difficult to define their present position, let alone their next action. All they stand for has been discredited through inappropriate forms of racism awareness training (see Gurnah, 1984). Activities aimed at combating racism have been exposed as either inadequate or positively damaging to black people when evaluated by them.

From a black perspective, white people's attempts to make black people feel welcome in Britain by assimilating them into the (white) 'British way of life' have been found wanting for being based on arrogant assumptions that white people and white culture have something to offer black people, whilst black people and their culture provide nothing in return (Gilroy, 1987). The assimilationist position has rendered black people's day-to-day experience of racism invisible, ignored the positive contributions they have made and are making to society, and denied their resistance to oppression. White people's efforts in overcoming the weaknesses of the assimilationist approach have led to the development of 'ethnically sensitive' perspectives which at least recognise some of the cultural strengths of black people's life-styles and their contributions to society. However, this has been downgraded as a diversionary activity focusing attention on black people and their communities rather than on white people and their power structures. This blames those at the receiving end of racism instead of the social relations creating it (Gilroy, 1987). The attempt to refine 'ethnically sensitive' approaches through 'multi-culturalism' and 'multi-racialism' as the embodiments of equality between different races and different cultures has also been found wide of the mark. Racial inequality has not disappeared because white people understand better the customs, traditions and religious activities of ethnic minority groups. Also the racial harmony which both black and white people have sought has proved singularly elusive outside the atmosphere of shared social festivities (Ohri and Manning, 1982).

Although our efforts at eliminating racism have so far, been ineffective many white people are still searching for solutions. Those of us struggling against racism from an anti-racist perspective are quite clear that, whatever we do, we must tackle racism at its core by combining change at the personal level with structural change to dismantle the organisational and cultural dynamics underpinning racism. Anti-racist approaches to countering racism have attracted those of us wishing to transcend the limitations inherent in the other approaches open to white people. I take the view that white people cannot have a black perspective because this is rooted in the experience of being black in a racist white society and challenges racism from that position. However, I do believe that white people can, nay must, become anti-racist.

I feel it is appropriate for me, as a white person of 'dark' European descent[2] writing this book from an anti-racist perspective, to address white people interested in anti-racist social work and to share the experiences gained from attempting to implement anti-racist practices in both my personal and professional life. Although my main audience will be white social work educators and practitioners, for I cannot and would not speak for black people, I acknowledge that the things I say carry implications for black people, whether it be exhorting white people to become involved in anti-racist struggles or demanding the establishment of egalitarian relations between black and white people as a precondition for our working together in non-racist ways.

Anti-racist perspectives focus on transforming the unequal social relations shaping social interaction between black and white people into egalitarian ones. Additionally, these offer white people hope – hope of changing society in egalitarian directions. In being committed to making racial equality a reality, white people working from an anti-racist perspective can build bridges between themselves and black people working towards the same objective from a black perspective.

Until recently, white social workers have adopted the view that racism is a societal problem requiring government intervention, rather than being a central concern of theirs as either practitioners or trainers (ADSS/CRE, 1978). Fortunately, this attitude is shifting. It is doing so whilst social work is both in a state of flux and under attack. Pressure for change is emanating from privatisation measures; managerial imperatives aimed at improving efficiency and coping with a situation of dwindling resources; legislative requirements, particularly in relation to child care, community care, mental health and social security; increasing public scrutiny of social work, especially around child abuse; consumer demands for more sensitive, unstigmatised and less oppressive services; and social workers' own emerging activism as they organise collectively to defend their rights as workers and improve the services they provide.

Meanwhile social work has been found wanting by critics from a variety of perspectives. The 'New Right' castigates it for its 'do-gooding' propensities and its failure in controlling people and ensuring their conformity to 'acceptable', i.e. white, middle class, heterosexual standards of behaviour (Gilder, 1982; Minford, 1984; Murray, 1990, 1994). The criticisms have also laid the groundwork for the white backlash against anti-racist initiatives in both Britain and America. The white Left criticises social work for being primarily about control (Bailey and Brake, 1975; Bolger *et al.*, 1981; Simpkins, 1980). White feminists take it to task for its sexist theories and practices (Brook and Davis, 1985; Burden and Gottlieb, 1987; Dominelli, 1986; Dominelli and McLeod, 1989; Hanmer and Statham, 1988; Marchant and Wearing, 1986; Statham, 1978; Wilson, 1977). Black women and men condemn its pervasive racism (ABSWAP, 1981; Ahmad, 1990; Devine, 1983; Manning and Ohri, 1982; Small, 1987). Facing attack on all fronts and the rupturing of established routines and assumptions about their place in the world, white people in social work teaching and practice have felt confused, deskilled, and uncertain about the direction they should now take.

White fears and anxieties about the process of becoming anti-racist rise to the fore. White professionals worry about making social work a 'political' subject, feel guilty about colluding with racism and seem powerless in the enormous task of struggling against it. They are concerned about the price they will have to pay, given their current unpreparedness and lack of skills, which might result in their losing out in the employment stakes. Whilst taking risks may be inevitable at some points in the anti-racist struggle, these have been exaggerated and ignore the heavy toll exacted from black people who daily pay the price for the continued existence of racism.

White people also have difficulty accepting their exclusion from activities which black people have redefined as theirs, for example working with black families (Stubbs, 1985) or teaching black students. Such exclusion is problematic because white people are not used to having their power challenged by black people in this way. They resent having discrete areas of their social order defined 'out of bounds' by those whom they 'rule', whose place in society they have designated as inferior, and whose activities they have sought to control. White people experience anger because normal power relationships between them and black people have been unilaterally ruptured.

Moreover, white people consider their intervention in black people's lives beneficial. To be told that they have no right to interfere in black people's lives in the pernicious ways to which they have grown accustomed comes as a shock to well-meaning whites, as does black people's directive that white people's priority should be to sort themselves, not black people, out. Encouraging white people to participate actively in the establishment of anti-racist social work is problematic. White people feeling tainted by the pervasiveness of racism in British society find the prospect of becoming involved in eradicating racism so daunting that they are tempted to ignore it altogether. Others are so consumed by guilt that they feel incapable of acting even though they are extremely worried about the continuation of racist practices (Powell and Edmonds, 1985). Moreover, the desire to 'get it right' can paralyse well-meaning whites. In this context, learning to accept responsibility for our mistakes and the lessons to be drawn from them can free us to move forward.

White social workers wonder how they can best respond to these criticisms whilst recognising the constraints of being state employees with legal statutory requirements to fulfil. Desperately seeking to resolve the tension between care and control in their work, they discover developing non-oppressive forms of practice in general, and anti-racist and anti-sexist practice in particular, to be complex and difficult. Without suggesting that there are easy solutions, I argue that we need not feel so helpless in the face of the challenge before us. Our feelings of powerlessness and inability to change things can be countered if white social work educators and practitioners accept the importance of struggling against racism and take up the issue of transforming social work education and practice to promote people's welfare and empower users. An anti-racist perspective in social work provides one avenue whereby such change can be achieved.

The anti-racist perspective may seem harsh in its negative judgements of many of our well-intentioned activities and motives. This is unavoidable when the measure of our endeavours is not what we think of them but the extent to which our efforts actually dismantle racism. We can make considerable progress in anti-racist directions if we are sufficiently motivated in wanting to change our world and organise collectively to do so. This book aims to help us in this task by providing an analysis that evaluates critically those practices which we consider to be indicative of 'successful' or racism-free social work and by suggesting principles on which future action for establishing anti-racist social work might be based.

Defining racism

The components of racism

Racism, the scourge pervading every aspect of social interaction, is 'the belief in the inherent superiority of one race over all others and thereby the right to dominance' (Lorde, 1984, p. 115). Racism consists of three main dimensions in dynamic interaction with one another: *individual or personal racism, institutional racism,* and *cultural racism* (Bromley and Longino, 1972). *Individual racism* is made up of those attitudes and behaviours depicting a negative prejudgement of racial groups. Individual racist attitudes without institutional backing constitute racial prejudice. Personal racism is the lament constantly emphasised in common-sense discourse about racist acts. Focusing on personal racism promotes the belief that racism is the prerogative of bigoted individuals indulging in overtly racist behaviour. *Institutional racism* consists of customary routines which ration resources and power by excluding groups arbitrarily defined as racially inferior. Relying on public power and authority for its legitimation, institutionalised racism pathologises excluded groups for their lack of success within the system and blames them for their predicament. The reproduction of racism through the interaction between individual behaviour and institutional norms underpins the dynamics of institutionalised racism. This concept is difficult to translate into everyday parlance. Hence, it is easy to miss its impact in daily, taken-for-granted routines. *Cultural racism* is centred around those values, beliefs and ideas endorsing the superiority of white culture. It provides the cement of popular racism which reinforces both institutional and individual racism. The impact of cultural, institutional and individual racism is felt by all non-Anglo-Saxon ethnic minority groups. The components of racism are depicted in the figure on the next page. At this level of abstraction, racism exists throughout the globe. However, its specific expression needs to be explicated in precise detail for each locality.

In other words, racism provides a basis for social exclusion on the basis of 'race'[3]. Explaining racism by trying to define the complex social relations it encompasses is tricky. There is controversy over the language we use. For example, the term 'black people' is contentious. Having begun as an inclusive political term to counter the divisive aspects of racism, it has become used by some to deny the heterogeneity and uniqueness of the many diverse groups potentially covered by the term. So, in Britain, Asian groups claim they are not 'black' as part of their struggle to assert their own particularity in historical, cultural, ethical and linguistical terms. In America, the expression 'people of colour' has been used for similar purposes. This has not solved the problem of which groups are encompassed by the terms or how the specificity of each ethnic grouping is best preserved. Nor do solutions focusing on identity politics and their capacity to fragment groups down to the level of the individual resolve the issue of simultaneously respecting differences within egalitarian parameters whilst highlighting commonalities.

The components of racism

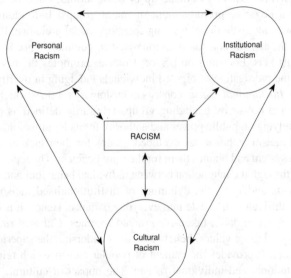

Our terminology is riddled with racism. For example, when white people, including social work educators and practitioners, speak of Britain, they usually mean white, 'English' Britain. Becoming aware of the implicit racism in the word makes white anti-racists hesitant in using it. But, as yet, we have neither reclaimed the word by divesting it of the racist ideologies and practices embedded within it, nor developed an appropriate alternative to it. Proposition 189 in California indicates similar forms of exclusion in the use of the word 'American'. White, preferably Anglo-Saxon Protestants are the preferred group, and there is great anxiety that in some areas they will soon be heavily outnumbered by Hispanics (S. Small, 1994). Hyphenated appellations like 'Hispanic-American' remain problematic.

The phrase 'multi-racial Britain', 'multi-racial Europe' or 'multi-racial America' does not meet anti-racist criteria because racism penetrates more than the cultural dimension of human organisation. It ignores hierarchies embedded in social relations which privilege one ethnic or racial group over another and reinforce disparities in power and access to social resources. Thus, 'multi-racialism' has become a concept through which white people obscure the real problem that needs to be tackled – racism – and focus instead on discovering one another's different life-styles, almost as if cultural interactions between black and white people were independent of structurally reproduced and reinforced inequality (CCCS, 1982). In other words, social relations are assumed to occur in a vacuum.

Racism is apparent in the minutiae of everyday life as well as in institutions and legislation. It permeates every aspect of our personal and professional lives whether we are black or white, making confronting it difficult and complex. British racism is about the construction of social relationships on the basis of an assumed inferiority of non-Anglo-Saxon ethnic minority groups, and, flowing from this, their exploitation and oppression. I use the term 'non-Anglo-Saxon ethnic minorities' to include all those people, black and white, who are not considered 'indigenous' British of white English and Nordic European origins, settled in Britain. The 1981 Census revealed that 4 per cent of the British populace is of 'New Commonwealth' or black origins. Ten years later, this had risen to 5 per cent. Other significant ethnic minority groups include the Chinese, Greek Cypriots, Jews, Poles, Italians and Irish. These groups constitute the non-Anglo-Saxon ethnic minorities found in British society, making racism more than a matter of black and white. Although there are significant sub-divisions within this categorisation, each of which justifies being written about in its own right, the discourse in this book is conducted largely in terms of black and white. I focus on this division because the groups currently being subjected to the most vicious and intractable expressions of racism are black people, of Asian, African and Caribbean descent (Brown, 1984; Bryan *et al.*, 1985; CCCS, 1982; Smith, 1976). Moreover, the racism being perpetrated against black people is such a fundamental and integral part of society that eradicating the racism that white people level against them will provide guidelines for countering the racism experienced by other non-Anglo-Saxon ethnic minorities.

Operating on a hierarchical continuum placing Anglo-Saxon Britons at the superior end of the spectrum and Asian and Afro-Caribbean Britons at its corresponding inferior point, racism politicises 'race' and ethnicity through relations of domination and subordination. The politicisation of human biology in white supremacist terms has enabled white people at the top of this racialised hierarchy to construct social relations imposing their definitions of the world over others, thereby maintaining their privileges and power. From the standpoint of those endorsing the biological determinism of racial inferiority, each person is endowed at birth with immutable characteristics based on white superiority and black inferiority (Eysenck, 1971; Gobineau, 1953; Jensen, 1972; Murray, 1994). Social organisation based on white supremacist terms has been perpetuated as a 'natural' state of affairs over which people have no control. Concentrating on the biological aspects of racism mystifies the social nature of the relationships embedded in racist practices and facilitates the scapegoating and instant oppression of those having easily visible racial and ethnic characteristics, for example skin colour, hair type, language and cultural traditions. The politicisation of these attributes indicates that racism goes beyond biological characteristics and is socially constructed. Rather than being 'natural' and immutable, therefore, racism can be dismantled and non-racist social relations can be created in their stead. The socially derived basis of racism has been acknowledged by some local authorities in their policy formulation. The London Borough of Lambeth, for example, has incorporated the social construction of racism in the definition of 'black' used in its child care policy document. It says:

'Black'. A description of any person whose skin colour renders them liable to the application of racism, irrespective of ethnic background, linguistic or academic ability, country of origin, or length of stay, in this country. (Lambeth, Social Services Committee, 1981)

In clarifying the social construction of racism, Stuart Hall posits racism as a set of economic, political and ideological practices through which a dominant group exercises hegemony over subordinate groups (Hall, 1980a, b, p. 338). Establishing hegemony or dominance means that the ruling group must capture people's hearts and minds in a common-sense, seemingly untheorised way which secures their consent to being dominated without being conscious of it. The unarticulated nature of racism makes it difficult for the majority of white people to see racism as an endemic feature of society which permeates all aspects of its social order and draws them into its ambit. It also enables white people to define racism as the crude, irrational beliefs and actions manifest by a few National Front supporters instead of a normal feature of social interaction between black and white people. This enables them to acquire a self-concept which is not racist. Hence, white people generally take exceptional umbrage at being called racist and become extremely defensive if it is suggested that they live in an inherently racist society. The Labour Party leadership's reaction to Sharon Atkin calling the Labour Party racist for its refusal to endorse autonomous Black Sections within it exemplifies this reaction (*Guardian*, 30 April 1987). The Labour leaders in turn nullified her prospective candidature for a Parliamentary seat. During this incident, the electorate of Nottingham East had Mohammed Aslam imposed upon them in her place. A similar scenario was enacted in social work in the early 1990s when the Central Council for Education and Training in Social Work (CCETSW) was manoeuvred into disowning Appendix 5 of Paper 30 because it stated that racism was an 'endemic feature' of British society (see Phillips, 1993; Pinker 1993; Appleyard, 1993).

Racism's adaptive forms: the 'new racism'

Centering social relations on asserting the supremacy of white Anglo-Saxon British, and ensuring that these views are accepted as 'common sense', provides racism with the ideological coherence that white Anglo-Saxon Britons use to maintain their position, deny non-Anglo-Saxon minority ethnic groups access to social power and resources, and trample on their racial integrity and dignity. 'Common sense' forms the basis of the 'new racism' (Barker, 1981) currently dominating Britain's political and social life.

The 'new racism' has developed as the response of white Anglo-Saxon Britons to Britain's declining socio-economic position and the existence of a settled, indigenous black population. Through it, white British nationhood is being redefined in cultural rather than biological terms. The 'new racism' has acquired legal force through the concepts of nationality and citizenship embodied in the 1981 Nationality Act. This uses patriality as an exclusionary principle in defining British nationals and has made 'repatriation' a respectable option for those denied British citizenship – mainly black 'non-patrials'. This new concept of nationhood excludes Black Britons whose culture the 'new racists' see as '*different from*', i.e. inferior to, that of the white 'indigenous' population. It also draws on a profoundly ahistorical notion of which group(s) of people are 'indigenous' in a country with a past peppered by various waves of newcomers, whether as conquerors or otherwise, who have settled. Similar kinds of selected history are evident within the white backlash in the USA.

Because what is at stake revolves around defining those whose culture is to be deemed insignificant and whose human status is diminished in consequence, the 'new racism' of today legitimates the continued exploitation and harassment of black people. It also indicates how racism changes its forms to adapt to altered circumstances.

Barker (1981, p. 18) contends that the 'new racism' is not based on white people claiming superior status. I challenge this assertion on the grounds that the new construction of racism has pushed underground overt statements of white Anglo-Saxon British supremacy. By affirming the Anglo-Saxon 'British way of life' because it is 'different' from that of others who are also entitled to defend their own way of life – in their own countries – the 'new racists' elevate the white Anglo-Saxon British way of life above all others. They speak from an anglocentric perspective[4] which confirms the supremacy of Anglo-Saxon life-styles rather than one which posits equality and the possibility of egalitarian co-existence between different ways of life. The black British way of life is specifically discounted as an 'alien' pollutant in their 'sacred' environment (Cohen and Bains, 1988). In describing black British ways of life in these terms, it is clear that the 'new racists' consider these inferior to the white Anglo-Saxon British ones which must be protected from being 'contaminated'. Margaret Thatcher best encapsulated these views when she spoke of white Britons' fears of being 'swamped' by alien cultures.

The anglocentric nature of the 'new racists'' position also appears in their demand for the 'repatriation' of black people to their 'inferior' countries of origin. Repatriation is being used to camouflage the 'new racists'' assessment of black people's ways of life as inferior; to resist the possibility of the black British way of life influencing the white Anglo-Saxon British one; and to prevent black people and white people from establishing egalitarian relationships with one another. Through repatriation, the 'new racists' proclaim a subtle form of apartheid which is concealed by sending black people 'back home' where their welfare needs become someone else's concern. The 'new racism' has to be understood as a white racist response to a settled black population in their midst. It also legitimates the exclusion of settled black people from welfare provisions. Evidence of the 'new racism' also appears in discussions about the exclusion of black people from Europe – a policy dubbed 'Fortress Europe' (Gordon, 1992).

Similarly, non-Anglo-Saxon white people are only acceptable as long as they assimilate into the white Anglo-Saxon British way of life. 'Aliens', i.e. non-Anglo-Saxon ethnic minorities from America and

Europe, are only marginally more desirable than those from India and Hong Kong. Through this particular political philosophy, the 'new racists' have found another way of restructuring social relations to affirm white Anglo-Saxon supremacy and ideological hegemony in a new but 'natural' and incontestable form. This has further mystified social relations between black and white people, facilitating anew the use of racism in reproducing a racially stratified population over which the dominant white group can rule (Cohen and Bains, 1988).

The social control of black people as *black* people occurs through the medium of racist social relations. Moreover, racism causes black people's experience of class and other social divisions to be mediated by and through 'race'. The intertwining of class and 'race' differentiates black people's experience of class oppression from white people's (Gilroy, 1987). Similarly, black women's experience of gender is mediated through and by 'race' (Bryan *et al.*, 1985; Carby, 1982; Lorde, 1984). Consequently, their experience of sexism differs from white women's.

Racism is a socially constructed and reproduced historically specific phenomenon whose form changes in response to transformations occurring within society's socio-economic base, altering between periods of expansion when economic demand for cheap labour results in policies promoting overseas immigration, i.e. the importation of labour with settlement rights, and the reverse during recessionary phases (Dominelli, 1978a; Gilroy, 1987). Racism in 1980s Britain has been restructured to take account of a declining manufacturing sphere within the context of international monopoly capitalism. In the 1990s the process of economic globalisation has intensified (Sklair, 1991). Moreover, it has meant that capital's capacity for transcending national frontiers has enabled it to move manufacturing jobs to Third World countries where production costs, including those involved in sustaining a welfare state, are substantially reduced or insignificant. This obviates the need for migrant labour to be located in Western countries.

Using immigration as the regulatory mechanism to attract or reject overseas labour (Castles and Kosack, 1972), the British state participates in this process as both formulator and enforcer of immigration policy, and as an employer in its own right. Layton-Henry (1985) gives an account of how immigration policy shifted from heralding an open-door policy in the 1950s to demanding strict control by the 1970s as British capital's need for labour declined. The current economic crisis in Britain requires a restructuring of its workforce and a realignment of the balance between an internally generated and an imported one. The existence of a large, internally generated labour force consisting of unemployed waged workers, women working in the home and unemployed youth reduces the need for importing workers.

These developments have moved British immigration policy closer to the continental European one. Indeed 'Fortress Europe' has led to the harmonisation of immigration policies throughout the continent so that, for example, the rejection of an asylum seeker's application by one country will have the effect of its being rejected by all the others (Read and Simpson, 1991).

Sivanandan (1976) attributes the state's increasing willingness to endorse repatriation to a way of substantially reducing the size of the workforce. Dominelli (1978a) argues that the need to limit the size of the labour force and decrease the costs of reproducing it pushes the state in the direction of converting immigrant workers to migrant or repatriated workers. The latter option is extremely attractive in a situation in which the government deems the welfare state a luxury wastefully consuming the surplus necessary for capital accumulation (Gilder, 1982; Minford, 1984). As a result of these forces, the conversion of immigrant labour into migrant labour is almost complete, and there is virtually no new immigration into Britain (Gordon, 1992).

The economic circumstances of late capitalism coalesce to make the exploitation of black ethnic minority groups different from that of other non-Anglo-Saxon ethnic minority groups of earlier periods. Besides the declining demand for their labour caused in absolute terms by globalisation and the penetration of new capital intensive technology into the economy, many avenues of upward mobility previously available to other non-Anglo-Saxon ethnic minority groups are now closed off, locking black people into a permanent reserve workforce unless there is a substantial transformation in social relations.

Whilst structural analyses of racism are gaining currency in British academic circles, the bulk of the theories embodied in the field of 'race relations' focuses on descriptions of black communities and their inherent pathologies. Publications by white academics, for example Rex, Tomlinson, Troyna, and Cashmore, have been criticised by Gilroy and others (CCCS, 1982; Gilroy, 1987) for presenting black people rather than racist social relations as the problem. Lawrence (1981) attacks black authors such as Foner, Khan, and Pryce for pathologising black cultures and reinforcing racist notions of black people as inadequate, unintelligent, 'rural and backward'. He also maintains that their writings condemn black people for being ill equipped to cope with white Anglo-Saxon British society and endorse expectations that black people be contained and controlled so as not to disrupt the smooth operation of society as a whole (Lawrence, 1981).

Social workers need to understand the structural basis of racism if they are to learn how to intervene in ways that do not reinforce racist dynamics. Moreover, an analytical grasp of the situation enables them to take action to eradicate both personal and structural racism.

The parameters of anti-racist social work

What role do white people have in getting rid of personal, cultural and institutional racism in social work? What policies and practices constitute the anti-racist social work which white people can follow? How do we overcome the obstacles to our progress without reinforcing and reproducing racist social work practice ourselves? How can we eliminate the institutional racism which bolsters and endorses our work? I address these complex questions by arguing that in Western societies, of which Britain is a key example, a commitment to countering racism becomes white people's starting point in acknowledging that they have a different relationship to racism from black people. From this, they can move on to recognise that they have different roles in the mutual project of dismantling it. White people's parameters are set by their position as perpetrators and beneficiaries of racist social relations, whether or not they engage directly in racist behaviour (Lorde, 1984). By denying black people access to goods and services and keeping them out of the competition for scarce resources, these become allocated to white people without their having to demonstrate merit or need. Thus, racist social relations have, for example, meant that knowledge, qualifications and skills held by black people have not been valued, and they are often overqualified for the jobs they hold (S. Small, 1994). In destroying the racist edifice they have constructed, white people will lose powers and privileges gained at the expense of black people.

Black people's relationship to racial oppression is a specific one in which they confront racism's razor-sharp edge, struggle against it to minimise its pernicious impact on their lives, and elaborate the theory and practice of a black perspective in eradicating it (Gilroy, 1987). Black people share common features of oppression which may unite them and facilitate collective action and solidarity between them. White people's common position as oppressors divides those fighting racism from white compatriots actively resisting anti-racist initiatives. Despite their determination to proceed with greater sensitivity and awareness than in the past, the difficulties white people encounter in tackling racism are legion. We will make mistakes because white supremacy has become such an integral part of our personalities and societal structures that we ignore its existence thorough our taken-for-granted assumptions about social interaction and perpetuate relations of domination when we are trying to eschew them. But we will know when we have erred, for our intuitive responses will signal it, other white people will tell us, or black people will respond in ways which reveal we have, yet again, been racist towards them. However, making mistakes and learning from them is preferable to taking no action. Owning our mistakes and taking their painful lessons forward can facilitate personal and spiritual growth, which will enable us to see more clearly how we can tackle racism in all its manifestations and relate more effectively to black people.

Racism endorses injustice and damages both black and white people economically, socially and emotionally. Socially, racism distorts human relations between individuals and social interaction between groups and makes all those involved poorer because honesty and openness are absent amongst them. The internalisation of supremacist ideologies causes deep psychological harm to white people who assume superiority by virtue of their skin colour, and to black people who continually encounter racist onslaughts through being defined inferior. Economically, racism legitimates the exploitation of black people, appropriates material gains for white people, and causes society as a whole to lose out through the misuse of resources rightfully belonging to black people. Culturally, white people lose out on the richness accruing from egalitarian relationships endorsing the celebration of diversity amongst peoples. Redressing this situation requires white people to counter the damage racism causes their personae and their relationships with black people by developing their role in fighting racism.

After taking responsibility for owning the monstrosity of racism, white people must actively deconstruct it. This constitutes the anti-racist struggle whereby white people can empower themselves. For me, this is a political, moral and socially necessary imperative. We must stop exploiting black people and desist from providing them with inappropriate services in exchange. In recognising the contribution black people make to our society and returning what is rightfully theirs, we become stronger and more complete people ourselves. For in getting rid of the injustice perpetrated by racism, we begin to reclaim our own humanity and establish egalitarian relationships between black and white people. Thus, we have much to gain by eradicating racism. Anti-racist social work forms the bridge that white people can cross to reach the competence necessary for beginning to work in non-racist, egalitarian ways with black people.

Although the processes whereby egalitarian relationships between black and white are achieved are difficult to develop, white people advocating anti-racist social work have a major input in redefining current understandings of social work along anti-racist lines. The lack of familiarity in working in egalitarian relationships and the loss of power over others will initially disorient and overwhelm white social work educators and practitioners. Neither our professional training, which presupposes hierarchical relationships between ourselves and others, nor our previous experiences will have prepared us for this. An acute awareness of our loss of power and privileges in the short term can obscure the long-term advantages that accrue from implementing an anti-racist stance. Yet white social workers will have to create egalitarian relationships with black people if they wish to work according to anti-racist tenets and become involved with black people working in similar directions. The bases on which white people can engage with black people in these processes will be qualitatively different from those currently defining the interaction between black people and white people, as power imbalances arising from relations of domination will have to be eliminated from the outset.

White social work practitioners and educators may find it useful to discuss their contributions to the anti-racist struggle in social work and share their anxieties about how to move forward with colleagues who have attempted to develop such working relationships. For example, white anti-racist social workers in Hackney, Lewisham and Brent, and white anti-racist social work educators at Birmingham Polytechnic, have learnt lessons and gained support from others through discussion (Stubbs, 1985; Willis, 1987). If white social workers start relating to black people on the basis of equality, not only will they be transformed into better practitioners, but their agencies' policies and practice will also be similarly improved. The same holds true for white social work educators.

White social workers' who sympathise with the hardships that poverty imposes on their white clients find it difficult to respond to their needs in ways that do not undermine anti-racist perspectives. For example, Emecheta (1983), speaking as a black woman, describes how easily her white social worker ignores the racial dimension in the interaction between them, and glosses over the issue when hearing her white clients making racist remarks. Looking at the problem in microcosm, Cohen (1985) reveals how difficult it is for white anti-racist youth workers to deal with racist white lads in a run-down working class community despite their being explicitly charged with establishing anti-racist youth work. Similarly, in community work, the account of tenants' associations striving to implement anti-racist practices in Tower Hamlets portrays the countless obstacles that white people have to overcome in establishing anti-racist relationships (THTA, 1987). In all these accounts, white social/community workers' uncritical acceptance of the premise that poor white people require a service makes them accord fighting racism a lower priority than meeting the needs of the white client when the two objectives conflict.

The dilemmas that white social workers encounter in these situations arise from their acceptance of white clients as the 'deserving poor' and the collusion engendered by their shared assumptions of white supremacy with casting black people as the 'undeserving poor'. Comments like 'You only get a ... service in this office if you're black', following the declaration of an equal opportunities policy, which go unchallenged by white social workers, illustrate this point. In such situations, white social workers have to find ways of acknowledging the disadvantages being borne by both groups, whilst at the same time being able to demonstrate that *racism* makes black people's experience of poverty different from white people's and that poor white people may, through their own racist actions, make the plight of their poor black neighbours even worse.

Ultimately, an anti-racist analysis implies that if changes in social work practice are to endure, society also needs to change. Societal change becomes particularly important in ensuring that scarce resources are equitably distributed. However, in the context of structural inequalities engendered by racism, poor black people may require an additional injection of resources to bring their situation up to the same starting point as poor white people. Moreover, changes must occur on two fronts – the personal and the structural simultaneously – if they are to initiate enduring improvements in the social order. Finally, the nature of such changes is so fundamental that ameliorating the position of poor black people by eradicating racism leads to a substantive improvement in the welfare of all poor people, irrespective of 'race'.

Consequently, to become fully human and live in egalitarian harmony with black people, white people have to become anti-racist. Anti-racism is a state of mind, feeling, political commitment and action. There is important work for white people to do. The days when we could assuage our guilt by employing black people to take up anti-racist struggles in social work on our behalf are over. Black people are refusing to endorse the tokenism of many of our gestures aimed at making good our inadequacies, and concentrating their energies on their own communities. In some instances, because of the very nature of racism, change from within cannot be commenced by black people because they have been excluded from the institutions and decision-making processes which oppress them. It is up to those of us who are located within them to change these by developing alliances and strategies which will foster anti-racist policies and practices.

In this book I examine what white social work practitioners and educators can and must do when struggling against racism in social work and developing non-racist social work in a number of settings – social services, probation, community work and the voluntary sector. I take the view that racism aimed specifically at non-Anglo-Saxon people forms part of a larger process of social control. Thus, it reinforces the controlling dimension of social work and intensifies the policing aspect of white social workers' relationships with ethnic minority groups. It also contributes to their exclusion from the creation and delivery of services relevant to their welfare. Whether acknowledged or not, racism becomes a powerful rationing device in the hands of under-resourced social work agencies and training departments.

It is vital that white social work practitioners and educators create a theory of racism which contextualises social work within the state apparatus; understands the dynamics in both covert and overt forms of racism; recognises how racism is legitimated through social processes and institutions outside social work structures; and relates these to everyday routines in social work. This includes what they do and do not do to become effective participants in the project of removing racism from society. Unravelling the dynamics of racism in social work practice becomes the preoccupation of Chapter 1. In it, I analyse both personal and structural racism and link these directly to the personal prejudice and institutional racism evident in social work training and practice. I demonstrate how definitions of social work tasks are imbued with and reproduce racism. Yet, these features are virtually ignored in social work training. Overcoming the limitations this imposes on teaching, learning and practice requires white social work practitioners and educators, as both perpetrators and beneficiaries of racism, actively to engage in anti-racist social work and bring about the demise of racism in their areas of competence.

Existing social work education has had a major role in perpetuating social work theories and forms of intervention permeated by racism. This state of affairs will end when social work training accepts its central role in establishing anti-racist social work as the form of social work practised by future generations of social workers. Similarly, it has a key part to play in retraining existing social workers. Chapter 2, therefore, examines the racist underpinnings of social work training and education and makes suggestions for reorienting training in anti-racist directions.

Social workers use their personalities, sense of self and experience in establishing relationships with users (Compton and Galaway, 1975). Because working in this manner is a significant aspect of social work practice, white social workers should question their cosy assumptions about their way of life, place in the world and views about black people. Embarking on and engaging in this process constitutes the anti-racism awareness or consciousness-raising stage in the struggle to establish anti-racist social work. White social workers need to participate in this process before proceeding to the next step of taking action to transform their racist beliefs and stereotypes, and agency policy and practice. Without promoting change which eradicates racism, anti-racism awareness is useless. It merely paralyses white social workers, leaving society's racist edifice intact. Chapter 3 considers anti-racism awareness training and its potential as a consciousness-raising activity which combines heightened personal awareness of racism with anti-racist action at both personal and structural levels.

Having completed this analysis, I focus the anti-racist perspective on a key *milieu* for social work intervention – the family. Chapter 4 examines the racist underpinnings of white social workers' current practice within black families, identifying the dilemmas they must resolve whether they are working with children, women, youths or elders. Using case materials, it provides guidelines for the limited interventions that white workers can appropriately undertake. Although I concentrate on the family as the prime site for social work involvement, the dynamics of racism operating in this context are replicated elsewhere. Thus, the lessons learnt in this arena can be transfered to other work with black individuals, groups and communities.

White social workers' anxieties about practising anti-racist social work become particularly frustrating when they struggle as isolated individuals or limit their activities to their particular agency. Overcoming the isolation of individualist responses to the eradication of racism requires white social workers to develop collective strategies coupling solidarity with material and emotional support from others. Forming support groups, networks and alliances is a prerequisite for implementing anti-racist organisational strategies in social work. Chapter 5 explores the implications of collective action by considering white social workers' involvement in eliminating racism in the workplace. It highlights the importance of reaching beyond their own agency to secure change there by forging alliances with people pursuing similar goals in other settings. Moreover, they will have to connect what is happening in their agency with central and local government policy and actions. Chapter 6 continues the exploration of organisational change by examining the role of white social workers in campaigning for anti-racist social work and laying foundations for transforming current practice. In Chapter 7, I conclude by considering the development of anti-racist/non-racist social work. Non-racist social work is about creating new forms of social work which transcend racism so that black and white social work practitioners and educators can work collectively together as equal partners in relationships free from racism.

This book is offered in the hopes of getting white social work educators and practitioners talking to one another individually and collectively about why they should engage in anti-racist social work and how they might best contribute to its realisation. It is not the final word in that process, merely a beginning whereby white people can undertake their own anti-racist initiatives instead of parasitically relying on black people to carry their burden of ensuring that good anti-racist social work makes its contribution towards eliminating racism from the face of the earth.

Notes

1   I use the term 'black people' to refer to any group of people who are at the receiving end of racism, regardless of the colour of their skin. It is a political phrase used to signify peoples who share racial oppression. It does not imply that 'black people' are a homogeneous group in religious, cultural, ethnic, national, linguistic or other attributes – be these physical or social. Nor does it suggest that one particular group's experience of racism is the same as another's. The forms through which racism against various peoples, for example Jews, Irish, Cypriots, Italians, Arabs, Bangladeshis, Afro-Caribbeans and Africans, is expressed are different. Moreover, the forms that racism assumes change over time even in respect of the same group.

2   The category 'dark' European is a Home Office classification used by the British police. Its recent introduction indicates a renewed desire for greater differentiation amongst the white population following the single European Act which ostensibly brought the European market together in 1992 and

reflects the insidious forms of racism levelled at people originating in the Mediterranean basin.

3   I have put 'race' in quotes to denote that I am using it as a socially constructed category and not a biological one. Biologically, all the world's people belong to one 'race' – Homo sapiens.

4   The term anglocentric was one I developed with the help of members of the White Collective for Anti-Racist Social Work when I asked for assistance in distinguishing between forms of racism that white people practice against other white people.

1

Racism Permeates Social Work Ideology and Practice

White social workers' fond belief in their liberalism and non-judgemental open mindness is endorsed in a study by Bagley and Young (1982). This suggests that social workers are more 'racially tolerant' than the general populace because only 3 per cent of them are racialist, i.e. hold crude racist views, compared with 20 per cent of the population as a whole. By identifying racism primarily in its overt forms at the level of attitudes, this definition of racism focuses on personal forms of racism and endorses its manifestation as the preserve of fanatical right-wing movements, groups and individuals. Making racism in social work practice a matter of individual import ignores the role of institutionalised racism and discounts the significance of indirect or unintentional racism. It pathologises the overtly racist few, ignores the subtle racism of the majority, and obscures the interconnections between structural forces and personal behaviour. Moreover, it converts racism into a matter which can be educated away, thereby ignoring the link between its eradication and the transformation of our socio-economic and political structures. Also, because only a 'few' white social workers are considered racist, it condones the belief that anti-racist struggles are activities which a small number of white social workers undertake as either educational exercises promoting understanding of other people and their cultures, or political activities undertaken outside working hours.

This chapter explores how racism is an integral feature of British society and permeates social work from its ideological underpinnings through to its practice. Conceptualising racism as the irrational beliefs of an evil few is, therefore, misguided. Racism, as the subtle playing-out of relations of subordination and domination in respect of 'race' in everyday routines and the minutiae of life, leaves no aspect of social work free of it. This makes it extremely difficult for white social work practitioners and educators to stand back from it and not become entangled in processes reinforcing its existence and endorsing its continuation. Colluding with racist policies and practices therefore, becomes the norm.

Racism in British society and social work: a theoretical and practical understanding

Racial inequality is the physical manifestation of the prevalence of racism in social relations. The structural nature of racial inequality and black people's plight has been affirmed through public inquiries (Gifford, 1986; Scarman, 1982) and research (Braham *et al.*, 1992; Brown, 1984; Rose, 1968; Smith, 1976). Inegalitarianism unfavourably distorts black people's access to social resources such as housing, employment and education (Home Office, 1986). Black people live in overcrowded inner-city areas, work in low-paid jobs without acquiring employment commensurate with their qualifications and skills, and experience higher rates of unemployment than their white counterparts, regardless of their age, gender or class (Brown, 1984). Racism's pernicious threads permeate the whole fibre of the welfare state (CRE, 1985; Gordon and Newnham, 1985) despite the welfare state's commitment to helping the disadvantaged and those in need. Black people's limited access to the personal social services throughout their life cycle has been well publicised. The report *Multi-Racial Britain: The Social Services Response* (ADSS/CRE, 1978) and Cheetham's (1981) report for the DHSS are only two of the numerous documents indicating that, despite known needs, black people are under-represented as recipients of personal social services. Others have demonstrated discrimination in health service provisions (Fernando, 1988; Littlewood and Lipsedge, 1982; Malek, 1985), social security (Gordon, 1986), immigration (Foot, 1965; Layton-Henry, 1985) and probation (Denney, 1992; Dominelli *et al.*, 1995; Taylor, 1981). Moreover, black people have been over-represented in schools for the educationally subnormal (Coard, 1971), criminal proceedings (AFFOR, 1978; Cook and Hudson, 1993; Hood, 1992; Tipler, 1986) and the higher echelons of the tariff system of court sentences (Dominelli, 1983; Home Office, 1986; Hood, 1992).

Black people have limited access to influential positions in the decision-making structures of both central and local government, trade union organisations, and prestigious jobs. After an absence of 58 years, four black candidates were elected to the British Parliament in 1987. Few councillors are black. For example, by the mid-1980s, although 11.4 per cent of Sandwell's population was black, only four black people had become local representatives. Moreover, its Council record as an equal opportunity employer was poor. Only between 1 per cent and 2 per cent of its employees were black, and few of these were located in the senior echelons (*Sunday Times*, 15 April 1984). This situation has changed little to the present day, and other large cities, including London, hold an equally abysmal record.

Although some authorities have encouraged black people to enter their ranks at the highest levels, these have had limited impact. Only a few social services departments – mainly in Greater London – have had black people reaching the highest management posts. However, their position is deteriorating. In contrast to the mid-1980s, no black person holds a director's post in the mid-1990s. There are many areas of public life in which black people are conspicuous by their absence. The picture is equally bleak in the higher reaches of the trade union bureaucracy, despite the disproportionately high number of black workers found within the trade union movement (GLC, 1984). By 1995, only one black man – Bill Morris – had succeeded in leading a major trade union. At the time of going to press, his position was being challenged by a white man. This in itself is highly unusual as sitting general secretaries are generally re-elected unopposed.

The experience of black people is that of welfare disenfranchisees being bombarded with systematic discrimination, the disparaging of their cultural achievements and humiliation if they dare rise above their allotted place (CCCS, 1982), despite assurances from government leaders guaranteeing them equality of treatment, justice and dignity.

Racism takes white norms as the measuring rod of life and accords worth and dignity to blue-eyed, blonde-haired, light-skinned individuals, granting those having these characteristics beauty, confidence and power. Those lacking these are made to feel ugly, dejected and powerless (Emecheta, 1983; Morrison, 1986). The social construction of black people's lives around their imputed worthlessness prepares the ground for their being pathologised and victimised. It can also lead black people to internalise white racist norms. Morrison (1986) traces the impact of these powerful motifs on the lives of black children in *The Bluest Eye*. Here, 'it is the blackness that accounts for, that creates, the vacuum edged with distaste in white eyes' (Morrison, 1986, p. 48) when black people and white people interact. Being rejected by white people because of her skin colour, one of the book's black protagonists becomes desperate to acquire blue eyes and with them, acceptance and fulfilment. Having internalised racism, she becomes 'A little black girl who wants to rise up out of the pit of her blackness and see the world with blue eyes' (Morrison, 1986, p. 161). Some of her companions refuse to be defined by the white yardstick, but they also find every aspect of their lives circumscribed by racism and have to exert considerable energy carving out the smallest space for themselves by opposing it. Speaking in oppositional terms when she is contemplating poverty and the destruction of black family life around her, one of these girls says, 'I felt a need for someone to want the black baby to live – just to counteract the universal love of white baby dolls, Shirley Temples, and Maureen Peals' (Morrison, 1986, p. 176).

These extracts reveal that racism damages oppressed people economically, socially, politically and psychologically, whilst at the same time eliciting resistance to its ravages (see Fanon, 1968; Bryan *et al.*, 1985; Collins, 1991). Meanwhile, racism operates to the economic and political advantage of the oppressors who are oblivious of the havoc they are wreaking. The vacuum in their eyes signifies the 'total absence of human recognition, the glazed separateness' (Morrison, 1986, p. 47). As a form of social control, racism keeps people in their place and rations social resources according to their position in the social hierarchy.

White social workers should bear in mind the psychological damage their racism imposes on black people who internalise the dominant values of a white society which labels blackness inferior. Such understandings become important, for example, when white social workers are confronted with black nursery-school children wanting to paint their skins white (Coard, 1971), black children in care demanding white foster parents, or black clients refusing to accept black social workers. They should not interpret these forms of behaviour as manifestations of white superiority or their desire to conform to white life-styles. Such responses are often survival responses aimed at retaining a sense of self in the context of internalised racism. They represent strategies that black people have developed for surviving the daily onslaught on their racial integrity (Bromley and Longino, 1972). If white social workers can see such conduct as part of black 'clients' as coping strategies or resistance to racism, they can take steps to protect these children from further racist damage and eradicate the racist practices which endorse and perpetuate such behaviour. Doing so prepares the ground for work to be done on enhancing the black person's sense of self.

Dealing with these situations appropriately calls for a proper assessment of the needs of black children. It also requires organisational change as well as changes in professional practice. These can include having black and white practitioners co-working to ensure that a black person's sense of self-esteem and identity can be addressed and reinforced in positive terms. For such action to be meaningful, white people can usefully adopt anti-racist forms of practice that engage with transforming the nature of social work, placing and supporting black children in black families living in black communities, and arguing for black social workers to be employed in non-tokenistic ways (BACSG, 1984). Making black dolls available to white children in nurseries, employing black staff in welfare agencies in significant numbers and in positions of authority, and developing services addressing the needs of black people are means to be used in tackling racism. They are not ends in themselves. The end of the anti-racist project can only be achieved through the elimination of racism and the establishment of egalitarian social relations throughout society.

Immigration policy has been the major public arena in which the politics of 'race' which impinge on social work practice have been officially played out. This process has shifted immigration policy from being a matter of concern to immigration officials at the point of entry, to a key mechanism for internal control (Gordon, 1984). It forms a bulwark on which institutionalised racism rests. These developments have subjected black people ordinarily resident in Britain and those born here to continual surveillance by the forces of 'law and order' and scrutiny by officers providing welfare services (Gordon, 1986; Gordon and Newnham, 1985). Immigration status is systematically used to deny black people living and working in Britain and paying its taxes 'recourse to public funds'. Only British citizens who have unconditional admittance to this country can draw benefits provided by the welfare state. Benefits from which they are excluded include national insurance benefits to which they have contributed, for example the disallowance of unemployment benefit to those on work permits, the ineligibility of children living overseas to child benefits and the denial of supplementary benefits to women whose husbands have gone on prolonged trips abroad to fulfil family obligations (Chapeltown Citizens' Advice Bureau, 1983; Gordon and Newnham, 1985).

The welfare state competes for governmental resources with capital accumulation and defence expenditure (Dominelli, 1978b). It loses out as long as the government defines public expenditure cuts in terms of limiting welfare provisions. In this context, stripping black people of their rights as citizens, curtailing the rights of 'immigrants' to welfare services, and encouraging the 'repatriation' of black people to Third

World countries which can foot the bill for their welfare, is an economically sound and integral part of Thatcherism's monetarist direction. This policy has been continued under various administrations and is evident in other Western countries, particularly the USA. The racialisation of the welfare state has become a major motif in 'New Right' ideology (see Glazer, 1988; Murray, 1990, 1994).

Social work's structural position submits the profession to bearing a share of cuts imposed on the welfare state. It also affects the roles that social workers undertake, distorts client–worker relationships by diverting resources to other purposes and skews the balance of power towards those providing or purchasing services instead of those requiring them, especially if they do not have independent means to pay for them. Black people, as an economically disadvantaged group, are at the sharp end of these processes. Depriving people of the resources they need to reproduce themselves as social entities when they are structurally excluded from doing so orients social work intervention more forcefully towards its controlling dimensions.

The high visibility of black people makes it easier for them to be targeted as objects whose eligibility to services must be authenticated above and beyond 'normal' standards. A white social worker put this to me as follows: 'I worry about whether or not I should provide welfare rights advice to Asian families coming into the office without asking for their passports first'. The possibility that these Asian families may be black British wholly entitled to welfare services is submerged by white social workers' anxieties that they are dealing with 'immigrants' who are not entitled to be here or receiving services. It is a racist position which gives black people the loud and clear message that they have not really been accepted as having a rightful place in society. In other words, black people's position as settled members of the community and contributors to its activities is being denied. The government's threat to withdraw entitlement to welfare benefits from refugees is likely to exacerbate and increase the number of such encounters.

Racism saves the government considerable sums of money. The mystification of the reprehensible connection between the exclusion of 'immigrants' from welfare provisions and the public expenditure cuts is reinforced when white social workers limit their intervention to those having popularly legitimated access to their services. The uncritical acceptance of common-sense definitions of those having access to welfare services leads white social workers to condone and confirm certain myths which are firmly embedded in racist immigration ideology and practice, for example that black people are in Britain on a temporary basis; black people are born overseas; black people provide their own welfare systems; and black people abuse welfare provisions by using them when they are not entitled to. Moreover, racist attitudes enable white social workers to participate in the provision of inappropriate services for black people, for example interpreters and home helps who are not matched for language, religion and caste. Racism also makes the Anglo-Saxon majority cautious about demanding welfare rights for themselves by fostering the view that individuals are solely responsible for their own welfare.

The endorsement of racism at the highest political levels, for example Thatcher's speech about British people being 'swamped' by an 'alien' culture (*Daily Mail*, 31 January 1978) and the 1981 Nationality Act (Gordon, 1985) have intensified the legitimacy of the view that black people *do not belong* in Britain as settlers with full citizenship rights. Making racism 'respectable' exacerbates black people's feelings of vulnerability and authorises *laissez faire* attitudes and practices endorsing inappropriate service provision and poor service delivery.

The British state has a contradictory position with regard to racism. It has made racism respectable by enshrining it in exclusionary nationality legislation enforced through immigration controls (CRE, 1985), whilst recognising 'race' as one dimension through which people can be disadvantaged. In this latter guise, it has tried to respond positively to its elimination by persuading people to accept equal opportunities for all, encouraging government bodies to become 'Equal Opportunity Employers' and promulgating legislation aimed at doing so, for example the Race Relations Acts. This legislation is difficult to enforce and does not merit the label 'anti-racist'. Legislative measures such as these can have only a limited impact on the issues they seek to address.

The state's role in the process of eradicating racism is neither a conspiratorial one nor a subordinate one in which it acts as the 'tool of the bourgeoisie'. Rather, the state as a whole is caught in the contradictory position of responding to the needs of the accumulation of capital on the one hand and the reproduction of labour power on the other (Dominelli, 1978b). This role has been intensified through the globalisation of the economy, increased international competition and the rise to power of the 'New Right'. These forces emphasise a reduction in state welfare spending, a rationing of welfare provision and the further residualisation of public social services. Racist discourses in this climate have facilitated definitions of service users which act against black people having unfettered access to welfare resources that are legitimately theirs.

Corrigan's (1977) argument that the class struggle mediates the outcome between the conflicting demands placed on the state by capital and labour is inadequate. The state, as one of Britain's largest employers and providers of welfare services, has a vested interest in the outcome of this struggle. Under a right-wing government, its ideological commitment to a 'withering away' of the state in matters of personal welfare worsens the situation. Its position is further complicated by the struggles that state employees have initiated and orchestrated over welfare provisions, for example industrial action by health service workers, fieldworkers and residential workers in social services, and teachers. Moreover, the relative autonomy confirmed on the state as mediator in these struggles gives it a certain independence from its role in guaranteeing workers their livelihoods and capital the conditions for accumulating wealth. The extent to which it can distance itself from key political actors and social processes and the direction this takes depend on who has control of the state apparatuses. Consequently, the capacity of ethnic minority groups to organise in pursuit of their specific interests and the influence which anti-racist white people can amass are crucial in affecting the decisions taken by government and the outcome of their struggle for power. The intractability of the problems posed by racism and the complexity of the political, sociological, psychological and economic forces embedded in racist social relations make a mockery of primarily economistic analysis condemning racism as false class consciousness (see Cox, 1970).

Social workers have an important role in facilitating the process of their own empowerment and that of consumers *vis-à-vis* the state by contributing to anti-racist struggles being conducted within as well as outside the social work arena. To achieve its objective of promoting people's welfare, social work has to transcend the contradiction of providing for everyone, whilst rationing resources to those 'deserving' help. Racism allows white social workers to straddle this contradiction by relegating black people to the realms of the 'undeserving' poor as welfare disenfranchisees whose access to welfare provisions is unfairly restricted.

In not confronting its own racism, social work practice belies the liberality of its ideology. Social work's failure to challenge its own racism can be attributed to its structural determinants. These are its allegedly apolitical professional stance; its emphasis on social control at the expense of caring; its role in rationing scarce welfare resources; and the way in which it problematises ethnicity.

Racism in social work practice

Racism exacerbates and extends social control in social work

At the present time, social work, like other elements in the welfare state, is being dismantled and restructured to exclude more and more people from receiving its provisions. This trend is a residualising one which will target public services on the most needy. Racist immigration laws, arbitrary checks on black people's entitlement to benefit, and the endorsement of a transient status for black people living in Britain, have seriously reduced the number of black people claiming their share of welfare resources, despite their entitlement to do so (Gordon, 1986). Illustrating this process, a study by Harambee in Lewisham revealed that despite being entitled to benefits, 50 per cent of black youth did not claim any (CIS, 1978). This attitude was exacerbated by the derogatory treatment of black youths at the hands of the then DHSS officers. As one young black man told me, 'I'm not going in there [the DHSS office] to be treated like shit. And they give you nothing'.

In a climate of public expenditure cuts which ration social services resources, the state becomes a force intensifying social workers' responsibilities as agents of social control whose tasks encompass that of reducing demands for scarce public provisions. The high visibility of certain ethnic groups, particularly black ones, makes it easier for them to be made scapegoats for the economic recession and to be targeted as subjects whose eligibility to services must be authenticated above and beyond 'normal' standards. This happens when black but not white people are required to produce their passports in order to send their children to school or receive medical care.

Public expenditure cuts reduce both the number of welfare workers and the material resources at the disposal of those remaining in the field (Loney, 1987). Meanwhile, demands for services are mounting through the pressures of unemployment and changing demographic structures. Consequently, social workers are more likely to be sucked into rationing resources to cover the largest number of clients, thereby improving efficiency, than to press for open-ended commitments to cover whatever 'needs' arise (Lowe, 1993). The criteria for determining provisions are led by economic considerations rather than human 'needs'. Social workers find they have to refuse aids and adaptations, telephones and home helps in implementing 'community care' for older people because money is tight even though they have assessed their clients as requiring them. The Social Fund further restricts social workers' response to one which can be covered by the monies at hand. Economic constraints and shifting eligibility criteria induce social workers and their managers, whether or not wearing a case manager's hat, to accept 'technical' rationing mechanisms which seem uncontentious, thus bypassing political questions embedded in resolving questions of 'need'.

The reduced availability of resources carries particular implications for black people whose specific needs receive short shrift because they have been constituted as the 'undeserving poor'. The additional resources they require to bring them to the same base line as poor white people are unlikely to be forthcoming during a period of cuts. Treating black people 'the same as everyone else' means that the deficit in resourcing going to black clients compared with white ones will not be eliminated but will remain unacknowledged. Abundant negative stereotypes of black people ensure that questions about their needs will not be raised. For example, not claiming help will continue to be interpreted as their not requiring services rather than as leading to an investigation of the relationship between white agencies and black clients; the nature and appropriateness of the services on offer; the methods of informing black people of their entitlements; and social workers' attitudes towards their demands for help. Unless they examine these areas, white social workers will carry on believing that black people do not request social services because their community networks look after them.

Within the framework of dwindling resources, the professional ethics and ideology of social work trap social workers in a further dilemma. How can social workers pay tribute to client self-determination, endorse needs-led assessments and empower clients in acquiring greater control over their lives when they operate under a state of siege? How can the conflict between black working class people's need for resources and that of white working class people be reconciled within diminishing resources? For example, how do white social workers adjudicate between the needs of a white older person needing sheltered housing and those of a black child requiring a day nursery place? It is much easier for them to avoid this quandary if they think that relationships in black communities are such that someone will step in to care for the black child. The failure of social work as a profession to confront this dilemma is problematic for both black and white workers. Concern over this issue compels black authors such as Gilroy (1987) to affirm the importance of black people controlling their own resources and autonomous spaces, whilst questioning the use of black self-help groups to perpetuate white people's view that 'black people can look after their own', thereby letting white people and institutionalised racism 'off the hook'. Thus, white social workers working in anti-racist ways have to consider racism in service delivery within a context in which the welfare state is being dismantled and restructured to exclude more and more people from receiving welfare provisions.

Social work as an 'apolitical' activity

The dilemma posed in choosing between the needs of a black and a white person reveals that social work is not an apolitical activity which can ignore power relations and the unequal distribution of resources in society. When developing anti-racist practice, white social workers have to take seriously the differential access that social groups have to these and become aware of the implications of power relations in their work with black individuals, groups and communities. This requires white social workers to recognise social work practice as a political activity in which power operates on a number of different levels, including the powers vested in them by society to allocate and distribute resources under their jurisdiction, their legal powers as social workers, and the personal power evident in their relationships with clients. Because power relations are multi-faceted and multi-dimensional, social workers may simultaneously feel powerless with respect to powerful others such as policy makers and managers.

In addition, white social workers need to be ethnically sensitive to the different meanings ascribed to social interactions by people who follow different cultural traditions from theirs and become attuned to the implications of their own dominant or majority ethnic culture on their practice. Furthermore, they need to be aware of the diversity contained within their own ethnic culture and that of other ethnic groups. Ethnic sensitivity does not mean accepting inhumane acts as 'normal' in any culture. Nor does it justify tolerating dehumanising behaviour in any given situation. Social workers will still have to exercise their judgement over contentious issues and not use 'culture' as an excuse for not doing so.

Not spotting child abuse in black families because they are perceived as disciplinarian is one example. By engaging with these issues, white social workers will acquire knowledge about themselves, their value systems and how they legitimate relations endorsing white supremacy. Moreover, white social workers have to grapple with the constraints imposed by their being state employees doling out scarce resources. These establish boundaries around the options open to them and are difficult to transcend

(Simpkins, 1980). Additionally, their vulnerability as employees is increased if they adopt overtly political stances at odds with either agency or state objectives. This latter becomes particularly problematic when the state furthers racist practices through specific social policy measures. However, taking risks lies at the heart of social work. Recognising that black people's lives are endangered through racist practices is another way of acknowledging that racism places black people's lives at risk. Tackling this may mean that social workers take risks with their own job security and career prospects, but it is unavoidable if their anti-racist initiatives are being opposed by those who hold power over them.

The obstacle of professionalism

Professionalism in social work practice has been elaborated on the premises that social workers have 'faith in the system' (Compton and Galaway, 1975, p. 34), maintain their distance from clients and do not get involved in 'political' issues. A professional social worker is not interested in challenging the social structures in which the social work task occurs and remains objectively neutral on the major social concerns of the day during work time. Sadly, these expressions of professionalism persist despite the existence of equal opportunities policies. Consequently, white social workers who subscribe to such views either ignore the presence of racism or do not concern themselves directly with it. Their work with black clients replicates that done with white clients, thereby inadvertently reproducing racist policies and practice.

Social workers are expected to deal with people by empathising with their condition, according them respect and dignity, and facilitating their access to the resources and expertise they need to assume control over their lives (Compton and Galaway, 1975). This position is difficult to achieve in normal relationships with clients. For example, Seebohm (1968) revealed that 60 per cent of social work clients had financial problems which social workers needed to address. However, social workers and probation officers lack the resources necessary for responding to cries for financial aid. As one angry woman on probation for shoplifting informed me:

> My probation officer's useless. I need money to feed my kids. Not tea and sympathy. But I know he's got none to give me. So he tells me to behave myself and not get into trouble again.

The arrival of National Standards has not improved this aspect of the worker–client relationship. As one young man on probation told me:

> He's [probation officer] just got time to see me the regulation 10 minutes every couple of weeks. We don't do much after we get past 'How're things going?' I asked him to help me get a job once and he gave me these papers for training. I'd already been on YTS – a worthless lark, and wasn't having more of the same.

Whilst social workers currently have access to limited amounts of money under discretionary budgets for the purposes of alleviating financial hardship, and the 1989 Children Act, these sources alone are incapable of meeting clients' monetary requirements. 'Befriending' offenders has been removed as an objective of supervision in a probation order. Thus, social workers and probation officers often find themselves in the frustrating position of knowing what clients need but feeling hopelessly unable to help them achieve it. Therefore, they continue as before to be involved in 'papering over the cracks' and making 'poverty seem the client's fault' (Bailey and Brake, 1975).

Additionally, social workers' position as professionals may undermine their capacity for empathy. They may be underpaid, but they do not have the same financial starting point as their clients. Power differences may also intensify the social control element in social work and thwart clients' aspirations for improvement. As their attention is deflected onto resolving 'clients' personal problems', social workers and probation officers expend considerable energy teaching clients to change their behaviour, making it conform more closely to 'acceptable' standards. For black clients, this has led white social workers to downplay the specific circumstances and avenues through which racism holds black people back and deprives them of resources, power, justice and dignity. As one young Afro-Caribbean man I interviewed said:

> I got done with TWOC [stealing a motor car] a few years back and sent to Borstal for 6 months. About a year later, this fancy Porsche was nicked not far from here. The police came banging on my door, saying I'd done it. I hadn't. I had me own car then. I'd got this job you see. But they keep coming round any time anything happens. And it's not 'cause they know me, it's 'cause I'm black. I was driving this brand new car once – a Rover I'd borrowed from a mate. And the police stopped me. Wouldn't believe my story. They said, 'People like you don't buy cars like this.' And they charged me... My probation officer said, 'I shouldn't worry about it. The police were just doing their job. They were wondering where people like you get money to buy expensive cars'. He then asked me if I sold drugs to get all the nice things me and my girlfriend had in the house. I got real mad. And he said he was joking!

The failure of white social workers to take on board the specific conditions affecting black people has meant that they have colluded with the continued denial of their access to resources, dignity and justice. The following example also exemplifies this problem:

An Afro-Caribbean woman left her two young children with their Afro-Caribbean father to work temporarily on the Continent. Shortly after her departure, the man also found a job. He tried desperately hard to get help with the child care, but was not successful. So he found himself juggling several timetables trying to manage on his own. After a while, the children started truanting from school and were eventually caught stealing goods from the local supermarket. A white social worker speaking to the father asked how he was going to ensure the kids attended school and did not get into trouble. Was he going to call his 'wife' back? He explained he could not and asked what facilities social services could offer. When he was told 'none', he insisted that he be given support. But the white social worker replied, 'Why don't you ask a member of your extended family to help you with them? You Africans are always looking after each other's children.'

Additionally, white social workers' concern to get clients behaving appropriately has problematised ethnicity by judging black people according to dominant stereotypes of their ethnic grouping. Belonging to an 'inferior' ethnic group means automatically being defined a problem by white social workers. The following illustrates the point:

A young Afro-Caribbean man was charged with 'causing grievous bodily harm' during an affray. The probation officer who was asked to complete a social enquiry report on him said 'Another one of those! West Indians are always getting into difficulties. They've such violent tempers. They flash at the drop of a hat. You've got to be ever so careful with them'.

Social work's poor showing on racism indicates the intractability of the problems confronting anti-racist social workers and trainers. It also means that to attack racism, white social workers and educators must adopt political and theoretical perspectives which are more than just ethnically sensitive. They must produce theories of welfare which acknowledge social work's social control function, recognise its dual position within state structures – a controller of substantial resources and the upholder of a caring ideology – and promote anti-racist social work practice. Thus, to ***develop anti-racist social work, we need to cut the Gordian knot of social work as a complex and contradictory form of social control***.

Anti-racist social work is not a case of simply adding 'race' to our considerations of a basically benign social work. What is required is the transformation of social work practice through the creation of social relations fostering racial equality and justice. To move in this direction, social work has to adopt a political stance against racism on cultural, institutional and personal levels within practice, social work education and the state apparatus more generally. This begins the process of ending racism perpetrated and legitimated by the state itself, and challenging a professionalism whose neutrality disguises support for the *status quo*. Professionalism would have to be redefined to enable white practitioners to transform their work by refusing to perpetuate practices which enclosed racial oppression.

Meanwhile, white social workers' failure to acknowledge the more subtle and covert forms of racism permeating practice has resulted in their unwittingly exacerbating black people's experience of racism. White social workers reinforce racism during service delivery through (a) the intentional and unintentional use of racism as a form of social control that keeps black people in their place, (b) the perpetuation of universalistic (the same service for everyone) treatment of all client groups, thereby ignoring the extreme hardship that racist treatment imposes on black people, and (c) overtly racist practices.

The colour-blind approach and the universality of treatment

Social workers have incorporated racist elements in their practice by adopting the view that black people are like white people. Referred to as the *colour-blind approach*, its dynamics cover far more than those whereby white social workers ignore the colour of black people's skin. It is not that white social workers are unaware of the colour of a person's skin, but that they discount its significance. Or, as two of them have put it to me:

Race is unimportant. Knowing them as people is.
I treat black people and white people the same. We are all members of the human race. There are no differences between people for me.

Colour-blindness is expressed primarily through the concept of 'universality of treatment', whereby *equality* is assumed rather than proven because all individuals and groups are treated as if they were 'all the same'. This assumption reduces everyone to the same common denominator, without regard to the material position they actually occupy either as individuals or as members of a specific social group. Little account is taken of the lower socio-economic positions that black people occupy; their different cultural traditions, familial organisation and obligations; their attitudes towards life, society and its social institutions; the variety and heterogeneity in their midst; and the systemic racism they endure daily. On occasion, these differences are recognised but judged as inferior to attributes held by white people or irrelevant to their concerns. So, pressure is put on black people to conform either to white people's standards or to their stereotypes of them.

Besides ignoring how structural inequality curtails black people's opportunities and access to social resources, this approach is rooted in white supremacy. Only those belonging to the dominant group enjoy the privilege of discounting the difference that 'race' makes to the quality of services available to them and their use of them. The colour-blind approach is conceptually linked to the 'new racism'. Both harbour the idea that individuals and groups need not specifically refer to 'race' because it is visually obvious which 'race' is being considered, and the underlying assumptions about 'race' do not need spelling out. The colour-blind approach also contains a dynamic which endorses white supremacy: the pressure placed on individuals and groups to conform to 'desirable' behaviour as specified by the dominant ruling group. The standards this exemplifies are compatible with maintaining bourgeois hegemony through the medium of white, middle class heterosexuality. In social work intervention with black people, this is evident when white social workers attempt to make black individuals, families or communities become white by adopting white life-styles.

White social workers' training, professional ethics and service delivery lend credence to the view that, apart from relatively insignificant individual differences which can be subsumed through individual casework, the British population is largely homogeneous and racial factors unimportant (see Cheetham, 1972). Practitioners assume that universalistic treatment is the best basis for preserving equality amongst individuals (ADSS/CRE, 1978). Differences and inequalities arising from the structuring of social relations to reflect the interests of powerful groups are discounted. Moreover, social workers seeking to achieve 'ethnic sensitivity' and reflect multi-cultural dimensions in their work have continued to treat individuals from a particular ethnic group as 'all the same'. The tendency to 'homogenise' black individuals and groups is reflected in their reference to '*the* black community', '*the* black family'.

They may be aware that the experience of a Jamaican is different from that of a Nigerian, but they perceive the experience of all Jamaicans to be similar. Besides 'race', 'universality of treatment' ignores the effects of other social divisions such as gender and class on individual circumstances. Moreover, the homogenising tendency also operates with respect to these. So, women clients' attention is focused on their responsibility to care for children and men (Wilson, 1977). Working class people are exhorted to emulate white middle class life-styles without having access to similar resources (Bailey and Brake, 1975). Convergence between these social divisions and the universality principle grant white, upper class, Anglo-Saxon males the most advantage and black, working class women the least.

The *universality of treatment* coupled with an uncritical casework approach to their task has resulted in white social workers contributing a further dimension to the racist burden already borne by black clients through discrimination in other parts of the welfare state and immigration controls. This forms the crux of the interaction between personal, institutional and cultural racism. It also ensures that black people's welfare is jeopardised by the very institutions whose responsibility it is to promote it.

Besides preventing white social workers from seeing for themselves the significance of bringing black clients to the same socio-economic starting line as white clients, the universality principle inhibits their ability to explain the need for doing so to others. Yet, identifying the gap between black and white working class people's access to power and resources is essential to stemming the backlash from poor, working class, white individuals who are also disadvantaged. However, although both black and white working class people experience deprivation through class, only black people are denied power and resources through 'race'. The connection between class and 'race' accounts for the disparity between them. Recognition of such differences and the points from which they emanate matters in promoting racial equality and preventing a white backlash which ignores the impact of racism by focusing only on undifferentiated class-based deprivation (see Morris, 1994). The formation of alliances between black organisations and white, working class ones is problematic because racism permeates the activities of white, working class people who also benefit from racism (CCCS, 1982). Working class racism has to be addressed as an issue because racism legitimates a rationing of scarce resources by excluding black people as 'undeserving'. Hence, white working class people get privileged access to resources and benefit from an unfair distribution system. As 'deserving' recipients, white working class people are allocated resources as individual members of a specific group with a recognised claim. Individual merit in these situations becomes secondary and at times irrelevant.

Systematic racism means that white social workers demanding resources for one black person are wide of the mark, even if they succeed in getting these. Every other black person facing racial discrimination will have to undergo a similar process of legitimating need by escaping the category of 'undeserving'. For example, a white social worker seeking housing for black families will repeatedly discover that their being a *black* family is crucial to the housing authority's response. Various assumptions about black families' immigration status, size and links with their communities impinge on their rights to public housing. These are taken into account in ways which exclude them from the best council housing stock, repayment mortgages and desirable residential areas (CRE, 1984; Jacobs, 1985). How these exclusionary dynamics operate is exemplified by Bangladeshi families in Tower Hamlets being denied council housing for making themselves intentionally homeless by emigrating to Britain (*Guardian*, 28 April 1987). The criteria regarding intentional homelessness in housing allocation policies were applied against these families as *black* families. Against a backdrop of systematic racism, white social workers appealing for 'positive discrimination' for black people confuse the issue. Black people do not ask for 'positive discrimination' because they lack qualifications and experience as white people frequently alleged. They demand the elimination of racism because they are systematically discriminated against and have both their qualifications and experience devalued. Systematic discrimination must be eradicated on the basis of redressing systemic unjust treatment and not special pleading for individuals or groups.

Racism in social work: a social issue

White social workers wishing to eliminate racism in their practice must redefine racism in social work as a social issue rather than just a personal one and ally themselves individually and as a group with progressive, anti-racist forces within both the central state apparatus and social work. They can develop initiatives for organising these forces directly, and use their membership of political organisations, trade unions, professional associations, employing authorities and training bodies to those ends. Some have already done so through NAPO and NALGO (now incorporated into UNISON). Only by continual vigilance and action against racism perpetuated by themselves and those organisations and bodies governing on their behalf, can white social workers begin to dent the racist bulwark underpinning social work.

White social workers adopting an anti-racist position have a consciousness-raising role to play in enabling white people to perceive racism as a social issue. Their day-to-day interactions with black people living in decaying urban areas, resisting poverty and coming to grips with hardship provides them with information for countering racist claims that black people are responsible for creating their own problems. White practitioners can challenge such allegations by using their practice experience to demonstrate the resilience of black people in overcoming adversity. This also gives social workers an edge in participating in public debates about poverty, its social causes, its debilitating effects on individual personalities, and its destructive impact on black–white relationships. Also, they can use knowledge so gained to argue for the transformation of social work practice in accordance with egalitarian anti-racist principles.

In making these comments, I am conveying a different message from the one that white people normally communicate to black people. I am saying that the responsibility for dismantling society's racist edifice belongs to white people who enjoy the privileges emanating from it. The primary task of white social workers wishing to implement anti-racist practice is to change their own racist attitudes and practices and those of the organisations within which they work. If they were to do this, black social workers could concentrate on getting resources to black communities instead of exhausting their energies helping white social workers to overcome their racism.

Meanwhile, white social workers need to acknowledge that black people have not been passive in the face of racist onslaughts. They have organised as black people to defend their interests, challenge white people's understanding of their oppression and demand an end to personal, institutional and cultural racism (CCCS, 1982; Gilroy, 1987; Moore, 1978). White people need to respond positively to the anti-racist agenda that black people have placed before them.

2

Social Work Training is Imbued with Racism

Social work educators have done little to challenge the racism inherent in their theories and practice. Although it had published several documents on the matter, the Central Council for Education and Training in Social Work (CCETSW) had failed to incorporate anti-racist measures as a compulsory part of the curriculum until the introduction of the Diploma in Social Work (DipSW) in 1990. This requirement has been highly controversial and poorly enforced. CCETSW's attempts to provide guidance on anti-racist social work in the form of publications written by the Northern Curriculum Development Project has backfired by prompting a backlash (see Pinker, 1993; Dunant, 1994; Phillips, 1993). By the mid-1990s, the backlash had led to the removal of Appendix 5 from Paper 30 and the disbanding of the Black Perspectives Committee. Academic disciplines are based on anglocentric models which take white British culture, history and achievements as the norm. Psychological theory and human development is considered largely in terms of the white British male standard. Discussions about the family centre on the white, middle class, heterosexual nuclear family as the favoured type. Variations from this are deemed 'deviant' and undesirable (Eichler, 1984; Lorde, 1984; Segal, 1983). Social policy is invariably British, glorifying white British processes and institutions.

Unacknowledged racism has been a central theme in the theories and ideologies used in setting up the British welfare state and characterises all post-war social policy (Williams, 1987). Law teaching ignores the racist dimension in the implementation of legislation (Gordon, 1984) and the racist bases on which it is formulated (Layton-Henry, 1985), or it treats it cursorily (Freeman, 1992). The epistemological base and political philosophy of social work education endorse the *status quo*, of which racism is an integral feature. Practice placements are also poorly equipped for training students in anti-racist social work. Work countering racism, if included, is badly integrated into the student's overall programme. Although anti-racist policies may be present in placement agencies, their implementation is inadequately resourced and imperfectly monitored (Ahmad, 1990; Dominelli *et al.*, 1995). White practice teachers often need greater support and expertise in delivering effective anti-racist practice teaching; black practice teachers remain few in numbers.

CCETSW has failed to make an anti-racist stance permeate its own structures by employing sufficient numbers of black staff in its key policy-making structures. At its most senior levels, its one black manager left in 1995 after a few years in post and has been replaced by a white man. In 1986, *one* Council member was black. By 1995 this had increased to *two*, even though CCETSW's advisory Black Perspectives Committee had been disbanded. More black staff have been employed in the Central Office, but their role is largely one of implementing policies formulated by others. CCETSW has not required teaching staff on validated courses to reflect the make-up of society. In the DipSW, the main arena in which black perspectives have been evident in any significant way is amongst the external assessors group, where black assessors have formed their own collective to exercise greater purchase on decision making. But even their influence on the outcome of the Review of Paper 30 in 1994 has been marginal (Black Assessors, 1994).

The social work curriculum: an analysis of the racism permeating the social work literature

The social work literature, although espousing a liberal democratic commitment to equality for all, has been remiss in its handling of racism. The failure of social work theories specifically to address racism has been reflected in the forms of practice they espouse. Jansari (1980) and Denney (1983), reviewing the social work literature, have indicated how limited the treatment of racism has been. By 1995 the picture they portray of the early 1980s has altered little. But the issue transcends this, for even literature aiming quite hard *not* to do so, *unintentionally reproduces racist stereotypes and biases*. Despite the authors' intentions, some publications suggest that black people's culture is responsible for the racist treatment they receive; see, for example, *Race and Social Work*

(Coombe and Little, 1986). Black people continue to be the problem, as the following quote exemplifies:

> Because of the nature of their employment and the cultural restrictions imposed on them, the majority of first-generation Cypriots – more women than men – have had little opportunity to mix with the mainstream society and learn the English language. As mentioned above, children with non-English speaking parents begin school at a disadvantage, which may impair their educational performance. (Orphanides in Coombe and Little, 1986, p. 84)

As the problem is located amongst Cypriot parents via their failure to learn English, the question of why English society failed to welcome Cypriot people into its midst and provide them with non-stigmatised resources for both learning English and retaining the Cypriot sense of cultural identity is never formulated. The identification of the problem in the terms evoked by *Race and Social Work* enables racism committed by omission to remain undetected. Despite their intention of espousing 'good practice' with black people, an examination of the theory and practice expounded in exemplary classic texts on social work with black people reveals that the impact of racism on black clients is largely ignored. *Social Work with Immigrants* (Cheetham, 1972) and *Social Work with Coloured Immigrants and their Families* (Triseliotis, 1972a) endorse the views that the number of black people in Britain should be limited and that helping them ought to be directed towards their assimilation into British society. The doctrine of assimilation assumes the superiority of the culture to which people are being assimilated, i.e. white British culture. Thus, these texts have encouraged white social workers to think of black people as *the problem* to be addressed, thereby unintentionally harming black people's interests.

Cheetham and Triseliotis define black people as 'reluctant settlers' who are imposing a 'burden' on social services, a claim feeding off the public's hysteria on 'race' at the time but unsupported by the facts. Black people have made a positive choice in coming to Britain, seizing it as an opportunity to *improve their lot* (Ahmed, 1984). The majority of black people are economically active, making few demands on social services (Ely and Denney, 1987). Besides, these texts ignore institutionalised racism in state policy and practice, for example on immigration issues. The 1971 Immigration Act, passed whilst these books were being written, systematically undermined the rights of black people to enter Britain as *settlers*. Earlier legislation had denied Kenyan and Ugandan Asians holding British passports settlement rights. The 1962 Commonwealth Immigration Act had imposed restrictions on the unfettered right of Commonwealth citizens to enter, settle and work in Britain (Layton-Henry, 1985).

These classic texts also reinforce racism through their conceptualisation of the social work task. Social work as casework is imbued with counselling techniques, focusing on individual clients and assuming that 'immigrant' clients are the same as other clients except for having more of the problems with which caseworkers are already acquainted (Cheetham, 1972). These similarities, (white) social work educators contend, make (white) practitioners' existing experience adequate preparation for working with black people.

The experiences of black people at the time and subsequently have denied the validity of this approach to social work (see Emecheta, 1983; Ahmad, 1990; Riley, 1985). From their perspective, understanding the social work task as advocated by Cheetham (1972) is misconceived. Firstly, it ignores the fact that it is primarily *white* social workers constructing a casework relationship with *black* people, thereby decontextualising 'race' and obscuring the power differential and privileges accessible to white professionals but not black clients. This criticism might have been less serious if white social workers had used it to create a breathing space for becoming aware of the significance of the racist dynamics operating in the casework relationship. Unfortunately, despite black people's endeavours in highlighting this point (see Gitterman and Schaeffer, 1972; Ahmad, 1990; Kadushin 1972; Mizio, 1972), this definition of the social work task remains dominant in the educational establishment and the field.

In treating black people in the same way as white people, white social workers ignore the impact of the power imbalance above and beyond that emanating from their position as professionals in the social work relationship. Its persistence reveals that those who are in power need neither justify their use of power nor spontaneously challenge it. Secondly, these strictures mystify the position of black people. Black people do *not* have the *same* problems as white people. *White people's right to be in Britain is not being questioned; white people belong here. Black people do not: they are guests.* Or so the thinking goes. The host–guest relationship underpinning black–white interaction reinforces the power of the former over the latter, who are in Britain on their host's sufferance. Moreover, although unrecognised in classic texts, such an unequal relationship between black and white people reinforces ideas about white supremacy. Research I am currently undertaking indicates that the host–guest basis of black–white interaction is a key motif informing the framework that white social workers throughout the European continent use in relating to black clients.

Having not experienced racialised rejection as an integral part of their society, white social workers are hard pushed to understand, let alone empathise with, the circumstances around which black people's lives are constructed. Moreover, since white social workers benefit from the existence of racism, they lack the material base from which to extend empathy to black people. The colonising experience in North America reveals how white settlers' assumptions about *racial and cultural* superiority facilitated the perpetration of cultural and racial genocide on First Nations peoples. Haig-Brown (1988) describes in detail how the policy of assimilating the indigenous population into white culture was systematically pursued in an Indian residential school in Canada:

> Their education must consist not merely of the training of the mind, but of a weaning from the habits and feelings of their ancestors, and the acquirements of the language, arts and customs of civilised life. (Haig-Brown, 1988, p. 29)

The failure of white social workers to appreciate the power and privileges they enjoy because they live in a racist society, and their fundamental misunderstanding of black peoples' experiences, facilitates the fostering of racist stereotypes in their practice. Abundantly interspersed throughout the social work literature, these include stereotypes of Asian women as passive and sexually repressed (Khan, 1979); Asian girls as 'caught between two cultures' (Triseliotis, 1972a); West Indians as sexually promiscuous (Moynihan, 1965); West Indian parents as over-ambitious for their children and over-disciplinarian in their child rearing (Triseliotis, 1972a); and West Indian families as unable to provide the environment for the nuclear family to prosper (Fitzherbert, 1967).

Social work texts are imbued with unexplored notions of white supremacy which are then translated into practice. The stereotypes they propagate provide useful motifs for pathologising black individuals, families, communities and cultures, and portraying black people as passive victims, taking whatever is hurled at them. For example, a Chinese student is considered 'blind to all expressions of anger and resentment' by her white placement supervisor because of the 'Chinese insistence on politeness and reverence' (Kent in Triseliotis, 1972a, p. 45). The possibility that this reaction is part of the young woman's coping strategy for surviving in a hostile, unsafe environment does not occur to the (white) practice teacher. Yet, if she had protested, the student would probably have been considered an aggressive troublemaker who had to be watched all the time.

Emigration is also deemed problematic. Firstly, it is termed 'migration', which suggests a temporal state of existence, i.e. black people are not here to stay. Secondly, 'migration' is blamed for the problems necessitating social work intervention. For example, the problems being experienced by Anthea, a West Indian child who skips school, and her family are assessed as 'the inevitable result of migration' (Cheetham in Triseliotis, 1972a, p. 63). The question of whether Anthea is going through a rebellious adolescent phase or whether the school system is providing Anthea with the type of schooling she needs is never raised. The problem is located within the child and her family for failing to adjust to the 'British' way of life. By presenting black people in this light, these authors endorse the implicit assumption that (white) British institutions and culture are superior. Thus, (white) social workers' task is defined as helping 'immigrants' to come to terms with limited abilities and employment opportunities (Cheetham, 1972, p. 53), thereby ignoring the damage that racism inflicts psychologically and materially on black people. Meantime, black people are compelled to endure these tribulations as the price they pay for demonstrating their abilities in 'coping' with life in difficult circumstances (see Emecheta, 1983). Racist policies and practices are camouflaged as the searchlight focuses on the qualities of black people themselves.

Whilst highlighting the racial origins of clients, these texts do not identify those of their social workers. I have added the word (white) in the appropriate places because it is clear that the 'race' being ignored is white. The fact that these authors do not consider it important explicitly to specify the 'race' of the workers in this context is racist. The powerful are conscious neither of their whiteness, nor of the privileges their position bestows on them (Katz, 1978). Yet, the failure to acknowledge racist dynamics in black–white interactions seriously hampers the possibility of establishing a real helping relationship between white workers and black clients (Gitterman and Schaeffer, 1972, p. 286).

Moreover, it is not simply white social workers relying on casework techniques who perpetuate racist practices. White social workers doing groupwork and community work handle racism equally badly. The community work literature, for example *Current Issues in Community Work* (Gulbenkian Community Work Group, 1976), focuses primarily on (white) community workers working in small groups and neighbourhoods which are treated as homogeneous (white) units. Black authors have complained that white community workers fail to appreciate that 'Their neighbourhood is invariably one which excludes "the blacks" who live next door or over the road' (Ohri and Manning, 1982, p. 6). White community workers trying to counter racism in their activities do not root their efforts in either social structures or the specific relationships they establish with black people. Rather, they marginalise racism, treating it as the product of racial prejudices held by a small number of individuals. Racism thereby becomes an issue to be educated away through Multi-Racial Festivals (Ohri and Manning, 1982). Moreover, the competencies for community workers produced in the mid-1990s take scant note of the anti-racist dimensions of practice (see ACW/Mainframe, 1994).

The problem that white practitioners and social work educators have to address is not simply that the skills and methods expounded by orthodox social work theories are inadequate, but that the concepts embedded in these theories themselves are fallacious. What makes this realisation more worrying is that anti-racist critiques of social work cannot be confined to orthodox theories alone. A range of progressive social work analyses has been found wanting when measured by the anti-racist yardstick. The integrated methods approach typified by Pincus and Minahan in *Social Work Practice: Model and Method* has been criticised by Dominelli and McLeod (1982) for failing to address racism. Amos and Parmar (1984) and Carby (1982) have highlighted the racist nature of white feminist theories. Feminist inattention to this issue in social work is exemplified in Brook and Davis' *Women, the Family and Social Work* (1985). Social work texts written from a Left and/or Marxist perspective have paid scant attention to racism: Curno's *Political Issues in Community Work* (1978); Simpkins' *Trapped Within Welfare* (1980); Corrigan and Leonard's *Social Work Under Capitalism* (1979) and Bolger *et al.*'s *Towards a Socialist Welfare Practice* (1981). More recently, radical authors have attempted to cover this gap by 'adding on' a chapter on racism, for example in Langan and Lee's, *Radical Social Work Today* (1989), Langan and Day's *Women and Oppression* (1989) and Thompson's *Anti-discriminatory Practice* (1993).

Examining the racism inherent in current definitions of social work

The problematic of the casework approach

Defining the social work task in casework terms is a barrier to white social workers confronting racist practice because, in ignoring the social context of social work, the significance of institutional and cultural racism or its structural components is lost. Looking at the interpersonal dynamics within client–worker relationships is important because workers reproduce racist practices through personal racism as it is reflected in their behaviour and collusion with racist policies by their silence over these. But simply doing this is insufficient. The white social worker–black client relationship does not exist in a social vacuum unrestrained by social, political and economic forces, although white practitioners operate as if it did. This is also a view virtually unchallenged in the literature that white social work educators write. Treated as being outside the scope of the casework relationship, policies are taken as given. Individual practice is evaluated only from within its own framework of the services available and those actually provided without considering the impact of policies on it.

Moreover, the casework approach pathologises white social workers who are held accountable for structural as well as personal failings if their services are judged by either supervisors or clients to be inappropriate. This makes individual workers feel vulnerable, defensive and powerless in initiating change. It also obscures white social workers' responsibility in challenging power relationships on the structural levels, and puts the focus for change on the wrong target – white social workers' failings, such as a lack of knowledge of other cultures. Overcoming white social workers' ignorance of non-Anglo-Saxon cultures is important in remedying cultural insularity. However, defining overcoming racism as the removal of cultural gaps is an inadequate solution to the immensity of the problem being tackled and its complexities. Knowing about others' cultures does not eradicate structural inequalities. Besides, cultural knowledge can become a further avenue through which black people are further pathologised by being measured against the 'white' yardstick (Ahmed 1978; CCCS, 1982; Gilroy, 1987). For example, instead of seeing black people's decision to leave dependants in their country of origin as a rational response to the lack of housing, child care and uncertain job prospects facing them on arrival, white social workers define it as a negative cultural trait with a propensity to cause problems when the family is reunited (e.g. Cheetham in Triseliotis, 1972a).

Moreover, casework professionalism portrays social work as a liberal profession graced with mutual tolerance and encourages white social workers to treat prejudice and discrimination as a matter of interpersonal dynamics, which can be quickly remedied by being educated away in classes describing the life-styles of different ethnic groups. But prejudice and discrimination feed off social conditions and their sanctification and legitimation in legal, political, social and cultural institutions. This makes for an interdependence and interconnection between the structural and the personal elements of racism, both of which must be tackled if racial oppression is to be eradicated.

Questioning the propensity of traditional casework to provide relevant services for black people, Cheetham subsequently moves away from casework-oriented 'social work with immigrants' to 'ethnically sensitive social work'. This includes other social work methods, such as community work and advice giving (Cheetham, 1981, 1982a, b). Although talking about (white) social workers' obligation to respond to the 'needs' of ethnic minority groups and bring about organisational changes to facilitate their doing so, Cheetham still ignores the significance of the workers' 'race'. An advance on her previous position, this shift remains problematic. Highlighting the marginal position that black people occupy, she continues to pathologise them by holding them responsible for it (Cheetham, 1981, p. 17), thereby blaming the victims of racism for their predicament.

Alhough carrying an expectation that organisational change will trigger off further changes, Cheetham's prescription oversimplifies the problem that is to be addressed. It fails to include those changes in national policies and attitudes necessary for securing anti-racist organisational change in social work, for example immigration policies restricting black people's citizenship rights. It also neglects the importance of incorporating personal change in the organisational change process. Without this, the commitment to ongoing reform will be lost amidst personal opposition emanating from racist white people. Personal change is essential for individual social workers fostering anti-racist social policy and practice. Furthermore, Cheetham (1981) naively assumes that the welfare state is there to *meet people's needs*. This view minimises forces undermining that objective. In recent years, these have been extended to include the welfare state's social control functions; the limitations imposed by successive waves of public expenditure cuts; the withdrawal of 'discretionary' payments; the intensification of cuts in social security provisions following the Fowler Review and subsequent Social Security Acts; the series of reductions in benefits initiated under Prime Minister John Major's administration; the application of a 'residence test' which will deny black people access to social security benefits; and a right-wing government ideologically committed to the dismantling the welfare state. With dwindling welfare resources on hand, (white) social workers will find Cheetham's suggestion of becoming welfare rights advocates a puny mechanism for dealing with racism in social work.

An analysis aimed at eradicating racism must examine the effects of cuts in welfare expenditure on the poorer sections of society. These must be balanced against increased public outlays on 'law and order', defence spending, subsidies to the private sector, tax relief for the better-off segments of society, and the hidden 'welfare' system of massive tax exemptions directing national taxation resources towards the wealthy. These reveal the class, 'race' and gender biases in the social control apparatus and demonstrate the inaccuracy of allegations that black people secure more than their fair share of resources through discrimination in their favour. Better-off white people continue to amass a disproportionate share of society's resources. White social work theorists going beyond 'race' and ethnicity to stress the total social construction of racism can expose the falseness of such claims.

By considering the impact of racism on black people's lives more directly, Cheetham's lengthy introduction to the more recent publication *Social Work with Black Children and their Families* (1987), edited in collaboration with Ahmed *et al.*, is a substantial improvement on her earlier material. However, the book as a whole fails to transcend the limitations of traditional casework approaches to social work and lacks a theory of racism which contextualises social work within the broader society (Ahmed *et al.*, 1987). Critical questions are not asked: Why does social work perpetuate racism when it is supposedly geared to meeting people's welfare needs? Why should social workers assume a political role by struggling against racism? What role can white social work practitioners and educators have in anti-racist social work? The contradictions between responding to individual distress and overcoming structural constraints ignored in casework relationships remain unresolved. Since then, a few texts have attempted to address both structural and personal racism, and posit more effective ways of working with black clients; take, for example, Bandana Ahmad's *Black Perspec-*

tives in Social Work (1990), Dominelli *et al.*'s *Anti-racist Probation Practices* (1995) and CCETSW's publications through the Northern Curriculum Project. Important as these texts have been in providing guidance on anti-racist policies and practice, they have had a limited impact on the dismantling of the racist edifice within which social work takes place. Structural change must accompany transformations in the intellectual terrain.

Cultural racism and the pathologising of individuals and cultures

The casework approach is riddled with cultural racism, i.e. the belief in the superiority of the Anglo-Saxon culture coupled with the disparaging of black people's life-styles. This is apparent in attitudes which belittle black people's behavioural norms and their expectations for improving their lot (Gilroy, 1987). Cultural racism is also reflected in white social workers' scepticism about black families' child-rearing practices, contempt for the close relationships between black parents and their children, and disdain in judging women's position within black families (Gilroy, 1987). Practices which white social workers find tolerable amongst white clients – for example inter-generational conflict between parents and adolescents – become alarming among black clients. Such behaviour, considered normal between white parents and their children, is defined as dangerous 'cultural conflict' in black families (Ahmed, 1984). As one white social worker told me, defining the problem in this manner legitimates intervention to 'free black children from the oppressive ties of their culture'. Healthy signs of black adolescents demonstrating independence and a questioning of parental authority are pathologised by white social workers (Ahmed, 1984), who subsequently subject black people to stricter surveillance and control, rapidly making clients of them as a host of welfare agencies descends upon them. Gilroy (1982b) refers to this as 'differential intensity'. White social work educators struggling against racism should cease endorsing such practices in their teaching.

Some writers, for example Husband (1980a), identify racism in social work practice as a white problem. However, this analysis lacks a historical perspective, fails to elaborate how class and gender interact with 'race', and provides social psychological explanations which include white social workers in the circle of pathology. They are blamed for not understanding the 'cultural traditions' of black people, not being sympathetic to their way of life, and not speaking their language. The onus is put on white social workers to change their behaviour and learn more about black people as *black* people. Whilst such measures are important in combating individual racism, it allows institutional racism to continue. Husband concludes that 'multi-racial social work is culturally competent casework, combined with organisational sensitivity to the needs of blacks'. Organisational change becomes a matter of 'sensitivity' grafted onto casework techniques. In failing to address the problem of racism as a construct of social organisation at the structural level, culturally competent casework enmeshes black cultures in a tangle of pathology and barely advances the struggle for developing anti-racist social work practice. Husband's approach, like that of earlier writers, does not ask for the transformation of social work. Nor does it enable white social workers to question prevailing definitions of the social work task and the structured inequality within which intervention occurs.

Social workers' willingness to practise culturally competent casework by learning about black people's cultures has also been redefined in negative ways by the 'new racists' (see Barker, 1981), who have pulled together the pathologising of black cultures with the pathologising of white social workers. In criticising white social workers' failure to deal appropriately with the social problems confronting society, and castigating social work's remote and bureaucratised professionalism, the 'new racists' have undermined social work's helping objectives and redirected service delivery towards control and containment (Gilroy, 1987). The white media's handling of 'race' and crime statistics contributes further to the pathologising process by conflating 'race' and 'crime' to endorse the view that black people are responsible for 'high crime rates' and economic decline (Hall *et al.*, 1977).

Consequently, the 'new racists' blame social work 'do-gooders' for helping clients, especially black clients, rather than being concerned with society's objectives of maintaining 'law and order' and aiding the victims of client aggression. The racialising of the 'dangerous underclasses' is particularly evident in America (Morris, 1994; S. Small, 1994). Moreover, racialised discourses promoted by right-wing thinkers use social work's general lack of support amongst the populace to link failed 'do-gooding' with permissiveness on 'race', scroungers and 'law and order' (see Murray, 1990, 1994). As a result of this linkage in Britain, anti-racist initiatives have been subjected to ridicule which has legitimated an intensive white backlash against anti-racist social work (see Pinker, 1993; Phillips, 1993). Concerned with countering this negative perception of their work, policy makers in the local state have pushed their local welfare agents, i.e. social workers, into more efficiently expediting their social control functions and containing the demands of more 'difficult' client groups. The emphasis on regulation and control has engaged social workers in 'policing' the black population, especially its problematic youth. Meanwhile, traditional social work values, such as respect for individual civil rights and safeguarding people's dignity as part of normal social interaction, are given short shrift. Social work educators should examine the gap between social work's espoused values and the realities of its practice as a central part of their teaching.

Multi-culturalism: a euphemism disguising racism?

The concept 'multi-racial society' purports to convey the idea of equality in a pluralistic consensus. Conceptualising society along these lines assumes that different racial and cultural groups have already achieved equality. It also neglects the contradictions engendered by social divisions, such as class, 'race' and gender. Assumed equality defines racism away rather than dealing with it, and obscures the necessity of having both black and white social workers confront racism as a structural and endemic feature of society. By focusing on personal racism, multi-cultural texts ignore structural inequality and present black and white people as already equal. The main problem then becomes one of not 'understanding cultural differences'. Khan's *Support and Stress: Minority Families in Britain* (1979), Foner's *Jamaica Farewell* (1979), and Cashmore's *Rastaman* (1979) suggest that in the process of 'understanding these differences', black people and their cultures move towards white people and their culture. Their underlying message endorses white supremacy, but each text handles it slightly differently.

Assuming that all members of society share the same political and economic troubles, Khan (1979) maintains that equal opportunities for black people are obstructed by individual attitudes, preferences and prejudices. Although she blames both sides for failing to advance the position of black people, she castigates Asian women for being 'backward', i.e. not sharing white values and traditions, and condemns them for being tied firmly to their roles as wives and mothers, even though this discounts their participation in waged work. Foner (1979) argues that Jamaican women prefer European physical features and habits and emulate these. This interpretation of Jamaican life devalues the day-to-day resistance offered by the majority of Jamaican women who do not follow white Anglo-Saxon fashions. Cashmore (1979) attributes the 'breakdown of law and order' amongst black youth to the disintegration of the West Indian family, thus adding to the chorus of voices pathologising this particular social unit. Moreover, he disparages Rastafarian attempts to establish autonomous black organisations and castigates them for encouraging Rastafarians to withdraw from mainstream society and thereby hinder integration. Thus, there is no serious consideration of the importance of these initiatives in withstanding the impact of racism on their lives. Instead, individuals who seek to resist the racist chaos of the world around them by establishing alternatives to it are held responsible for their predicament.

The development of an anti-racist social work practice means taking on board the structured inequality existing between different racialised groups and working on ways in which equality between them can be achieved. It requires white social workers to consider a multi-racial society as something that must be achieved rather than an entity that already exists. Treating British society as currently multi-racial means staying at the level of biology. Britain is multi-racial only in so far as it contains people with a variety of skin colours. It is not socially and politically multi-racial. Making British social work multi-racial requires white practitioners to move away from seeing black clients as pathological individuals and acquiescent victims of social work. It also requires white social workers to acknowledge the politicisation of black people. Black people know who they are and what is happening to them. And they are refusing to accept social work interventions which exacerbate the intrusion of the state into their lives and exert greater control over how they lead them.

Pathologising black resistance to racism

Other white authors have developed their understanding of social work's relationship with black people by looking more extensively at their responses to racism, at both individual and community levels. Whilst only a few, for example Wood (1974), focus on reintegrating black people into the majority community, both white and black writers sharing a white perspective seize on cultural explanations to demonstrate that black people's resistance is the problem. For example, in *Black Youth in Crisis* (1982), Cashmore and Troyna consider the inappropriateness of black youth rioting in response to unemployment. Even the title suggests that the crisis is occurring amongst black youth rather than within society and how it organises social relations. This line of thinking is also evident in Pryce's *Endless Pressure* (1979), in which he talks about 'the problem of the second generation, alienated black youth'. While raising the legitimate issue, at least by implication, of how to best protest against discrimination, such explanations convert the social problem of racism to the problem of the response to it, thereby giving a new twist to pathologising black people – *pathologising black resistance to racism, whatever its form.* In belittling black critiques and responses to their treatment, such interpretations of black activism allow white social workers to continue not taking seriously black people's critique of their work. This enables them to perpetuate racism through their daily practice.

So, when hundreds of black youths arrested after the 1981 rebellions, had their rights of *habeas corpus* and civil liberties bypassed by courts convened specifically to deal with them, white social workers and probation officers offered few objections. As one white social worker in Leeds told me, 'Rioting is not the sort of thing done in British society'. Yet if white youths had been treated *en masse* in this way, public outrage would have been ignited. This process is replicated in white social workers' responses to individualised forms of black protest offered by Rastafarians. The Rastafari stance against white racism is ignored by focusing attention on an individual's illegal use of *ganja* (marijuana).

Within the probation service, matters are substantially worse. Social enquiry reports (now pre-sentence reports)[1] are littered with racist comments and stereotypes which do little to secure justice for black individuals (Denney, 1992; Dominelli *et al.*, 1995; Whitehouse, 1986). White probation officers feel unable to recommend sentences to courts because they 'do not understand black people and their ways'. They are afraid they 'cannot work with them on probation orders'. The final outcome of these positions is that black clients experience harsher sentencing (Pinder, 1984). Thus, black people are disproportionately represented in custodial settings (Home Office, 1986; Hood, 1992). Young black men are less likely to receive cautions and be kept out of the processes leading to penal sentencing (Tipler, 1986). Even in the non-custodial area, Dominelli (1983) finds that black people are more likely to receive community service orders for first and second offences, and be breached sooner for being absent from placements.

Respecting autonomous black organisations

Anti-racist social work recognises the importance of black autonomy in enabling black people to develop their own structures and organisations against racism. It is important that social work educators and practitioners understand this issue and the distinction between separatist and autonomous organisation. Staff in autonomous black organisations will be articulating stringent critiques of current social work theories and practice. They also supply the black practice teachers and lecturers used in training. Autonomous organisation is essential if oppressed black groups are to exert their power to redefine their situation in society and take control of the process whereby solutions for their welfare are proposed. Black people have consistently lodged the legitimacy and appropriateness of their desire to organise autonomously in order to safeguard their interests in a racist society; white people respond to these suggestions with fear and label them 'separatist' (Phillips, 1982). White people's conflation of autonomous organisations with separatism arises from their attempts to resist moves which exclude them from controlling, i.e. subverting by incorporating into white supremacist structures, black people's reality. A white social work assistant on a training course clarified this issue for me when we were divided into a black group and a white group by saying:

> 'I don't understand why we [black and white people] can't join the same group. With them in their black group and us in our white group, it's like having apartheid in the classroom. It's another form of racism. We have the same aims in common. Why do they [the course tutors] want to separate us?'

Further discussion with this person revealed the anxiety that 'I won't know what's going on in that [black] group and I can't influence it.' The point that black people have little power in shaping the outcome in white groups never crossed this individual's mind. Yet, she was aware of the limits that autonomous organisations placed on her power to shape the agenda for black groups. Similar observations occurred during Gitterman and Schaeffer's analysis (1972, p. 282) of working relationships between white workers and black clients: 'the white professional has the upper hand – both in the larger society and in the specific encounter between them'. As power dynamics are a crucial aspect of black–white interaction, white social workers must respect developments fostering black autonomy. Autonomous black organisations, as oppositional forms facilitating black resistance to incorporation, play a significant role in challenging existing service provisions and social relations in social work. White social work educators should be aware of such developments and reflect these in their teaching. Black professionals working from an autonomous base, but integrated into mainstream services, can both monitor provisions for black people and operate as a pressure group for change in mainstream social work.

Models for activities attempting to redress traditional power imbalances between black and white social workers have been provided by a range of black organisations such as the Black Families Unit in Lambeth and the Black Social Workers' Group in Hackney. The models these supply resemble apprenticeship learning. They require white social workers to subject their work to scrutiny and evaluation by black social workers operating as a group (Stubbs, 1985). The black social workers' monitoring group monitors and assesses the work of white practitioners for its racist content. White social workers have the task of working out how to change their practice, seeking help in developing anti-racist work from both black and white colleagues.

The contribution of black social workers towards such training should be recognised as an integral part of their workload and not taken for granted as an extra goodwill input into the agency. Trade unions have the responsibility of ensuring that black workers are not exploited by having this work included in black social workers' employment contracts. This requires NALGO (now UNISON) and the other unions negotiating contracts for social workers to include countering racism in their collective bargaining process, thus redefining the tasks appropriately undertaken in workplace negotiations. Such initiatives also reveal how fighting racism carries implications for areas other than those being directly addressed. Countering racism by having autonomous black organisations flourish within the existing welfare state is not the same as agreeing to the creation of separatist facilities for black people. Arrangements based on separate provisions for black people carry the danger of condemning black people to an under-resourced and under-financed second class service. Moreover, separatist provisions would involve black people in paying twice for services which are theirs by right – once through the general taxation system and once in direct payments to black organisations.

As the Lambeth and Hackney experiences demonstrate, autonomous black groups operating from within the framework of mainstream social services offer black professionals a collective identity and support networks through which they can enhance their power, facilitate their critiques of white colleagues' work, and effectively monitor and evaluate it (Stubbs, 1985, 1987). Such organisation reverses the customary flow of power between black and white professionals, and allows black people to demonstrate in practice their ability both to hold positions of authority over white people and to work co-operatively on a more egalitarian footing (Dominelli, 1979). Moreover, by organising their work in this fashion, black social workers avoid becoming trapped in the negative individualism and professionalism characterising much of white social workers' casework approach to social work (Stubbs, 1985). It also ensures that eradicating racism becomes a central concern of social work, rather than being added on as an afterthought.

White social workers can feel threatened and uncomfortable when placed in the unusual position of being judged by their black colleagues. They will feel vulnerable and demoralised if their work is found wanting. These feelings will be even more intense if the person believes that he or she is committed to anti-racist social work and has worked very hard to realise it. Thus, it is important that employers provide supervision, training and support for white social workers to explore their anxieties, resolve the issues entailed in their role reversal and ensure they are motivated to improve their work instead of wallowing in a morass of guilt and paralysis. Group supervision based on consciousness-raising techniques can move white social workers out of the trap of being pathologised as racist individuals by acknowledging the validity and worth of the steps they have taken. Similarly, white social work educators whose work is criticised from a black perspective will need support in enhancing the quality of their teaching. Having opportunities to develop in anti-racist directions should become an entitlement for every worker if anti-racist social work is to become part of the normal working environment.

Improving facilities for black people has positive implications for the quality of services more generally. For example, the critique that the Black Families Unit made of fostering arrangements has both challenged the criteria that white social workers use in determining which families are suitable as foster parents, and improved Lambeth Social Services Department's relationship with black communities. This includes the ways in which it informs black people of services available and encourages their use. Rating Lambeth's practices as unsatisfactory on these counts, the Black Families Unit has revealed that black families have been excluded from consideration by the white, middle class, heterosexual norms which have underpinned the procedures for communicating with them and used to judge them. In questioning the set-up for black families, black social workers have also exposed the systematic exclusion of white working class families, single parent families and homosexual people for not conforming to white, middle class, heterosexist criteria of having large homes, a comfortable income and a stable, traditional family life.

Following their analysis, black social workers have exerted pressure to make the Department more responsive to the needs and life-styles of all the people it purports to serve. Thus, the Black Families Unit has improved fostering services for both black and white children. Its activities demonstrate that anti-racist practice promotes good practice for all clients irrespective of colour. White social work educators need to become familiar with the work of autonomous black groups and include it as an integral part of the social work curriculum. Doing so challenges the anglocentric nature of social work teaching and presents models of good practice endorsed by black people.

Moreover, autonomous black organisations enable black people to examine their position with their specific needs in mind without having these subsumed by those of others. Phillips (1982) argues that the Left, for example, continually subsumes black working class people's priorities under those of the white working class in theory and practice by maintaining that economic issues always take precedence. This stance negates the significance of 'race'. Or, in Stuart Hall's words, such analyses 'ignore capitalist dynamics, for capitalism reproduces the working class in a racially stratified and internally antagonistic form' (Hall *et al.*, 1978, p. 346). Similarly, black feminists argue that white feminists subsume their specific interests under the notion of sisterhood. But their experiences are not the same. White women enjoy power and privileges accruing to them as white women; these are denied to black women (Carby, 1982; Collins, 1991; hooks, 1981; Lorde, 1984; Parmar, 1982). For example, white women's right to have families is not questioned, although their right to control their sexuality and fertility is. But, as black feminists have pointed out, in the National Abortion Campaign, black women's right to a family and sexual expression has constantly been questioned by white people. Black women have been forced into unwanted abortions and sterilisations because white doctors believe they should control their 'rampant fecundity' (hooks, 1981). The immigration system persists in dividing black families, thereby enshrining the denial of their right to familyhood in a respectable institutionalised form. Parmar (1982) and Lorde (1984) also highlight the heterosexism in both black and white communities and argue strongly for the recognition of the specific forms of oppression that black lesbians endure. Nasira Begum (1993) has also identified the specific forms of oppression that black disabled women endure. This gives them a different agenda on certain issues from either black or white able-bodied women.

Changing directions in the social work curriculum

Altering the social work curriculum in anti-racist/non-racist directions means removing its anglocentric bias and accompanying arrogance to affirm black people in terms they define and present. Shifting the political bias in this social work curriculum away from favouring the *status quo* towards one seeking to secure justice for oppressed groups will accord priority to social work's traditional caring values rather than its controlling ones. However, since the question is one of balance, the duty of social workers to be controlling in certain situations, cannot be avoided, for example in safe-guarding the rights of a black child or confused black elder. Ultimately, an anti-racist curriculum lays foundations for a new type of social work – one that is not simply casework oriented, although it will still have to deal with individual difficulties and suffering, but which also challenges structural constraints. A new social work agenda will have to incorporate the dictum 'the personal is political' to take on board the fact that our individual experiences reflect the social position within which we find ourselves. Moreover, egalitarian relations acknowledging the power differentials and different life experiences that exist amongst individuals and groups will have to be included in the redefinition of the social work task whether white social workers are working in one-to-one counselling, with groups, or through community action and organisational change with either black or white people.

Transforming the social work curriculum and the structures supporting it is only one of a number of changes which social work education must initiate. This action has to be combined with changes within CCETSW and its governing council. CCETSW's regulations governing social work education and training must actively foster anti-racist objectives. This includes providing the additional resources required to create an anti-racist environment in both colleges and agencies. In responding positively to demands for changes which have already been articulated by both black and white people, through the Mickleton Group, the White Collective for Anti-Racist Social Work and its Black Perspectives Committee, CCETSW needs to ensure that it carries people with it. Its failure to do so was a major factor in the backlash against Appendix 5 of Paper 30, which focused on the need for anti-racist measures to be covered in the curriculum. Instead of imposing its will in a vacuum which can be filled by those opposing anti-racist social work, CCETSW has actively to involve practitioners and educators in anti-racist social work initiatives at grass-roots and managerial levels. Black people have to be included in all of CCETSW's structures in significant numbers so that they can be empowered as a group rather than being individualised token solutions to institutionalised racism. Social work courses themselves need to attract black students and black teachers in substantial numbers so that they do not become isolated examples of white benevolence.

CCETSW and central government must release sufficient resources to ensure that anti-racism is handled appropriately. These resources need to cover grants for black students, additional funding for recruiting black staff in educational institutions and the field, and further in-service training for existing white teaching staff and practitioners. CCETSW's failure to date to do this has undermined its desire to make anti-racist teaching mandatory under the DipSW. Also, CCETSW must ensure that anti-racist social work is adequately assessed in both written and placement work on qualifying programmes. This requires assessors who have the expertise for doing so. CCETSW also has to demonstrate more action and commitment than simply issuing an edict that makes working in anti-racist ways a requirement for the satisfactory completion of courses. What is taught, how it is taught, what is assessed, how it is assessed and by whom are matters which must be openly discussed and resolved. Teaching and assessing anti-racist social work involves acquiring knowledge and expertise which cannot be transmitted by osmosis.

The employment of teaching staff with a black perspective

Besides the racism evident in student recruitment and selection, course content and practice placements, educational institutions embrace racist employment practices. Black supervisors and lecturers are under-represented on courses. Experienced black practitioners are drafted onto programmes on poor conditions of employment as sessional teachers, filling gaps left by white colleagues rather than being employed on career grades with mainstream terms and conditions of work. White trainers can play a significant role in reversing this situation by promoting organisational change in employment policies and practices.

To address the issue of providing students with more than an anti-racist reading list, white social work educators need an environment which frees them to acknowledge that there are teaching processes which are beyond their expertise. White lecturers' limitations in teaching anti-racist social work include being unable to substitute for black people in giving white students the experience of working with black teachers who have the power to evaluate their achievements. White tutors cannot provide black students with either positive role models of black people or experiential knowledge of the skills necessary for black people to survive in a racist society. Neither can white educators form black support networks with black students. Consequently, courses lacking staff with a black perspective seriously handicap all students. White educators must confront the thorny question of providing both black and white students with the experience of working in an environment where black people occupy positions of authority (Dominelli, 1979). That white social workers recognise the complementarity of the tasks white anti-racist educators and practitioners can play with respect to those holding black perspectives is important in establishing non-antagonistic relationships between black and white colleagues.

By openly acknowledging their inability to provide black and white students with the full range of required educational services, white teachers can pave the way for the employment of black academic staff. White educators may perceive this suggestion as reinforcing competitive and conflictual relationships between black and white persons applying for the same jobs. As a number of them have said in discussions with me, 'I am not prepared to give up my job for a black person. I have my mortgage and my family to think about'. Defining the problem in these terms is misleading. Redefining the situation to clarify the nature of the issues being addressed empowers white anti-racist social work educators facing this analysis to move forward. For, as the discussion above reveals, designating white teachers as 'race experts' disguises the absence of black teachers in carrying out essential anti-racist teaching which cannot be provided by white tutors. Work currently being undertaken by white educators but which should be being done by black people can be shown to be complementary to the work they ought to do.

Individual white social work tutors concerned about the failure of social work courses to address the question of racism have placed themselves in a competitive relationship with black teachers by trying to provide *all* the 'anti-racist' teaching in the absence of black colleagues. Their single-handed attempts to challenge racism often confound anti-racist practice, contrary to their expressed intentions. Having little understanding of racism or training in fighting its myriad manifestations that white trainers unwittingly perpetuate racist practices in their work. By becoming 'race relations experts' overnight, they unhappily fall into the trap of speaking on behalf of black people, whose voice continues to be either unheard or absent, both physically and metaphorically, from courses.

With declining funding, the well-meaning intentions of white social work educators have been unintentionally subverted by their employing institutions. These have found their white employees' willingness to act as 'race experts' to be an easy solution to the problem of inadequate resourcing for tackling racism. Instead of employing additional black staff to bring black perspectives into the pedagogic processes, establishments redeploy existing white staff regardless of their expertise in anti-racist teaching or ability to undertake the entire range of such teaching. By covering gaps in service provisions in this way, agencies exploit their white personnel, abuse their humanity and turn their professional ethics of meeting students' needs against them. In acquiescing to this state of affairs, white tutors have personally, if unwittingly, colluded with institutionalised racism. Once embarked upon this process, feelings of powerlessness and isolation within their institutions have made it difficult for white educators and practitioners individually to resist pressures for their continued involvement on this basis. Black people's critique of their work has made white trainers realise how their humanity and generosity have been hijacked by racist policies and practices which have kept black people out of academe (Dominelli, 1987).

Moreover, the more junior members of staff whose teaching is marginalised are more likely to have their humanity so compromised. Although taken from Britain, the following vignettes illustrate processes and situations replicated in universities throughout the English-speaking world:

In one university department, a white woman lecturer, appointed to teach community work, became appalled at the course's failure to address racism and initiated an option on it. Attempts to make racism a more central issue on the course where thwarted by cries of, 'We already have an overburdened timetable, we can't add more to it'. These objections were strengthened by the lack of resourcing within the department. This point was articulated as, 'We have no black members of staff and no money to appoint any'. Returning from a prolonged absence, the lecturer discovered her teaching had been restructured. Her normal areas of teaching had been dropped whilst her 'race options' teaching had increased. Despite her protests, this situation remained and the staff group congratulated themselves on 'doing as much as they could in the circumstances'.

In another university, a newly appointed white male research worker complained about the absence of teaching on racism in the social work course and was given the task of offering students an option on it. His pleas for the appointment of black staff went unheeded.

Although polytechnics (now called 'new' universities) currently continue to lead ('old') universities in their preparedness to appoint black members of staff, their record in abusing white staff is equally abysmal:

For instance, in one (former) polytechnic, a white woman lecturer teaching community work made it her responsibility to foster teaching on ethnic minorities in the department. As a result of her concern, she was forced to adopt the mantle of 'race expert' for 10 years before convincing her colleagues that they should convince their 'equal opportunities' employer to appoint the first black lecturer.

This abuse of white staff by employing authorities must end. CCETSW has a role in putting pressure on educational establishments to appoint black staff and helping them to acquire the financial resources necessary for realising this objective. White educators can promote movement on this front by organising collectively to expose the nature of the problem confronting them. By collectively refusing to continue being misused as 'race experts', white educators can empower themselves in challenging the exploitation of their labour. Redefining the problem to be confronted as institutionalised racism, i.e. their employers' failure to demand anti-racist teaching and practice from all existing staff and employ substantial numbers of black staff, can be very liberating for white educators and practitioners. Besides exposing their employers' insistence that they perform work they cannot do, redefining the problem stops white practitioners and educators feeling guilty about working in 'anti-racist' ways without success. This can in turn strengthen their resolve not to accept the label of 'race expert' inappropriately.

Moreover, once they see clearly the issues at stake, white social work educators and practitioners can take action, not as individuals who can easily be picked off through allegations of breach of contract, but as a group of concerned professionals acting in concert effectively to resist being abused by employers. Through collective action, their individual plight of feeling compelled by their institutions and personal consciences to teach the impossible will be both resisted and made visible in an extremely powerful way. By organising collectively through their unions, professional organisations and anti-racist support networks, they will become pivotal in securing much-needed changes in employment policies and practice. Moreover, in taking the risks entailed in this stance collectively, they will reduce the vulnerability each will encounter.

Anti-racist practice placements: the anti-racist apprenticeship model

Training does not prepare white students to be effective anti-racist practitioners in an ethnically diverse society. They are seldom actively encouraged to confront racism in either the classroom or their practice placements. Their performance in these settings is rarely adequately evaluated. If white students are in an office having neither black workers nor black people using its services, the fact is either ignored or interpreted as a comforting validation of the irrelevance of the personal social services to black people. White students are not required to work under the tutelage of black supervisors to experience directly a situation in which black people occupying powerful positions help them to unravel their prejudices about black people's social status.

As white students are being trained to practise anywhere in Britain, with all client groups, anti-racist practice ought to be a central feature of all placement work, whether or not black people are directly involved in an agency. Since challenging their stereotypes about black people and their role in society is an essential part of the anti-racist social work curriculum, all white students should have the opportunity of working under black fieldwork supervisors or practice teachers. This would help them to acquire the skills of working in anti-racist ways and gain the cultural and ethnic sensitivity they need to work with black colleagues on an equal basis once they become paid employees. Their placement practice would also prepare them for intervening more appropriately and relevantly in their subsequent work with black people. The possibility of white students having direct experience of working under and being evaluated by black practitioners constitutes what I have called the 'anti-racist apprenticeship model' of teaching.

The suggestion that white students' practice placement is influenced and assessed by black practitioners should not be used to 'dump' the responsibility for teaching anti-racist social work onto black practice teachers' shoulders, or to deny black students access to them. Black students also need black practitioners, but for different reasons – as positive role models and to help them to acquire the skills they need to work in the racially uncongenial environment of social work. That both groups of students require black professionals to complete their educational experience underlines the importance of drawing substantial numbers of black people into these positions.

For the opportunities in the 'anti-racist apprenticeship model' of teaching to be made available to white students, several changes have to take place in current practice. These include the large-scale employment of black people as practitioners in mainstream activities, training black practitioners as practice teachers, counting student supervision in the normal workload of black workers, and providing them with the time and resources necessary for carrying out this work effectively. Universities and colleges would have to develop extensive links with black communities to ensure that they draw substantial proportions of academic staff and practitioners from these. Moreover, social work authorities and educational establishments together would have to convince CCETSW to amend its requirements concerning the accreditation of practice teachers and eliminate one which acts as an obstacle to their recruitment. In its current formulation, this one insists that all practice teachers be experienced, formally qualified practitioners who have recently supervised students in mainstream agencies.

This requirement indirectly discriminates against black people because it does not recognise experiences and qualifications obtained in countries other than Britain; accept that black people acquire expertise in the voluntary sector amongst black community groups whose concept of social work does not necessarily match that depicted in mainstream white agencies and endorsed by CCETSW; and acknowledge institutionalised racism in the field and education (ALTARF, 1984; Stone, 1981) as it denies black people the opportunity to acquire the qualifications and experience demanded by CCETSW. For example, many black practitioners in statutory settings assist their white colleagues in the supervision of black and white students. Yet, this work is invisible or discounted because credit for the supervision is only given to the white practice teacher who formally holds the contract with the student. Seeking a change in this requirement does not constitute an attempt to dilute the standards to be met by practice teachers. It is, rather, a suggestion about ways of bridging the gap in opportunities that black people experience and validating the expertise they already have so that they can begin from the same starting line as their white colleagues. Finally, CCETSW should fully endorse working in anti-racist ways by making it a compulsory aspect of placement assessment and supporting those involved in implementing such a requirement with both moral and material support.

Black students and social work training

Black students' specific needs continue to be virtually ignored in social work training (NISW, 1994). Few resources are earmarked specifically for them (De Souza, 1991; Willis, 1987). Black students experience considerable discrimination in getting accepted onto social work courses, recruitment and selection procedures work against them (CCETSW, 1985) and they are failed in disproportionately high numbers (NISW, 1994). Their experience of working in black self-help groups is devalued and downgraded because it is different from that obtained in social services departments or probation offices. Considering only the experience gained in mainstream or statutory agencies as *real practice* reinforces racist definitions of social work. Black people working in unpaid capacities in voluntary agencies using a variety of social work techniques are also doing social work. Black people seldom sit on the interviewing panels making decisions about admissions to courses. This means that white definitions of what constitutes social work practice go unchallenged in the interviewing process and black candidates are rejected as having 'unsuitable practice experience'. White candidates find their racist definitions of social work unquestioned and their commitment to working in anti-racist ways inadequately checked out. Rules regulating the funding of courses, especially those concerning secondment and discretionary grants, also operate to the detriment of black applicants (Duffield, 1985).

Once on courses, black students need to be supported by both black and white staff so that they do not feel isolated and vulnerable in a predominantly white setting. Their raising questions about teaching methods, course content and interpersonal relationships is important. Treating their point of view seriously validates their concerns and ensures that white staff do not respond in defensive or negative terms.

Mechanisms geared towards getting black students together as a group so that they can offer each other support against the racist practices that impinge daily in their lives as students remain missing from courses (NISW, 1994), yet black student support groups are an important learning resource. The shortage of black tutors in educational establishments denies black students access to positive models of black people working in authoritative positions. Their absence also means that black students do not receive the support they need in discussing the problems of black people living in a racist society and in considering their position as black students with those in authority who have also experienced racist courses and survived. Furthermore, having black tutors enables black students to receive support in challenging racism on courses, for example assessment criteria which discriminate against them – an issue raised by black students at Bristol Polytechnic and confirmed elsewhere in subsequent reports (DeSouza, 1991; NISW, 1994), and the use of black students as the 'race' experts.

Support networks of this form are crucial in challenging a trend towards disproportionately high failure rates among black students (NISW, 1994; Willis, 1987). In addition, few practice placements allow black students to work with black people under the supervision of black practitioners so that they can fully explore questions relating to their needs as black workers in a predominately white society. Nor do they get access to black supervisors who can help them deal with the racism they encounter from white clients and white colleagues. The appointment of sufficient numbers of black staff would also help to pre-empt the 'ghettoi-sation' of black students as the 'experts' dealing with all the issues concerning 'race' on their courses. Black consultants can be appointed in the absence of black staff employed on permanent contracts, but these should not be considered to be substitutes for permanent staff. Consul-tants may themselves be disadvantaged in the work they do by not being familiar with organisational procedures and routines. Their distance from its day-to-day regimes, however, can be beneficial.

Guidelines for white educationalists

This chapter has highlighted the weaknesses of social work education and training in countering racist policies and practices. It has identified the need for white social work educators to come together collectively as a group and commit themselves to anti-racist social work in fairly practical ways. These can be summarised as follows:

1. developing anti-racist social work curricula;
2. replacing anglocentric concepts in social work theory, practice, law and policies with anti-racist ones;
3. transforming current definitions of what constitutes social work practice;

4. changing course selection and recruitment procedures so that only applicants committed to anti-racist social work are admitted;

5. having selection panels which include black people who can ensure that non-racist definitions of social work are used in evaluating the suitability of black and white applicants for courses;

6. having recruitment and publicity materials geared towards encouraging black people to apply for courses;

7. employing a substantial proportion of black academic staff, administrative staff and practitioners;

8. developing links with black communities to provide a substantial pool of placements through which black practitioners can evaluate the competence of students working with black people;

9. providing black students with the space and resources to develop autonomously as black students;

10. challenging CCETSW's current assessment criteria and replacing these with adequately resourced enforceable anti-racist ones;

11. demanding that central government releases resources to employ black people throughout social work education and retrain white staff already within it in anti-racist directions;

12. challenging institutionalised racism more generally by making explicit the gains accruing to white people by virtue of its existence and incorporating the exposure of these in their teaching;

13. getting white social work educators and practitioners to refuse to accept roles as 'race experts' who can offer black and white students the teaching and skills which can only emanate from a black perspective; and

14. making the commitment to working and teaching in anti-racist ways a criteria of employment in social work education.

Notes

1. Social Enquiry Reports (SERs) became Pre-Sentence Reports (PSRs) when the 1991 Criminal Justice Act was introduced.

3

Deconstructing Racism: Anti-Racism Awareness Training and Social Workers

Conscientisation (Freire, 1970), as the processes individuals use to make connections between the social relations they personally perpetuate through their attitudes, values and behaviour and the social positions they hold, is an essential feature of anti-racist social work. White people's innermost concepts of positive selfhood rest on a fragile sense of being non-oppressive. Becoming conscious or aware of the processes whereby they personally collude with institutional racism can make them feel extremely uncomfortable with and dispirited by the realisation that they are playing the role of oppressor. They are more likely to experience this and feel guilty if they are oppressed along some other social division themselves.

Casting the role of oppressor in biological terms having a 'natural' immutability can be incredibly disempowering. Similar dynamics operate *vis-à-vis* those who are being oppressed. However, this sense of powerlessness can be overcome if individuals can take action which enables them to change situations for the better, by devoting energy to eliminating oppression. The means whereby white people, as the beneficiaries of white supremacy, embark on this process are not easy to discern. The complexity of the enterprise and our inadequate analyses of racism make it easy for white people to collude with one another and avoid confronting racist practices directly. This collusion becomes systematised through what I call *avoidance strategies*. Key to our collusion with racist dynamics is our failure to take seriously the interlinking of the three forms of racism (personal, cultural and institutional). Their combined interaction gives racism its subtlety when practised in non-physically violent and covert ways. White people use a variety of avoidance strategies which draw upon institutionalised racist norms, policies and practices. Linked to personal racism, these interact with each other to stifle the development of action necessary for eradicating racism. By perpetuating individual, institutional and cultural racism, strategies of avoidance work against the establishment of anti-racist social work.

Barriers to anti-racist practice: avoidance strategies

Avoidance strategies

I have identified these avoidance strategies as follows. They may overlap with each other and a particular behaviour may incorporate several of them. Moreover, these barriers to anti-racist social work practice are interdependent:

1. *Denial.* The refusal to accept that racism exists, especially in its cultural and institutional forms. People using denial strategies ignore research evidence indicating the widespread prevalence of cultural and institutional racism and at best think of racism as personal prejudices held by a few extreme and irrational individuals.
2. *Omission.* The racial dimension of social interaction is ignored. Individuals subscribing to this view do not see the relevance of 'race' in most situations, and relate to others as if racism did not exist. A social worker's comment of 'There is no racism here', in describing a district office located in an area with a high proportion of black people living in it, but employing no black workers, depicts a situation which reflects the failure to acknowledge the existence of racism, particularly in its institutional form. It also contains elements of denial.
3. *Decontextualisation.* Persons decontextualise racism by accepting that it exists in general terms, 'out there', for example in South Africa under apartheid. However, they refuse to believe it permeates the everyday activities they undertake. The crucial feature in this strategy is that it denies black people's individual experience of racism.
4. *The colour-blind approach.* Black people are treated as if they were the same as whites. People holding this position negate black people's specific experience of racism. The statement, 'I treat everyone the same' is a common formulation of this strategy.

5. *The 'dumping' approach.* The responsibility for creating racism and getting rid of it is placed on black people. Individuals acting on this basis blame the 'victims' for what happens. Thus, black people are held responsible for racism. Expecting black employees to deal with all issues to do with racism is indicative of this approach.

6. *The patronising approach.* White ways are deemed superior, but black people's ways of doing things are tolerated. Black people are considered to be entitled to their 'quaint ways'. Multi-culturalism which does not address unequal power relations and structural inequalities typifies this strategy. In other words, there is a superficial acceptance of cultural difference.

7. *Avoidance.* There is an awareness of 'race' as a factor in social interaction, but opportunities for confronting it are avoided. This usually means flinching at racist behaviour but keeping quiet about it, for example ignoring racist diatribes which colleagues or clients might make.

8. *Exaggeration.* This entails an awareness of the existence of racism in everyday life and an acceptance of the necessity of doing something about it. However, it involves exaggerating or magnifying the value of even minimal (from the point of view of those at the receiving end of racism) steps taken to address it, for example thinking that racism can be eradicated *simply* by introducing an 'equal opportunities' policy. The wheel of avoidance strategies below depicts these in graphic terms.

Figure 3.1 The wheel of avoidance strategies

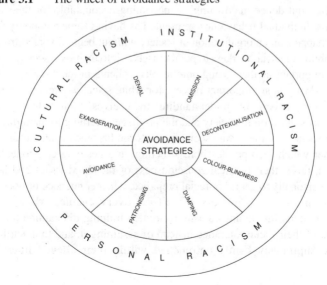

Anti-racism awareness training

Unearthing the ways in which these strategies prevent white people from initiating and realising anti-racist action is the aim of anti-racism awareness training. Anti-racism awareness training is geared specifically to raising white people's consciousness of racism in all its manifestations, helping them to define the issues and then take action to counter racism. Anti-racism awareness training of this form is not necessary for black people. Black perspectives on racism and assertion training are more relevant to their needs. This chapter explores the strategies that white people use to avoid challenging racism, the implications of this for social work practice and the role that anti-racism awareness training can play in tackling racism.

Anti-racism awareness training is not predicated as a personal quest which assumes that individual practitioners as state employees are free from structural constraints. Anti-racism awareness training connects the individual and structural (organisational and cultural) elements of social interaction. Taking changing the system so as to eliminate structural inequalities as its central point, anti-racism awareness training attempts to deconstruct racism by demonstrating how personal change affected through increased consciousness of what one does as an individual fits into changing organisational and societal policies and practices. Besides making connections between the three different forms of racism and their interaction with each other, anti-racism awareness training helps individuals to acquire confidence in 'owning' or becoming accountable for their own actions. Individual behaviour is presented as having some autonomy from what happens in an organisation or society without being divorced from it. The ability of social workers to put themselves into their own social context is as important as their being able to place clients in their social setting. *Know thyself* is an important precept for white social workers to apply to their own racism. By understanding themselves, their value system, prejudices, position in society and the privileges accruing to them through racist social relations, white social workers can become racially aware in a manner which incorporates both structural and personal components of racism, raises their political consciousness of racialised issues and helps them personally to get rid of racial prejudice, whether intended or not.

Embarking on a process of self-discovery enables white social workers undertaking anti-racism awareness training to examine the real extent of their racial tolerance instead of assuming it, and to unearth the white supremacy firmly entrenched within their alleged liberality.

Gaining insights into their behaviour which unravel their self-concept as decent, tolerant human beings makes white people uncomfortable. In these circumstances, it is easier to be kind to oneself and often unintentionally end up colluding with strategies which camouflage this unpleasant reality. This is illustrated in the comments made by a white person employing black trainers to run anti-racism training courses for white social work educators and practitioners:

> Racism Awareness Training is a sensitive area. Many white people have had a bad experience of it, and so we have to consider carefully who we bring in to take charge of these courses. Originally, I agreed to go along with black trainers being bought in to do this teaching. I wanted someone who was good, but who would be sensitive to and careful with our feelings. I didn't want an 'uppity black' to take control of the thing.

Notions of white supremacy and commitment to having white people define the basis on which black people are employed are obvious from this account. So is the white person's fear of being exposed in a way that did not allow him or her to 'save face', i.e. to retain a modicum of self-respect and the ability to continue. The importance of challenging white people in ways which do not humiliate them in the process cannot be over-emphasised. Without respect being accorded to individuals involved in a change process, real change will not ensue. Instead, people become wrapped up in a vicious circle of constantly proving their superiority rather than seeking ways of establishing relationships rooted in equality. An irony in the above quote is that the white person seeks a precondition which is not being granted to the black trainer.

There are other situations in which white people's beliefs in the correctness of having status, power and control are more subtly expressed. The subtlety of the dynamics involved came across when I used an exercise to explore the views of people who did not consider themselves racist. Those of you who feel this applies to you should undertake the following exercise and consider your answers in relation to those that came up in groups I have run.

Exercise:

A. *Write down your reasons for thinking you are not racist.*

B. *Then examine your answers in the light of the following questions:*
• How many reasons dwelt solely on your personal attributes, i.e. failed to contextualise your views in structural terms by taking

account of your position as a white person in a predominantly white society?

- Have you identified those forces and relationships conferring power on you and those making you feel powerless?
- To what extent did you think about black people's experiences?

Most white respondents do not identify themselves as white. Taking our white identity for granted is part of the privilege of belonging to the dominant group (Fletchman-Smith, 1984). If your replies indicate that you have taken your position as a 'white' person for granted, you are presupposing white supremacy. This is racist. Whilst white people can ignore their racial origins, black people are not allowed to forget theirs. The colour of their skin becomes the initial basis of white people's reactions to them. White social workers ignoring the significance of 'race' for black people in their intervention are denying a crucial aspect of their existence including their identity. Doing so creates a major obstacle to effective social work with them (Gitterman and Schaeffer, 1972). Moreover, white people relate to black people as *black* people, who are expected to behave in certain deferential ways and occupy inferior positions in the socio-economic hierarchy. Not taking such dynamics into account means that white social workers reinforce racism by decontextualising black people. White people may have the luxury of 'forgetting' that they are black; black people themselves do not (Riley, 1985).

White people also provide a catalogue of anti-racist activities, particularly campaigns in which they participate, to demonstrate their lack of racism. This suggests that racism is irrelevant in their everyday routines or has nothing to do with them personally. Whilst supporting anti-racist activities alongside others, white people must tackle the ways in which their own day-to-day behaviour affirms institutionalised racism. It may be difficult to acknowledge culpability in this area if our analyses focus primarily on the *intended* consequences of personal racism, as these play down the connections between personal and structural racism. Minimising the interaction between them gives the impression that personal racism takes place in a vacuum, independent of the political, social and economic forces within which it occurs. Anti-racist social work can assist in this process of recognising collusive practices because it does not separate the person from their social situation. On the contrary, anti-racist social work aims to unpack the dynamics whereby institutional and cultural racism buttress personal behaviour, and personal behaviour feeds off institutional and cultural racism. It also clarifies the interconnectedness between these three dimensions.

Becoming racially aware as individuals is essential for white social workers countering both institutionalised racism and racial prejudice amongst the broader public they meet during the course of their work. The objective of becoming racially aware can be achieved by engaging in a process combining anti-racist struggles with anti-racism awareness training. This message may strike readers as overtly political. It is. But all social work is political, regardless of the perspective from which it is practised, because all social workers make decisions affecting other people's lives, and have the power to allow or deny people access to social resources. Social workers making these decisions within the parameters of the dominant ideology are not acting apolitically: they are *reinforcing* the *status quo* (see Lorde, 1984). The fact that decisions predicated on this basis are less likely to be questioned than those emanating from a perspective challenging established practice should not obscure the political nature of such acts. In a racist society, it is all too easy for white social workers to remain oblivious of the racist nature of their intervention. For unless they are racially aware, both they and their white colleagues can unknowingly be colluding with racist policies and practices through their shared ideology of white supremacy.

Ignorance of what constitutes racist practice is not a valid justification for its perpetuation. All white social workers practising in an ethnically pluralist society are morally as well as socially obliged to raise their consciousness, personally take steps to eradicate racist practice, and encourage their organisation to do so as well. Racist practices are those actions, decisions and policies which either directly or indirectly ascribe an inferior status to black people and deny ethnic or racial groups access to their share of society's power, resources and dignity. In social work, this includes the failure of service delivery to meet the specific needs of ethnic minority groups, to provide employment and training opportunities commensurate with their numbers in the population at large and to validate black people's resistance to oppression.

Furthermore, in a climate of public expenditure cuts, state attempts to ration social services resources intensify pressure on social workers to act as agents of social control by reducing demands for scarce public resources. The high visibility of certain ethnic groups, particularly black ones, along with their being perceived as 'undeserving', makes it easier for them to be targeted as objects whose eligibility to services must be authenticated above and beyond 'normal' standards. This is usually achieved by white professionals who are gatekeepers to social resources demanding that black people produce their passports before being given access to services when they do not impose similar requirements on white claimants. The possibility that these families may be black British, and therefore wholly entitled to the services available under the welfare state, is submerged by white social workers' anxiety that they are dealing with 'immigrants'. It is a racist position which gives black people the loud and clear message that they have not been accepted as having a rightful place in society as a settled population with full citizenship rights.

Anti-racism awareness training as consciousness raising

By becoming an integral part of social work education and in-service training, anti-racism awareness training enables white social workers to examine their internalised racism and unpack the myriad ways in which their social interaction utilises racist behaviour to disparage black people during teacher–student, practitioner–student, social worker–client and worker–worker relationships. Becoming racially aware is not an exercise in guilt expiation but a first step in developing anti-racist practice. It proceeds through consciousness raising, which makes individuals aware of the connections between personal, institutional and cultural racism, and how these operate in and are reinforced through everyday actions and attitudes. The next stage concerns the individual making a commitment to struggling against racism, knowing that the process may well be painful, and developing strategies of action for individually and collectively combating racism. Having worked these out, the individual embarks on implementing the action. This section contains exercises aimed at exploring racist assumptions held by white social workers and helping them become more racially aware in the process.

'Race' awareness training

I draw a distinction between race awareness training, racism awareness training and anti-racism awareness training. Although only one part of it, language is an important aspect of the oppression process because it contains within it cultural expectations, social norms and power relations which, whilst remaining implicit, key into stereotypical views and taken-for-granted assumptions about others which the speaker holds (Spender,

1980). *Race awareness training* as an expression, therefore, is problematic because it defines 'race' as the problem to be tackled. In practice, this leads to practitioners being sidetracked down the path of biological determinism searching for a mythical black 'race' and a mythical white one, whereas we have seen that 'race' is a social construct embedded in all aspects of human relations. *Racism awareness training,* in defining racism as the problem to be addressed, focuses on the social processes and the power differentials existing between different ethnic minority groups, but limits these to interpersonal interaction. *Anti-racism awareness training* goes one step further by linking personal racism with structural racism. It also legitimates combining action aimed at eradicating racism with an appreciation of its effects. Because it combines understanding racist dynamics with action countering them, I believe we should shift from race awareness and racism awareness training to anti-racism awareness training.

Race awareness training developed in the aftermath of black criticism of white involvement in the Civil Rights Movement in the USA. White liberals became perplexed when black militants accused them of being racist and of becoming involved in anti-racist struggles to assuage their feelings of guilt and complicity rather than to liberate black people (Cleaver, 1971). As the black critique increased in strength and popularity in black communities, black-only organisations replaced mixed ones and white progressives were left out in the cold, feeling confused by the message given by those whose aspirations they endorsed (Adamson and Borgos, 1985).

Some 'progressive' whites have interpreted black people's call as one requiring them to do nothing since fighting racism is the prerogative of black activists. Others have felt discomfited by this interpretation and have probed deeper to find a significant role for themselves in the struggle against racism. The central message that black people have given progressive white people is that we are so conditioned by living in a racist society and imbued with privileges stemming from it that we cannot see our own racism, the benefits accruing to us because of its existence and our role in perpetuating it. We use 'race' in a highly politicised way but are racially blind when looking at ourselves and our behaviour. Anti-racism training enables us to transcend this limitation.

Moreover, black people's own consciousness and sense of self-worth had, at this point, reached the stage at which they were no longer prepared to tolerate white patronage, condescension and paternalism, whether or not it was well intentioned (Cleaver 1971). Standing up against white liberal intentions of 'doing good' is essential for black people's own social growth and development, and for reclaiming their autonomy and self-respect. Their taking this stance has been crucial in steering white progressives into anti-racist directions and compelling them to focus their energies on white racism. White progressives culling this message from black people's rejection of their earlier contribution to the anti-racist struggle have turned to examining themselves and the social relationships mediating their interaction with black people. This exercise has unearthed the material basis for black people's allegations. The complexity of the project that white people are embracing and the myriad subtle ways through which racism operates and is perpetuated have been quickly appreciated. The attempt to become racially aware has brought humility amongst progressive white people, who now wonder at their earlier arrogance in thinking they had all the answers. As one practitioner on an anti-racism awareness training course said to me, 'Humility and the realisation that I'm not so superior is what I take from this'. White social workers need to make humility part of their approach if they are to indicate their willingness to listen to black clients and learn to treat seriously their view of a situation. This awareness must be coupled with using the power they wield as white social workers to undertake anti-racist action.

There is a paradox in this position, for white social workers retain the power to decide whether or not to participate in anti-racist struggles. This position is, however, consistent with white people accepting the notion that racism is their problem and taking responsibility for dismantling the racist edifice which they have created. In assuming responsibility for their actions, white people can enact human intentionality, exercise agency by taking control of events, and ensure that these unfold along liberating lines, i.e. those endorsing racial equality and justice. Or they may decide to leave things as they are. Both choices depict white people's ability to act (show agency) in accordance with their own perceived interests and priorities. Both actions carry implications for black people, who also respond to this by exercising their own agency.

Judy Katz's book *White Awareness* (1978) was amongst the first American publications in the race awareness training field and has contributed considerably to its discussion in Britain. Katz's contribution to race awareness training has been critiqued by those attempting to transcend the limitations of her pioneering efforts. Gurnah (1984) criticises racism awareness training, including Katz's seminal work, for diverting the energies of black activists; being colonised by the state, which uses racism awareness training courses to give an illusion of tackling racism when it is giving priority to controlling both black and white opposition to it; lacking a clearly articulated theoretical analysis of racism; failing to initiate change which would benefit black communities; and reducing racism to an abstract entity contained within the person. To this list, I would add further reservations. These are: (a) a naïve view of power; (b) a failure to root racism within patriarchal capitalist society, although Katz acknowledges that racism occurs within a social context; (c) an end product of paralysing guilt rather than a spur to action; and (d) an over-emphasis on what *individuals* can or must do.

Whilst to a point sharing Katz's definition of racism I draw a deeper distinction than she does between racial prejudice and racism (Katz, 1978). In Katz's framework, individuals hold racial prejudice, but it requires the exercise of power to make it racism. This has given rise to the slogan that racism is 'prejudice plus power' (Katz, 1978). In my view, *all* white individuals in Britain exercise some power over black individuals by virtue of their being *white* people in a predominately *white* society. Even in one-to-one interactions between black and white people, that power balance hangs in the air by an invisible cord and shifts in favour of the white person. Hence, I would argue that in a white capitalist society all racial prejudice is tinged to varying degrees with racism. Thus, change at the personal level must be accompanied by societal change, a factor which Katz (1978) underplays. By becoming aware of this factor, white social workers developing anti-racist practice with black clients can take it into account in their work.

Power relationships predicated on membership of the white community are reflected in the assumptions that white social workers make about black clients. These include the belief that black people are recent immigrants. Yet black people have been settling in Britain for over 500 years (Fryer, 1984). Furthermore, the majority of black people are now black British people born here. White people's failure to incorporate this knowledge into their everyday interactions with black people is illustrated by the following. When white social workers ask black children they are placing in a nursery, 'Which part of India are you from?', the message being conveyed to them is, 'You don't belong here. You are not one of us'. Underpinning this statement is the view that the black person is not entitled to this service (or can only have it on sufferance). The message is a racist one.

The communication of such messages in a climate endorsing repatriation for black people exacerbates a racist situation. That white social workers intend to welcome black people into a white *milieu* through such statements does not, if this is the nature of their initial greeting, make vulnerable individuals feel less anxious. White social workers facing such predicaments should give priority to establishing their friendliness and commitment to fighting racism by ensuring that the appropriate services are made available to black clients. Questions about origins can be asked later when a climate of safety and trust prevails. White social workers should then feel able to reveal their ethnic origins and talk about these too. Being open about their own racial and ethnic identity and considering its strengths and weaknesses constructively can empower white social workers. Recovering the positive aspects of Anglo-Saxon ethnicity, for example its collectivism via extended kinship and community ties, can be a vital step in the process of reclaiming their own humanity.

Racism awareness training

The emphasis on individual racism in both race awareness and racism awareness training is problematic in terms of the processes in which they lock white participants. Their individualistic approach emphasises the need to resolve personal hang-ups about racism and hinders the realisation of the collective responsibility that white people have in eradicating racism as a system. This has led to conflicts between white people who are newcomers to the issue wanting to concentrate on discovering what 'racism' is, and those who have worked on this aspect for some time and are impatient to develop strategies which bring about structural change. Their diverse expectations create frustrations which pit white individuals who are at different starting points in the conscientisation process against one another.

White participants come to race awareness and racism awareness training courses already divided by a number of hierarchies, including employment status and gender. Sadly, these features are set aside as diversions allowing white people to avoid the task of confronting racism. Whilst trainers need to be cautious in responding to these divisions and ensuring that they do not divert their attention from tackling racism, they cannot ignore them. These divisions can lead white people to compete against each other to establish who is the least racist of the lot, thereby exacerbating divisions between them and setting in train rivalries which are destructive to collaborative work aimed at fighting racism. This discord feeds on individual fears and insecurities sparked off when their self-concepts as non-racists have been undermined and challenged. These anxieties immobilise white people through the guilt and shame they feel at having undesirable facets of their behaviour publicly exposed without their being able to replace them with acceptable ones.

Personal approbation and a strong sense of self-worth are important attributes for anti-racists, whether black or white, to satisfy. Without these, white people will not overcome their feelings of powerlessness and guilt. Others are paralysed by being fearful of challenging authorities on which their livelihood depends. Some people are frustrated by their failure to make the links between personal awareness and social action. Others are incapacitated by the insistence of race awareness and racism awareness training that they bare their feelings. Focusing on one's emotions is difficult for people who believe in maintaining 'a stiff upper lip'. It is, therefore, a matter which must be sensitively addressed and handled if the individual is to move beyond resistance to engaging in anti-racist work.

Anti-racism awareness training and difference

Anti-racism awareness training grapples with these differences within a group by establishing relations based on acknowledging and respecting the *different social positions* occupied by its various members and undertaking steps to reduce power differentials between them. Only when this has happened can real social change affecting the individual and society take place (Lorde, 1984). Anti-racism awareness training takes these dynamics on board, not necessarily by addressing each one specifically, although individual interventions outside the actual training session should be established for those requiring them, but by directing white people's energies towards achieving personal change and transforming the systems in which they operate. This process commences with personal commitment to change coupled to a redefinition of the problem that takes it away from individual pathology and onto inadequate social structures and oppressive social relations. Ultimately, anti-racist action aims to establish egalitarian social relations which combine both personal and societal responsibility towards others.

Anti-racism awareness training starts from the premise that society's social organisation is responsible for creating racism. Individuals perpetuate it in their actions because the social relationships they enact reproduce racist structures and patterns of behaviour. Individuals are crucial in perpetrating racism, but racism transcends their individual actions and behaviour. That our social organisation creates and legitimates racism does not absolve individuals from taking a stand against it.

Social organisation is created by people. People can change society if they have the will and collective organisation for dismantling society's racist bulwark and eliminating institutionalised racism. The forms that racism assumes vary over time as socio-economic conditions, and our understandings of the steps necessary for its elimination, change. White social workers can become involved in the struggle to eradicate racism by:

- becoming racially aware individuals;
- working to eliminate institutionalised racism in their agency and in their practice; and
- taking up the anti-racist struggle more generally through political activity.

Exercises aimed at examining personal awareness of racism

The connections between individual, institutional and cultural racism can be explored by examining how these are embedded in our perceptions of black people and the statements we make about them in performing our daily work.

Exercise 1: Examining our views on who holds power

This exercise explores white social workers' unconscious endorsement of relations of subordination in their understanding of black people's location in the labour hierarchy and the status they hold.

A. *Imagine yourself and your reactions in the following hypothetical situation:*

You are a white social worker and have been talking on the phone to the Head of a residential home about getting a place for one of your clients across a period of a couple of weeks. You eventually meet the person when you go to take the client there. You discover that person is black. (You can imagine yourself talking to any other highly placed person elsewhere if this facilitates your thinking about it.)

B. Then answer the following questions:

● Did you expect the Head of the home to be white?
●. How did you react to the discovery that s/he was black?
● To what extent were you surprised to see a black person in charge?
● Why were you surprised (even if only ever so slightly)?

To understand the racism latent in this situation, we have to consider the responses ranging from a low degree to a high degree of surprise in terms of our assumptions and expectations about who holds power in society. The norm is that the powerholder is a white, middle class male. Our acceptance of this state of affairs as white social workers is revealed through: (a) the surprise, albeit well disguised, when we encounter black people in decision-making posts; this is particularly evident when a black person is in charge of a home with mainly white residents, or a district team in a predominantly white area; and (b) not questioning the lack of black representation amongst fieldworker grades, the upper echelons of management and the decision-making apparatuses. Expectations about black people being 'in their place' result in white people being taken aback *even when* black people are found to be in charge of institutions that white workers have little enthusiasm for. Yet, organisations which white workers eschew are more likely to provide sites in which black people will be given the chance to rise to a position of prominence through their own efforts.

White social workers' assumption that white people are the legitimate holders of society's resources is indirectly revealed when they express surprise that black clients have 'nice homes', 'nice cars', etc. Implied in these statements is the view that they have goods which are inappropriate for those in their place, i.e. 'they have risen above their station' (Comer and Poussaint, 1975). Such judgemental comments have often appeared in reports prepared for the courts (Denney, 1992). Sometimes racist comments are made when attempting to counter racist expectations. The following example taken from a social enquiry report written by a white probation officer on a black man is indicative of this:

> The probation officer wrote, 'Mr K has a brand new Rover, which he paid for in cash'. Since Mr K had not been charged with stealing a Rover (or any other car), anti-racist social workers would question the relevance of this information. When asked, about this, the probation officer concerned replied he wanted to pre-empt the court's expectations about Afro-Caribbeans. He thought that showing Mr K's diligence might secure a more lenient treatment

from the court. Mr K had been charged with assault. He claimed he had been defending himself from a racist attack by a group of white lads who were not facing charges.

This short extract exposes a number of racist stereotypes and assumptions revolving around black people's immigration status; black people's capacity to work and save money; black people's right to defend themselves against racist attacks; and white people's privilege in defining the situation. Whilst the intention is to the contrary, the net effect of this approach confirms racist stereotypes. The individual concerned is made to appear an exception, i.e. he is not like other black people who, it is assumed, fraudulently own 'nice' things. Black people in general are thereby pathologised without cause, and white people's definition of their position reigns supreme.

Exercise 2: Examining 'hidden' racism

White people's assumptions about and perceptions of black people and the allocation of power and resources to them can be usefully explored in a group setting. The following exercise is aimed at doing this and can be undertaken in an area team. However, black members of the team should not participate in this exercise in the same session(s) as their white colleagues. The hurtful nature of the comments expressed makes it inappropriate to use black people as enablers in getting white colleagues to deal with their racism. The statements should be read out and responses made initially in a *brainstorming* format. Brainstorming allows all participants to make spontaneous statements which are written down when they are made without being evaluated for merit. The responses are subsequently analysed and assessed by the group, highlighting the racist elements contained within them. The advantage of doing this exercise in a white people only group is that it allows individuals to appreciate the complexities of racism and compare their perceptions, attitudes and understanding of structural constraints with others like them and spare black people the pain of having to listen to racist comments, intentional or otherwise. It also allows white people to get on with addressing the issue instead of 'dumping' it on black people.

The statements below reveal both the subtlety and the variety of ways in which racism is expressesed in the actions and attitudes of social workers. They also show how these are underpinned by policies and practices which have racist effects. These statements, made by white social workers, form the basis of the brainstorming session.

Statements:

1. Black clients come to the office with so many conflicting demands. What do they *really* want?
2. Racism is rare amongst social workers.
3. Other ethnic minority groups have settled in this country and improved themselves without 'positive discrimination'. Why shouldn't black people do likewise?
4. When black clients get angry, I feel so helpless.
5. The problem isn't racism. It's just that social workers don't feel good about themselves and what they are doing.
6. I'm not racist, I just think each ethnic group is different and should keep itself to itself. Black social workers should deal with black clients.
7. When a black client complains, hundreds of white people rush in to help. If a white client complains, everyone turns deaf.
8. How can I be pro-black clients without being anti-white clients?
9. I personally have no say in the formation of this Department's policies, racist or otherwise.
10. How can social workers solve *the black problem*?
11. Every individual client should be judged on his or her merits.
12. Black clients and community groups could do more for themselves by using the anti-racist legislation available in Britain.
13. Black clients should acknowledge social workers' efforts in dealing with the black problem. They are doing all they can to help.
14. I know these clients so well that I never think of them as black.
15. Some of my closest social work colleagues are black.
16. Black clients are over-sensitive. They over-react by reading more into a situation than is really there.
17. Home Office statistics have shown that there is a higher crime rate in black neighbourhoods.
18. For white social workers to progress in their anti-racist work, groups examining racism in their departments must include black members.
19. Black clients shouldn't be expected to integrate into British society if they don't really want to.
20. Black clients who show an interest in their affairs don't want us to deal with their problems.

Now examine your replies. You will discover that the statements cover racism in a number of different guises. The key ones which should be highlighted are: the variety of ways in which black people are blamed for creating racism; holding black people responsible for eradicating racism; devaluing black people's contribution to society; pathologising black people and their culture; exaggerating the progress that white people have made in eliminating racism; assuming that white ways of doing things are superior; believing that 'race' is not a crucial social issue in this society; and over-emphasising the powerlessness of the white individual in initiating social change.

Although there are a number of aspects of racism which can be identified in each statement, the key ones are:

1. White people assume that black people do not know what they want. It's a way of trivialising their demands and struggles for racial justice. White people from their superior standpoint do know.
2. Racism is defined as crude, irrational behaviour, thereby ignoring the significance of institutional and cultural racism on personal attitudes and action.
3. The person making the statement has failed to grasp the specific conditions surrounding black people's experiences of life here. Structurally, it is not the same as that of earlier groups of settlers.
4. The statement blames the victims of racism for their plight.
5. This comment attempts to avoid the issue.
6. Black people are held responsible for racism and for doing something about it. It suggests there is no role for white people in deconstructing racism.
7. The impact of anti-racist measures thus far is being exaggerated.
8. By assuming that black and white people are at the same starting points, and in competition with each other, the person is making inappropriate comparisons.
9. In externalising racism, such individuals are abrogating personal responsibility for what happens in a racist society, and denying their role in perpetuating racism.
10. This statement pathologises black people, and separates social work off from what happens in society, seeing it as an apolitical activity.
11. By looking at the situation in universalistic terms, the person is not recognising the specificity of the black experience. It is structurally different from that of white people.

12. Responsibility for eradicating racism is shunted onto black people's shoulders. It also ignores the weakness of legislation such as the Race Relations Act, affirmative action and contract compliance in enforcing anti-racist measures.
13. This comment reveals how white people exaggerate their efforts and their impact in eliminating racism.
14. This statement depicts the *colour-blind* approach. In it, black people are turned into honorary white people.
15. By treating black people as if they were white people, this comment is assimilationist. Black people with their specificity washed out are acceptable to white people who can make exceptions for the few who are not like the rest, i.e. *black*.
16. This statement blames the black victim.
17. The white person is pathologising black people.
18. In this comment, white people shunt responsibility for eliminating racism onto black people.
19. By presenting racism as a matter of personal choice, this statement ignores the institutional and cultural dimensions of racism.
20. The responsibility for eliminating racism is placed upon black people.

Anti-racism awareness training and organisational change: changing employment policies

Black people's employment prospects in social work reflect institutionalised racism. They are generally employed in small numbers in the low status echelons of the labour hierarchy, particularly in residential work and, in Britain, on Section 11 contracts. Black people are largely absent from prestigious posts and the range of work. White people take this situation for granted, assuming that black people are suitable only for a limited number of jobs. Anti-racism awareness training engages white social workers in organisational change, opening up opportunities for black people. This they can undertake by confronting agency policy and practice in terms of (a) the resources made available to black people; (b) the employment of black workers within that agency; and (c) the position of black people within the agency's decision-making structures. White social workers should look at their agency policies and practice and ask the following questions:

- In which services are black people either under-represented or over-represented?
- What are the reasons for their being either under-represented or over-represented?
- How can either their under-representation or their over-representation be rectified so that racial justice and equality is ensured?
- What positions do black people hold within this agency?
- . Are black people found proportionately at all levels of the agency's career ladder?
- If black people are either absent as workers or disproportionately represented at the lowest rungs of the career ladder, what steps need to be taken to correct this?

The following exercise sensitises white social workers to some of the issues they will confront when undertaking organisational change. A fuller discussion of this takes place in Chapter 5.

Exercise 3: Simulation/role-play

You are a white social worker in Middletown District Team A. The area's housing stock is fairly run down; employment opportunities are few. Middletown's population contains 15 per cent black people. The black population has been there for a very long time, and two-thirds of the young people under 30 were born in Middletown. They are descendants of people whose origins were in the Indian sub-continent, Africa, the Caribbean and China. Your team is located in the middle of an area inhabited mainly by black people, but few of them come to you for services. None of the workers in your team is black. There is, however, one black home help, a Muslim woman born in the Gujerat in India. The cleaning lady was born in Jamaica. You have been on an anti-racism awareness training course and the extensive racism in the situation strikes you on your return. You raise the matter informally with your colleagues, but they think you are exaggerating the problem. You discuss it with your senior during a supervision session and agree to raise the issue in a team meeting. There are so many aspects you want to take up, you don't know where to begin. You decide it might be simplest if you tried arguing for the employment of a black social worker. Role-play your team meeting.

Take 10 minutes to assign roles and have individuals prepare themselves.

Characters

You can base the role-play on the following characters, or vary them to resemble your own team more closely if you wish:

District Manager: S/he tries to be helpful, but is fairly muddled in her/his thinking on this issue.

Principal Social Worker: Her/his main interest is in child abuse cases. S/he doesn't think much of this happens in black communities.

Home Help Organiser: S/he thinks s/he has 'done' her/his bit by having one black home help already when there are few black elderly clients on the books. For this, s/he blames the social workers. Anyway, white people have complained when Mrs Kahn went to them. She kept coughing over everything.

Social Worker, Level 3: S/he doesn't think black people should be 'given' social work jobs. They should be properly qualified for them and get them in competition with others.

Social Worker, Level 2: S/he has much sympathy for your views, but doesn't see how the situation could be changed. S/he is the NALGO team representative.

Social Worker, Level 1: S/he came on the course with you and agrees with your analysis. S/he thinks you are 'brave' to try and do something about it.

Social Care Assistant: S/he thinks you are coming up with another of your 'new-fangled' ideas. You get one every time you go on a course, but they never amount to much. Mind you, s/he's never seen you so 'het up' about things before.

Several Observers: To watch the role-play and take notes.

Duration of role-play: 20 minutes

Discussion: Guideline Questions. Take an hour for the discussion. Spend a few minutes after the role-play talking about how each person felt in his/her role. Then consider the following questions:

1. What aspects of each character in the role-play did you identify as racist?
2. What aspects of the organisation's policies and practices did you identify as racist?
3. What strategies can you develop for changing some of the attitudes and understandings of your colleagues?
4. How can you develop support for your ideas?
5. What measures can you take to stop yourself from feeling isolated, frustrated and bad about what is happening?
6. What organisations, groups and individuals could you contact to help you change agency policies and practices?
7. How can you get your union to adopt anti-racist policies?
8. How could you develop more appropriate relationships with the black communities on your doorstep, bearing in mind their heterogeneity?

Introducing organisational change is a difficult and challenging process, made even more problematic because those initiating change are simultaneously struggling with their own racist stereotypes and expectations. This becomes especially relevant in responding to the 'black community' as a homogeneous entity, and perceiving the employment of a few black workers as solving the problem of racism.

Anti-racist awareness training and trainers

The previous exercises show how difficult and complicated the business of becoming racially aware and moving into anti-racist practice is. Although not the ultimate word on the issue, they highlight how much work remains to be done to function appropriately as an anti-racist practitioner on the personal, interpersonal and organisational levels. I strongly recommend that all white social workers participate in anti-racism awareness training, bearing the following in mind.

Firstly, anti-racist awareness training, if done properly, will not be an easy undertaking for white social workers. It will profoundly challenge your concepts of self, of others and of your relationships with them. So, prepare yourself for an emotionally draining time. Secondly, the question of whom you should approach to do this work with you is not easily answered. There is considerable controversy about who should be involved in teaching on these courses and whether white trainers can perform an adequate job. I take the view that talking about the experience of black people is a matter that only they can address. Hence, only black trainers should be used in this context. However, there is a role for white trainers in talking about how we utilise racist practices to reproduce and perpetuate both individual, institutional and cultural racism; discussing what racism does to us; asking questions about what we can do to carry on the anti-racist struggle in our organisations and amongst our colleagues; and considering the steps we need to take to achieve this. White trainers can also help to develop support groups for white anti-racist social workers struggling with the resistance emanating from white colleagues and the exasperation of black colleagues for their failure substantially to progress their implementation of anti-racist practice.

4

Social Working Black Families

Problematising black families

The white supremacist ideology deeply embedded in social work practice can be explored by examining white social workers' intervention in black families. The family, as the raw material of practice, provides the major backdrop against which social work intervention occurs. White feminists have criticised at length white social workers' involvement with white families (Dominelli, 1986; Wilson, 1977). When it comes to intervening in black families, white social workers pretend that there has been no such critique and that 'the white family', unlike 'the black family', is the source of all that is wonderful. Intervention in black families becomes problematic because white social workers treat black family forms as pathological and deviant for transmitting traditions differing from white, middle class, heterosexual ones. As one white social worker involved with an Afro-Caribbean family informed me, 'They are not like us. They're more strict with their children. They're more ambitious for them'.

Handling black families in these terms is racist. It enables white social workers to problematise black families by classifying their relationships, expressions of concern for each other's welfare, and child-care methods as inferior to white ones, and label them inadequate and inappropriate (Bryan et al., 1985). Such labelling undermines the confidence of black parents and black children (Comer and Poussaint, 1975). Black people's aspirations for improvement in their status through upward mobility has been stigmatised as being over-ambitious (Ahmed, 1984). Black people's rejection of the inferior status allocated to them has been castigated by white social workers as poor socialisation for the roles they can occupy in Britain. As one white social worker put it:

94

Asian families are not preparing children for the jobs they can take in society. They refuse to allow their youngsters to join YTS schemes preferring them to go on in school and train to be engineers!

Black families are generally presented as breaking down and in crisis by white people who do not see their dynamic presence and positive influence in black peoples' lives (Bromley and Longino, 1972). White social workers constantly belittle black families by pathologising them, seeing in them only weaknesses and ignoring their strengths. Black family forms have shown remarkable resilience, enabling black people to survive society's racist onslaughts and offering their members a positive sense of identity which contrasts strongly with the negative ones posited by white social workers (Amos, 1984; Bromley and Longino, 1972; Bryan *et al.*, 1985). White social workers' pejorative assessment of black families and the reinforcement of racist stereotypes through their intervention are central to the 'social working', i.e. the social control of black families, and form the major avenues through which they 'clientise' black people.

Thus, the personal social services, like the educational system and the criminal justice system, reinforce racist stereotypes which pathologise black people and confirm their subordinate status. The dynamics of pathology underpin the 'clientisation' of black people. The 'clientisation' of black people is the process whereby black people having 'client' status are systematically belittled and have their contribution to society devalued, and their access to their share of social resources, including the personal social services, blocked. Black people become 'clients' through referrals from welfare organisations, including the health services, the agencies of law and order, and themselves.

The social working of black families by white social workers is particularly evident in their handling of child abuse in black families, the fostering and adoption of black children, and issues affecting black women, black youth and black elders. This chapter examines the ways in which white social workers pathologise black families through their interventions.

The myth of the 'black family'

White stereotypes of black families are rooted in social relations founded on arrogant and racist notions of white cultural supremacy. These begin with the idea that there is one black family type which acts as the norm whereby all black families are gauged. Except that 'the black family' exists primarily in the perceptions of and is reinforced through the practices of white people, there is in reality, *not the black family, but a rich and diverse variety of black family forms,* each with their own specific set of relationships, obligations and networks.

The myth of 'the black family' has been given a significant measure of respectability and credence through academic works such as Moynihan's *The Negro Family* (1965), which assembles 'facts' substantiating white people's stereotypes about black families. Although this book was quickly and thoroughly discredited by black authors in America where it was written (e.g. Ryan, 1972; Hill, 1972; Rainwater, 1966), it has entered the gates of academe to become a 'classical text' on 'the black family' in both Britain and America. The analysis that the black American family:

> has been forced into a matriarchal structure which... seriously retards the progress of the group as a whole, and imposes a crushing burden on the Negro male and... Negro women (Moynihan, 1965)

confirms white people's view of black families as deviant and unstable. Usually used in teaching without reference to black writers' critiques, this book reproduces these myths in generations of young scholars who go on to become social workers and community activists.

Common stereotypes of the black family, particularly of African or Afro-Caribbean descent, cover the sexual prowess of black men; the lack of sexual morality amongst black women, as evidenced by a high ratio of single parenthood; the absence of a stable family tradition; the lack of family bonds between family members; and the power of strong, domineering matriarchs complemented by weak black men incapable of sustaining stable relationships (*Ebony*, 1986; Staples, 1988). These myths reveal that black families are being measured against the norm of the ideal, white, middle class, heterosexual nuclear family. Asian families are portrayed as more controlling, particularly of their womenfolk, and sexually repressed (Wilson, 1978). Other ethnic groups, for example, First Nations people in America, also have their family forms problematised by being measured against the white, two-parent family yardstick and being found deficient through the construction of similar sorts of myths, which aim to devalue their culturally specific child-rearing practices and expressions of sexuality in particular (Haig-Brown, 1988).

The stereotypes described negate the living reality of black people, but judge it in negative terms which problematise 'the black family'. White racism is more complex and contradictory than its myths on 'the black family' imply. As Amrit Wilson demonstrates, sexism, racism and ignorance combine to condemn black people whatever they do. For example, a white male psychiatrist accused a young Bangladeshi woman he was allegedly treating for depression of being morally 'loose' because she wore beautiful saris (Wilson, 1978, p. 24). Moreover, white people draw distinctions between different ethnic groupings within the black population, although these differences are likely to be construed in negative ways. For example, in Britain different stereotypes apply to the 'West Indian family' and the 'Asian family'. Thinking of the range in family forms which exists amongst people whose origins are in the Caribbean Islands and the Indian sub-continent in these terms creates subdivisions in the myth of 'the black family', turning the myth on its head whilst still drawing on the stereotypes contained within it. West Indian families are deemed unstable because 'they are run by domineering women who are morally loose'. The strength and unity of the Asian family is problematised. Asian women are too docile and sexually repressed (Wilson, 1978). Asian men are too powerful. From this we can conclude that whatever living arrangements black people make, white people will find them wanting. In other words, a 'deficit' model of human relations is the outcome of these (racist) evaluations.

Moreover, white people ignore the fact that legislation actively curtails black people's right to a self-defined family life (see Plummer, 1978). In Britain, for example, immigration controls since 1962 have made it virtually impossible for black family units to be reconstructed in their traditional totality as is demonstrated by the following case study:

A Pakistani Muslim man was made redundant and sought advice from an Advice Centre on making a claim for supplementary benefit. He had two of his children living with him and his wife in England. His other two children, one aged 12 and the other aged 15, were living with relatives in Pakistan. Before becoming unemployed, he used to send money to his relatives for their care. Now, he was having problems making ends meet. His wife did not get child benefit for his two children resident outside Britain because this is prohibited by the legislation governing entitlement to child benefit.

The welfare rights worker, a white man, felt unable to offer the claimant any support for his claim. This case exemplifies how white workers collude with institutionalised racism. The white worker was placed in this position by the way his job was defined, i.e. giving advice on the existing legislation. Advice work predicated on responding to individual requests does not facilitate challenging the racist bases of its provisions. The white worker wanting to respond to the obvious needs of the black man in meeting his responsibilities to his dependants, felt powerless and hamstrung by the framework in which he operated. When telling me of his predicament, he said: 'There was nothing I felt I could do. I didn't know how to give him what he wanted. And, I'm not very good at challenging racism, though it was clear to me this was what I was up against'.

Had this white advice worker been working in anti-racist ways, taking on institutionalised racism would have been central to his response. To do this, he would have had to redefine his task and work simultaneously on several levels, drawing on the help of others: colleagues, his own organisation and people in other organisations – trade unions and professional associations, campaigns and networks. On the individual level, he would have sought to relieve the client's personal distress by facilitating contact between him and black organisations experienced in dealing with similar situations. Besides ensuring the claimant was getting everything to which he was entitled, the advice worker could have investigated other sources of financial aid and helped him expedite his application to bring his children to Britain, by calling on other organisations and resources, for example the Joint Council for the Welfare of Immigrants (JCWI) and the United Kingdom Immigrants Advisory Service (UKIAS), various immigration campaigns, MPs and the Commission for Racial Equality (CRE).

Dealing with institutionalised racism in the child benefit legislation would have required the white worker to involve himself and others in a campaign exposing the injustices perpetrated by the existing provisions and putting pressure on the government to change the legislation on child benefits. Thus, the white worker would have been challenging the view that the claimant was creating a problem by having his children in Pakistan, and focusing instead on an iniquitous system. Similar legislation limiting the rights of black people to bring in dependants exists in other countries in Western Europe and the USA (see Read and Simpson, 1991).

Poor employment prospects and bad housing also deny black people choices in establishing their preferred family forms. White social workers continue to divide black families by taking disproportionate numbers of black children into care by 'inappropriately intervening in the family process' (Brummer, 1988; Lambeth Social Services Committee, 1981). Revealing that black children are more likely to end up in care than white children when white social workers intervene in their families, the Lambeth child care study exposes a further disturbing trend. Whilst white children in care come from families which are 'atypical' of the white families in the borough, black children come from families which are 'very representative of black families in the borough, covering a wider range of income, employment and housing situations' (Lambeth Social Services Committee, 1981, p. 7). In other words, white social workers are pronouncing the whole spectrum of black families inadequate. The high-profile intervention that white social workers adopt in reaction to black families reveals that although their intervention in general compels white families to stay together, it forces black families apart. It has led black people to perceive white social workers as child snatchers (Wilson, 1995).

White social workers' intervention with black children

White social workers are anxious about the appropriateness of black families' child-rearing practices, relationships between black parents and their children, and women's roles within black families. These anxieties are central in the social work equation of pathologising black families. White supremacist values channel white social workers' thinking along the lines that the welfare of black children is better served by their being either fostered or adopted by white families or brought up in predominantly white institutions. Conceptualising their interventions in these terms has led to poor services being delivered to the individuals concerned; a failure to place either black or white children in care with black foster and adoptive families; not staffing residential institutions with black employees at all levels; and not creating an anti-racist environment capable of nurturing black identity and psychological development in residential establishments. Meanwhile, white people congratulate themselves on doing a good job because 'the children suffered no obvious harm' (Gill and Jackson, 1982; Tizard and Phoenix, 1993). This usually means that black children have been successfully indoctrinated into thinking they are white (BCSG, 1984). That is, they have had to either repress or reject their black identity and become colour-blind, reflecting the nature of the white families into which they have been placed (Maximé, 1986).

A one-way traffic in children

In keeping with the white supremacist belief that white child-rearing practices are superior to black ones, white social workers resist the idea that black families can appropriately foster and adopt white children. They are reluctant to accept black parents as *bona fide* fosterers and adopters by placing white children with them. This traffic in children has been criticised by black practitioners for being one way: black children going into white foster homes (ABSWAP, 1981; Devine, 1983; Small, 1987). The lack of mutuality in the placing of children in care has caused black professionals to define such practices as another form of cultural imperialism in which black children become commodities of exchange (ABSWAP, 1981; Comer and Poussaint, 1972).

Whether white people agree with this interpretation of the transaction is irrelevant. The important questions that white social workers have to consider are why so few prospective black parents for fostering and adopting black children are on their books and why virtually no white children are placed with black families. White social workers who justify this situation by saying that children are best placed with those who share similar racial and cultural backgrounds still have to explain why this axiom does not apply to black children. An honest answer is better than one camouflaging racist practice as it at least allows organisations and individuals the possibility of undertaking action to reverse their position. White social workers attempting to blame black communities for the lack of black adoptive and fostering families also need to explain why authorities such as Lambeth Social Services Department, acting under pressure from black social workers to alter their procedures and criteria for selecting black foster parents, have few problems filling their books with potential black foster families (Small, 1987).

The inclusion of other important criteria – the ability to love and relate to a black child as a *black child*; skills in handling racist onslaughts; knowledge of black people's cultures, languages, religions and ethnicities; a sense of positive black identity (all essential to the full development of black children); and links with black communities on the social work agenda, did not occur until black practitioners criticised the previous criteria. Their challenge has yielded better practice in fostering and adoption and opened the field so that those now accepted are more representative of the families found in the community (ABSWAP, 1981). Moreover, ongoing pressure from black people has been influential in ensuring that the 1989 Children Act includes a commitment to take racial, religious and cultural factors into account (see section 22 (5)(c)). Other countries have also begun to address this issue. For example, New Zealand has passed legislation in the form of the 1989 Children, Young Persons and their Families Act which is based on recognising Maori traditions and is more ethnically sensitive than previous legislation. This Act signifies a response to Maori critiques that (white) social workers in New Zealand had imposed anglocentric models of child welfare on them.

Transracial adoptions

Despite legislative initiatives, transracial adoptions remain controversial, as do policies endorsing same 'race' placements. In Britain, the Norfolk case that hit the papers in the summer of 1993 involved a couple consisting of a white (English) man and an Asian woman. Their application to adopt a black child was allegedly refused on the grounds that the black woman claimed never to have experienced racism. Although this allegation was later proven to be unfounded, the media had a field-day using it to undermine 'same race' policies and belittle white social workers' attempts to take seriously black people's criticisms of *colour-blind* practice.

White social workers working on an individualistic basis have become immobilised and cannot easily perceive and confront the negative features in their practice identified by black social workers in places like Lambeth. Trapped by institutionalised racism, a conviction about the superiority of their own culture, ignorance about other people's culture, personal anxieties about risk taking in complex situations which become open to public scrutiny if they are mishandled, and powerlessness in changing policy and practice, their reaction is to stay clear of what they perceive as a 'minefield'. Feelings of entrapment ensure that white social workers minimise the risks they take by playing a cautious role or going by the book instead of either using their discretion or challenging the system. In this context, placing black children in white families becomes their safest option. By exercising choice or judgement about the appropriateness of intervening in this manner, they pathologise black people and limit their right to self-determination.

White social workers should beware of promoting an individual black person's right to self-determination without putting in place support networks and structures provided by other black individuals and organisations. Placing black people in unsupported environments, lacking clarity about the objectives they seek to achieve through their interventions, and not having the resources to implement their intended plan of action, can be counterproductive and increase the black person's vulnerability in racist situations. For example, having a white family foster a black child because the child and its parents wish it, without exploring the reasons behind their request, is not encouraging client self-determination.

Many black people have internalised racist values which pathologise black families (Lorde, 1984). They may be colluding with a white social worker's own racist view that white families provide superior care, so black parents would 'naturally' want their child to be reared by them.

Instead of acting on the basis of taken-for-granted assumptions, an anti-racist social worker would explore the motives of both parents and child by carrying out a full assessment of the family. Equally, white social workers who pounce on black families to care for 'difficult to place black children', leaving the family unsupported in doing so, are not providing an anti-racist service. They are being racist in so far as their actions depict an uncaring attitude suggesting that second-rate families are appropriate for second-rate people. They are also being racist in expecting a black family to do whatever work is necessary without considering its needs for additional resourcing and support. This latter response poignantly highlights their racist assumptions about black families.

White social workers' handling of the Jasmine Beckford family reveals a further salient point; that it was white social workers in a predominantly white department working with a black child and her black family is seldom mentioned, even in Blom-Cooper's report, *A Child in Trust* (1986). Yet 'race' is a crucial aspect of the dynamics in the case, not only because racism adversely affects black people, but also because white people are afraid to confront the issue. They are scared stiff of challenging black people's statements or behaviour because they might be accused of being racist (Banks, 1971; Comer and Poussaint, 1972). This fear makes them feel unable to take control of the situation, assess it fully and reach a well-founded professional judgement about the appropriate action to take in the circumstances. Knowing oneself – one's fears, aspirations and values – and using this knowledge in the casework relationship is central to traditional concepts of good social work practice (Compton and Galaway, 1975, p. 143). Failure to deal with this fear through a lack of self-knowledge can produce appalling practice. It is important therefore, to address it through anti-racist staff development and training.

Addressing white social workers' fears

In short, if white social workers do not address racism directly, they cannot come to terms with their fears about working with black people. Moreover, not doing so actively blocks effective interaction between them and black people and leads to poor practice. If racism is not considered relevant when it undoubtedly is, detrimental consequences are unavoidable. Black people may pay with their lives for not getting the services they require, as Jasmine Beckford did (Blom-Cooper, 1986). Or, as Banks (1971, p. 137) warns:

In the effort to help the black man [*sic*]... the issue of black and white becomes significant. Indeed, if this issue is not considered, much of the new effort to help the black man may go astray.

Meanwhile, white social workers and their social services departments carry on ignoring the problems engendered by racism. When this happens, both the department and the white social worker have failed black clients. The department has also failed white social workers, as their difficulty in confronting racism, including their own, is not being addressed. If white social workers can acknowledge racism as an issue or problem they have to deal with, it is easier for them to refer black clients to other black people or organisations who can provide the relevant services whilst they seek support for overcoming their racism and anxieties about it. Staff development and training geared to the individual worker's needs may be helpful here.

In other situations, 'race' may be acknowledged slightly, but as a problem which cannot be tackled. Sometimes, lack of resources is used as a reason for not doing so, for example not providing Sikh elders with Sikh home helps because departments do not employ the relevant employees and additional home helps are unavailable as services are being cut back. In other instances, statutory agencies transfer their obligation to provide facilities for all client groups onto the voluntary sector. Social services departments often use voluntary organisations run primarily by white people to avoid establishing their own anti-racist services. In Britain, this is more likely to occur now that the National Health Services and Community Care Act compels local authorities to spend part of their budget in the voluntary and commercial sectors. Social services departments have at times formed poorly funded voluntary agencies to provide cheap 'band-aid' services for black people.

By evading their responsibilities, management in statutory agencies colludes with and perpetuates racist social work policies and practices. In so far as voluntary organisations plug gaps in statutory provisions, they collude with institutional racism and enable social services departments to continue avoiding the development of adequate facilities for black people. Voluntary bodies are, however, usually poorly equipped to work in anti-racist ways. Hence, black clients continue to receive inappropriate services. Presented to me as an example of 'successful intervention in a black family', the following case makes this point and demonstrates the process whereby black families are clientised.

A health visitor referred Indejit, a Sikh woman who spoke Punjabi but virtually no English, to the local social services district team because she was 'suffering from post-natal depression after giving birth to a girl-child'. As there were no Punjabi-speaking black social workers in the team which had few referrals involving black people, a white English-speaking social worker went to do a home visit. She was welcomed into the home by Indejit and her eldest daughter, aged 9, whom the white social worker used as a translator. Following the visit, the white social worker decided that the social services department had nothing to offer: 'Indejit seemed alright. She was merely experiencing the "normal let-down in Asian families after giving birth to four (successive) daughters". But the white social worker thought 'Indejit was lonely', so she asked a voluntary agency to see her in a 'befriending way and help her learn English'.

The voluntary agency in question operated on a shoe-string budget, including some funding from social services which had initiated its formation several years earlier. It did not have any black Punjabi-speaking workers either. But it wanted to demonstrate its lack of prejudices by making itself available to the black community, so they sent along their best worker, Sue – a sensitive older white woman who 'would be a friend to Indejit and teach her English'. The white worker and Indejit 'got on well'. Indejit learnt some English and Sue got invited to many of the family's festive occasions. Although Sue noticed Indejit looked neither well nor happy, she did not broach the subject of Indejit's 'depression'.

She felt she need not worry about it because Indejit had been seeing her 'GP who had put her on tranquillisers'. Yet when Sue left the agency and another worker, Ros, took her place, she discovered, quite by accident, that Indejit was being regularly physically abused by her husband. Yet she did nothing to ensure Indejit's safety. Ros claimed 'There was nothing I could do. There's no women's refuge in the town, let alone an Asian women's one. And social services said there was nothing they could do since the children were safe'.

This case is one in which collusion with institutionalised racism and sexism is occurring on a massive scale. Within this social services department, institutionalised racism flourishes because management has abrogated its responsibility with respect to black clients, for example providing Punjabi-speaking black workers who can make a proper assessment of Indejit's needs. No one else in the department is taking up the issue of the lack of services appropriate to the needs of black people in general and black women in particular. The voluntary agency colludes with this institutionalised racism by accepting responsibility for the case when it is not equipped to do the job. The white social worker personally colludes with institutional racism by (a) making an assessment visit knowing she is unable to communicate with Indejit, and not taking steps to overcome this problem by demanding the employment of a Punjabi-speaking black social worker; (b) passing judgement on the nature of the problem without sufficient evidence; (c) using racist stereotypes to justify further inaction; and (d) keeping quiet about the department's general failure to address the needs of black men and women. The white voluntary workers collude with the racism displayed in the handling of the case by accepting the white social worker's assessment of the problem, and not responding to the issue of domestic violence. Moreover, the social workers have been entrapped in reinforcing racist practices in this situation through the best of intentions – wishing to demonstrate their lack of racial prejudice by providing a service to this black family.

Indejit needs someone she can speak to directly and who would understand her specific situation in the langauge in which she as the client is fluent. To make possible an adequate response without the requisite skilled personnel in place, the social services department should have made additional arrangements to bring in a Punjabi-speaking Sikh social worker. In the short term, Britain is not so vast a country that a social services department which argues that having 'few black families' living in its area makes it 'uneconomic to employ black workers' cannot develop links with other authorities which do recruit black staff to purchase their services. Regional links between several authorities to facilitate such arrangements and authorise extra payments for black workers with mobility across the region could be set in motion easily and quickly by management were it so inclined. Authorities located in areas where communities of black people live should employ sufficient black staff to provide the services these communities need. In the long term, black social workers should be found in all parts of Britain, irrespective of whether or not black communities are located within a social services department's boundaries. Any black person is entitled to walk into any office in the country and receive a service which meets his or her specific needs. Knowing their limitations in providing the services relevant to black clients should encourage white anti-racist social workers to press their departments to develop links with relevant black organisations and acquire the resources they need to ensure that they provide black people with the appropriate services. It is also important to acknowledge the skills that black workers bring to the job by paying for these and budgeting for their use.

Moreover, Indejit's case illustrates how employing institutions ride on white workers' sympathies and 'desire to offer something' to those whom they know would not otherwise get a service, whatever their needs. Employers exploit white social workers' humanity by forcing them to provide inadequate and inappropriate services, thereby making them poor practitioners and less human in the process. Meanwhile, agencies are saving money. Compelling poorly equipped workers to do tasks they cannot handle has become one way in which employers use racism to ration their resources and give black clients the message that their needs are no great concern of theirs.

Both the white social worker and the white voluntary workers responding to Indejit are reinforcing institutionalised sexism by not making available specific provisions to meet women's needs as women, or considering Indejit's personal needs to be important enough for intervention in their own right. Instead, they relate to her as a mother who has to be kept 'coping' with her family responsibilities, responding only to those aspects of her situation they deem potentially disruptive of her ability to look after her children.

The use of interpreters

White social workers should also appreciate the power structures and dynamics within black families and the alterations engendered in these by racism. Their failure to do so in the case above has been triggered by the lack of interpreting facilities and is manifest as the inappropriate involvement of black children as interpreters to plug gaps left by inadequate service provision. The use of children as interpreters has been questioned by black writers like Ahmed (1978). Such exploitation of black children is racist because it facilitates the continuation of inadequate services for black people. When this happens, the black child becomes an integral part of the interaction between black people and powerful white agencies and bureaucracies which hold direct power over them. The black child's knowledge of English also becomes a tool through which parental authority can be undermined. Additionally, the child might not understand either the nature of the problem under discussion or the subtleties of the language being used. His or her help may, therefore, exacerbate the difficulties already present.

Inappropriate interpreters, translators and volunteers have been used for several decades to cut costs because they are cheaper to employ than qualified black social workers skilled in English and other languages. Translation is a highly skilled task if done properly. Using inadequately trained volunteers or makeshift methods relying on whoever is available for this delicate work is a racist crisis response to the lack of appropriate services. It trivialises and devalues this activity. The development of a comprehensive translation service is necessary in establishing anti-racist social work. White social workers can more effectively invest time and energy in fighting racism by refusing to exploit black children for translation purposes and demanding appropriate facilities instead. Translation services should be publicly funded and provide interpreters matched to clients' ethnic grouping, language, religion, class and gender. The provision of interpreters is not an alternative to employing black social workers. Establishing a good translation and interpreting facility provides a venue through which white social workers can contribute to ensuring that black people have equal access to mainstream facilities rather than 'ghettoised' ones.

The convergence of white sexism and racism in social work practice

Institutionalised sexism – the casting of women in the role of carer; the definition of men as breadwinners and 'head' of the family; and the placing of children in a dependent status – combines with white people's racism to subordinate black family forms to the white, middle class, heterosexual nuclear one. Institutionalised sexism also fuses with racism to ensure that black women's specific needs are seen as secondary to their responsibilities to their families. White social workers' stereotypes of black women make them particularly prone to integrating sexism with racism when intervening in the lives of black women and girls. Here, too, racist assumptions that white ways are best underpin white social workers' handling of black women.

White people use white cultural supremacy when judging Asian 'arranged' marriages as inferior to Western 'romantic' marriages. This enables them to redefine 'arranged marriages' as 'marriages of convenience', i.e. phoney marriages. By not facilitating the acceptance of arranged marriages as the expression of loving relationships endorsed by a larger collectivity than the two individuals entering the marriage contract, the idea that arranged marriages are phoney marriages legitimates their being treated as inconsequential by white people and their institutions. This in turn allows white people to start treating black families as if there were no marriage contract and no family to preserve. Conceptualising black families in this fashion makes it easier for white people to ignore the extended ties and relationships existing among them. This includes deprecating black families for preferring boy children, even though white families express similar preferences (see Oakley, 1972) and ignoring the ties which black fathers have with their children (*Ebony*, 1986). It also legitimates the use of immigration laws to keep black families apart (Bryan *et al.*, 1985).

Acting as if women in the West have achieved full liberation, white social workers end up 'putting down' other people's achievements. In saying this, I am not suggesting that sexism should be condoned in any culture. But when white social workers work with black women and black girls wishing to escape the bounds of their particular form of sexism, they should not assume that black women demanding action in their specific situation are rejecting their culture and opting for an Anglo-Saxon life-style. Nor should they convey the impression that white women are free from gender oppression and can tell others what to do. It is not up to white men or women to tell black men and women how to run their lives (Amos and Parmar, 1984; Carby, 1982; Lorde, 1984).

Sexism is already an issue that black feminists are pursuing in their communities as a matter for them to resolve (Carby, 1982; Collins, 1991; hooks, 1989; Lorde, 1984). Meanwhile, black feminists have exposed the racism underpinning white feminists' presentation and understanding of gender oppression within black communities (Amos and Parmar, 1984; Bhavani, 1993; Bryan *et al.*, 1985; Carby, 1982; Parmar, 1982). Black women have condemned the ineptness of white women's demands for reproductive rights, and stances against violence against women. These have been particularly insensitive to the specific needs of black women because they have ignored the racist context within which black communities are situated (Bryan *et al.*, 1985; Collins, 1991). White anti-racist social workers should take seriously how gender oppression operates in white communities (Brook and Davis, 1985; Dominelli, 1984; Dominelli and McLeod, 1989; Hanmer and Statham, 1988; Marchant and Wearing, 1986), leaving black women to address this issue in theirs. This approach does not exclude white women from supporting black women in their endeavours against sexism, provided that black women set the agenda. Moreover, in raising gender issues when uncovering racist practices in social work, black women have unearthed the sexism generally prevalent in social work practice and raised the issue of improving the position of white women as well (hooks, 1989).

Ideally, until white social workers become anti-racist and anti-sexist, they should not intervene in the lives of black women. But, if white social workers find themselves supporting black women who have taken decisions to break from their community, they should explore with them the consequent impact of white racism upon them. Of particular importance is that of preparing them for the isolation, sexual harassment, racial harassment and lack of resources they will encounter. Being aware of the disruption that such action causes black women's relationships with their families and communities, white social workers' task is to facilitate contact with other black women and black support groups sharing their particular views or needs, for example Southall Black Sisters. Although they may encounter opposition from their own communities, black women's support networks and resources can provide the space within which black women can decide what they want to do with their lives and receive support in maintaining their decisions. White social workers facilitating such contacts should know about the existence of support networks and resources aimed specifically at black women and the work these do, particularly in the areas of domestic violence and sexual abuse (see Mama, 1989; Wilson, 1995).

The expression of white sexism in a case involving a black woman

Such knowledge is important if white social workers are helping black women to escape difficult domestic situations, for example black women wishing to leave battering husbands. Simply encouraging black women to leave and take their chances in white society would constitute racist practice. White social workers must discuss with black women the racist white society they will encounter alone once they leave the protection of their community, its familiar surroundings and support networks, unless steps are taken to counteract this. The following account gives an indication of the difficulties that black women face when they are 'helped' by well-meaning white social workers who have not thought through the implications of their interventions to address the broader social context black women live in and the subsequent isolation they encounter and have to deal with.

A young, British-born Muslim woman, Fatima, asked a white social worker to help her leave her arranged marriage because her husband refused to allow her to go to college and pursue a career. Fatima insisted on total secrecy for fear that either her husband or relatives would find out and prevent her from leaving – with force if necessary. The white male social worker agreed because 'Here was a woman crying to be free of an arranged marriage'. However, he was only able to organise accommodation for Fatima in a town far away, where she knew no one. Her first encounter with the DHSS – claiming supplementary benefit – was a nightmare, riddled with racial harassment and racist and sexist innuendo. Whilst queuing, she was told, 'Go back to your husband and let him keep you. We don't want you... scrounging on the state'. The poor woman was devastated by the ordeal. She felt lonely and homesick and missed contact with her mother.

This is an example of white naïvety reinforcing and exacerbating this Muslim woman's experience of both racism and sexism. The sexism that the white social worker has tried to avoid has been intensified through his racism.

The tasks for white social workers working with black women are being sufficiently aware of black women's networks and resources to be able to refer black women to those that are relevant for them, and forming alliances to endorse black women's demands for funds to develop their own support groups and networks. For anti-racist relationships to flourish, black women should control both the funds and the campaign for which the alliance has been created. Guru (1987) presents a powerful case for making more welfare resources – refuges, workers and funds – available to Asian women challenging oppression. White social workers can endorse these activities and put pressure on their authorities to release funds without strings attached. They can also campaign against the law depriving voluntary organisations of their charitable status if they promote issues challenging institutionalised racism because the state considers such action 'political' (Guru, 1987). White social workers can expose the political nature of a law which allows racism to persist by (re)defining situations in these terms. The interventions depicted above demonstrate how white anti-racist social workers need to bring community action and campaigning techniques into social work and facilitate combining personal with structural change.

The expression of white sexism in a case of child abuse

White social workers' views of the black family as pathological can lock black families into disadvantageous long-term intervention. The following case study involving child abuse highlights the variety of ways in which sexism interacts with racism. The case material below is suitable for clarifying issues and identifying:

- sources of cultural, institutional and personal racism, including the links between them; and
- elements of bad practice, including sexism and racism.

A white health visitor referred the Patel family to the social services department shortly after the birth of twins – a boy and a girl – because she considered the care of the girl twin inadequate. She thought the girl child was being rejected and neglected by her mother because the family 'had wanted more sons'. The Patels had two other children, a boy aged 3 and a girl aged 2. A white social worker who did not speak Gujerati, the language the family used in communicating with each other, visited regularly to:

a. advise the mother generally on caring for her babies; and
b. check and discuss the mother's relationship with the girl twin.

Her involvement with the family continued for one year, when Mrs Patel became pregnant again. When she was due to give birth, the twins were received into care. The male twin was returned home promptly following the birth of the third son, but the girl twin remained in care for a year whilst white social workers made intensive visits to the Patels to encourage the mother to prepare for her daughter's return. Meanwhile little contact occurred between mother and daughter, for she was being fostered by a white family some distance away. When the girl twin was returned home, the white social worker provided a day nursery place for her, a home help for her mother, some financial assistance for her unemployed father, accommodation advice for rehousing the family whose two bedroomed terrace was too small, and a white voluntary worker to 'befriend Mrs Patel' by providing language tuition. The 'support of the mother' lasted four years. During this time, the mother's relationship with the girl twin improved, and the case was closed. Three years later, the case was reopened on suspicion that the girl twin was being physically abused. She displayed 'problem behaviour' at home and school. The family requested she be taken into care. The social work intervention this time consisted of:

a. intensive home visits;
b. counselling and advice for Mr and Mrs Patel regarding the 'care and control' of the girl twin; and
c. liaising between the school and parents.

This intervention continued for two years. The situation improved and the case closed.

White social workers saw the Patels two years later when writing reports for the Juvenile Court for the girl twin and her youngest brother. Both had been truanting. This time their intervention focused on:

a. regular home visits;

b. advising and counselling Mrs Patel; and
c. helping the girl twin to organise her leisure time more effectively.

The girl twin was received into care for three weeks to provide the family with space for re-evaluating their views of her. The parents subsequently discharged her from care. The case was closed anew.

This was followed by intermittent involvement at the family's request for advice regarding care and control of the girl twin whose behaviour continued to deteriorate. Meanwhile, the police became concerned about her behaviour, as did the school. She was subsequently moved to a special school with smaller classes offering firm control over its pupils. The girl's behaviour improved slightly. A short time later, the Juvenile Court requested further reports, as the girl was being charged with theft and criminal damage. After the report was completed, further social work intervention seemed unnecessary. So the case was closed.

This case study is riddled with instances of personal, institutional and cultural racism interconnecting with each other, sexism and bad practice. Illustrating the social working of black families, it provides a horrific example of the processes involved in their 'clientisation'. Although discussion on it can cover a number of aspects, I will focus on only a few. Cultural racism is evident in defining black families' child-rearing practices as inferior to white ones, particularly in the handling of girl children. This is particularly evident in the instruction of the mother in 'approved', i.e. white, child-care practices and the child being fostered in a white family without due regard for her cultural and religious heritage. Cultural racism is also expressed in the white social worker's request for a white voluntary worker to 'befriend' the mother and teach her English. The white health visitor's individual racism is conveyed through her assumption that black families treat boy children better because they are preferred to girls. Yet, as she neither spoke Gujerati, nor used a competent interpreter, it is hard to visualise how she acquired the evidence to reach this conclusion. Ignoring communication needs is shoddy practice without the addition of racism. Institution-alised racism is evident in the social services department's failure to provide a black Gujerati-speaking worker who could have properly assessed the problem(s) that needed to be addressed instead of immedi-ately tackling the 'presenting' one. Also, the unspecific nature of the department's responses suggest its workers do not take seriously the needs of black clients.

Racism in these varied forms was integrated into the work to produce a catalogue of bad practice spanning thirteen years. It included not having an adequate system for evaluating, assessing and processing the referral; the failure of both health and social services departments to provide language facilities in the appropriate mother tongue; not providing the family with a black worker to communicate effectively with them; concentrating intervention on the (twin) girl child and her mother, ignoring the needs of the unproblematic sister, the boy children and the father's involvement in their upbringing; not facilitating contact between the girl twin and her parents when she was in care; emphasising the desirability of the family keeping their children well behaved and under control rather than looking at their needs for growth and development; and ignoring the identity needs of the children and limiting the resourcing of the family to advice and practical help in areas compatible with their analysis. Thus, for example, the father's employment prospects are not specifically considered. Instead, constantly reinforcing labels of inadequate mothering, despite the evidence which showed some 'good enough' parenting was taking place with regard to the other three children, emphasising control, and opening and closing the case without due regard for the actual needs of the individuals concerned, mark the poor practice here. Consequnetly, poor practice meant that the social workers involved also missed the opportunity to explore areas of the family's strengths, such as their adequate care of the girl twin's siblings, and use these to promote growth in more problematic ciricumstances.

Good anti-racist practice would have ensured that both the health service and social services department employed black employees who could have spoken directly to the family and addressed their actual needs. Had this occurred, they might have challenged the assertion that preferring boy children leads to the mistreatment of girls and discovered what the real problems were. The case before us would then have been very different.

Multiple oppression: the case of a First Nations woman

White supremacist views, in their more extreme forms, aim to obliterate cultures deemed to be 'inferior' or 'deviating' from the white yardstick whilst simultaneously compelling those at the receiving end of their racist practices to emulate their allegedly superior ways. In some cases, for example Nazi Germany, social work becomes abused as a tool justifying the oppression of vulnerable groups like the Jewish people. In other situations, social work promotes assimilation by another name. Social work intervention became harnessed in pursuit of this end vis-à-vis the aboriginal peoples of North America, Australia and New Zealand. As a result, social work practice became deeply implicated in this form of racist practice and played a key role in dividing black families. Thus the First Nations peoples of North America were subjected to assimilation in the form of cultural as well as physical genocide (Haig-Brown, 1988). By way of illustration, the case study below indicates the multiple ways in which a First Nations woman in Canada was subjected to this particular process of oppression. In it, Joan is initially forced to lose her identity as a First Nations person. The destruction to her sense of self leads to further psychological damage and she is unable to fulfil her responsibilities as a mother. Yet, throughout her tribulations and suffering no one takes the time to find out what she wants, help her acquire the skills to live as an independent being and make real choices about what she wants to do with her life.

Joan was a First Nations woman, aged 21. She had spent much of her early life in care, after the death of her mother from a drug overdose. Once in the residential Home, she was encouraged to 'drop her Indian ways' and adopt 'English' ones. Any lapses on Joan's part were derided. Joan hated her life in the Home. She was constantly 'in trouble' with the white staff who had nicknamed her 'Smoke'. This was not only because she was constantly engaged in the unauthorised smoking of cigarettes, but because her persistent denial of wrong doing when the white staff were looking for culprits was countered with 'there's no smoke without fire', which usually brought forth loud guffaws and lewd looks form the white male members of staff.

When Joan left the care establishment, she was given a small grant to get her started on her new life, but no other form of support. Joan sought employment but was unsuccessful. She became very depressed. She started doing drugs, drinking heavily and engaging in unprotected sex. She soon found herself in a vicious circle of decline which she found impossible to get out of. Any attempts to get support from the white staff at her former residential Home were rebuffed. 'You're not our responsibility now', she was told more than once.

At one point she became pregnant with a white man and gave birth to a daughter who was very fair like her father. After several months of unsuccessfully attempting to look after her, Joan decided to give the child up for adoption.

She rang the social workers in her previous Home and asked them to help her get her child adopted as soon as possible. The social worker who spoke to her suddenly became amenable and said she had a young white couple who could adopt her daughter straight away. They would care for her properly and would not object to her having regular visits to see the child. The two made arrangements to meet the following day. When Joan got to the residential Home, the (white) social worker sat her down and immediately gave her the papers she needed to sign for the adoption to proceed. Without any counselling or discussion, Joan signed the documents, handed over the child and went home.

She spent the next three days in a drunken stupor crying over the loss of her child and wondering if she had done the right thing. Joan never saw her daughter again and no one contacted her to make any arrangements for her to visit the adoptive parents. Indeed, the white social worker overseeing the adoptive process had told the white adoptive parents about Joan and the long history she had of 'doing' drugs and being deviant. This convinced them that making contact with Joan would give them 'more problems than it was worth', so they declined the offer of help in getting in touch with her.

This case study reveals how stereotypes about the 'inferiority' of First Nations peoples and their cultures resulted in Joan losing much of her cultural heritage by being made to adopt 'English ways'. Thus, she is stripped of her dignity and identity on both personal and cultural levels. The impact of such treatment on her personal growth was disregarded without thought. Assimilationist ideologies and practices are also used to exclude Joan from the social work decision-making processes. Moreover, having been labelled inadequate and blamed for her predicament, she is given neither the space nor the support to prove otherwise. Her mothering skills were deemed so lacking that she was not given support to explore the decision to give up her baby for adoption, prepare herself for it emotionally in the first instance and come to terms with it subsequently. Joan's needs as a First Nations person with a right to her heritage are ignored. These same rights with respect of her dual heritage appear to be being violated in relation to her daughter. A cycle of multiple oppression is well on its way and was still being played out in the early 1990s.

An anti-racist social worker would have to begin where Joan is 'at' and work with her to undo the damage caused by the institutionalised as well as personal abuse she has endured. Intensive one-to-one work with the aid of a First Nations woman social worker and group work with others with similar experiences would be essential in this case. Treating Joan with dignity and respect would provide an initial step in focusing on her specific needs as a First Nations woman. Addressing the issue of insititu-ionalised abuse in the residential home would have to be pursued alongside this and would require the assistance of others to bring about the necessary organisational changes. This might include linking up with First Nations action groups already campaigning on such issues (see Haig-Brown, 1988) and initiating demands for legislative changes.

White social work intervention with black youth

Youths in general, and black youths in particular, currently have few opportunities for contributing to society in significant ways and acquiring a sense of belonging to it. Society's major concern with youth has been to control the rebellious elements threatening its fragile stability (Dominelli, 1983). This task has become increasingly difficult as the 'crisis of policing [the] working class city has become a crisis of legitimacy for the bourgeois public realm as a whole' (Cohen, 1980, p. 136). Black youth, carrying white society's stigma for causing inner-city malaise, are considered its greatest threat (CCCS, 1982; Murray, 1990). Everything about them – their life-styles and relationships with one another and authority – is defined as problematic by white people. White social workers working in inner-city areas incorporate these definitions of 'the problem' into their work, thereby pathologising young black populations.

White people pathologise black people by treating them rather than racism as the problem. Black people's resistance to racism is similarly pathologised. Young black men are penalised for having 'deviant' life-styles when they reject racist definitions of their situation and propose positive self-identification as *black* men, for example Rastafarianism. White social workers pathologise such behaviour to justify their racist stereotypes and institutionalise young black men within the welfare and 'law and order' apparatuses.

White people's perceptions of black youths are largely influenced and defined by their contacts with the 'law and order apparatus' and the moral panics arising out of their alleged relationship with crime (Hall, 1978). Central to these is their expectation that black youth will be effectively contained and controlled by their own communities. As Rex puts it in respect of one group: 'Asian youth... have ready to hand a highly effective communal economic, social and political system to help them cope with the exigencies of life in an alien land' (Rex, 1982, p. 62). Points at which black youth either individually or collectively reject white demands for such conformity trigger white responses aimed at reasserting both external control initiated by the white community, especially its police force, and internal control imposed by 'the black community' through family ties and allegiance to its 'leaders'. White people's views that black communities are inadequate and pathological are reflected in their demand that black communities contain their young people when black youth 'get out of control'. Black youth's rebellion over the police's handling of social relations on the Broadwater Farm Estate in the 1980s is one illustration of this state of affairs (Hutchinson-Reis, 1986). The failure of the black community and its leadership to discipline its youth and keep its activities confined to those acceptable to white authority resulted in the whole estate being stigmatised, labelled inadequate and subjected to intensive policing and external control (Loney, 1986b).

The relationship between black youths and the police is highly problematic because the police, in upholding racist societal norms, amplify black youths' 'deviance' and exacerbate the difficulties they endure when they refuse to comply with 'soft' forms of social control (Moore, 1975). The police differentiate between categories of black youth and claim that 'West Indian boys get into trouble because they are out of control'; Asian lads do so as a result of problems 'arising from violence and the enforcement of discipline or fighting for the control of institutions' (Rex, 1982, p. 61). Nonetheless, the overall impact is similar. Reinforcing notions of being out of control and blaming black youth for resisting institutionalised racism become the means whereby the forces of 'law and order' instigate tighter surveillance of black youths and their communities as an avenue through which their activities may be curtailed. Consequently, black youths are viewed as 'dangerous' and therefore requiring even more stringent measures of control. They are given fewer 'cautions' by the police, and are more likely to appear disproportionately more often in criminal courts and in custodial settings (Hood, 1992). These reactions add a further twist to the mechanisms used to stigmatise and socially control the reactions of black youths and black communities. Yet, official measures such as those proposed in the Scarman Report have failed to tackle institutionalised racism because they place undue emphasis on pathologising racist individuals within the police force. Hood's (1992) findings and those of others, for example Cook and Hudson (1993), and Dominelli *et al.* (1995), indicate the dreary persistence of racism in the criminal justice system and stand as testimony to the failure of proposed interventions to reduce its impact.

In social work, the expectation that black communities exercise internal control, display docility and look after their own means that activities that white social workers would tolerate in white clients become alarming in black families. Juvenile crime and adolescent struggles for individual autonomy are seen as particularly threatening. Thus, black people's alleged deviance is amplified to allay white people's fears about them. White social workers encase black people in a web of stricter surveillance and control, rapidly clientising them as a host of welfare agencies descend upon them.

The idea that black youths are constantly out of control and liable to get into trouble accounts for white social workers' and probation officers' failure to ensure that the black youths referred to them for a variety of offences receive equality of treatment compared with white youths. Institutionalised racism in the procedures adopted for handling black youths who come into contact with the law causes their civil liberties to be more easily disregarded than for white youths and leads to their being 'clientised' at the heavy end of the sentencing tariff (Tipler, 1986). Hutchinson-Reis (1986), describing his work as a social worker on the Broadwater Farm Estate, depicts the difficulties his team had in protecting the rights of young black people charged with offences following the 'uprising' there. He makes it clear that young black people needed social work intervention aimed at securing justice from both the police and courts. As he says:

> Juveniles were often intimidated by the thought of murder or affray charges being brought against them if they did not co-operate with the police investigation. (Hutchinson-Reis, 1986, p. 76)

Moreover, in that situation, both black and white social workers who followed casework models of intervention were unable to stop the blatant disregard of black youths' rights because they were being 'severely obstructed' and 'denied the opportunity to perform that function' (Hutchinson-Reis, 1986, p. 76). Black social workers involved in these attempts have found that institutional restraints adversely affect them by compromising and negating their racial and political integrity (Hutchinson-Reis, 1986, p. 79).

Unfair practices compelled social workers on the Broadwater Farm Estate to work collectively to empower themselves and deliver a more appropriate service to clients. By challenging individualistic casework approaches to their work, racist dynamics were initially modified and elements of them subsequently ruptured. Hutchinson-Reis (1986) calls their new techniques 'community social work'. His description of their new methods highlights the team's efforts based on community action principles. These transcend one-to-one methods of responding to individual clients' needs. Using new forms of organising, 'the social workers responsible for the arrested juveniles began to meet weekly to share information and discuss issues and arrangements for working with the large number of young people being arrested, detained, charged, remanded into care and needing placements' (Hutchinson-Reis, 1986, p. 77). Collective action amongst social workers, regardless of whether they are black or white, is indispensable in tackling institutionalised racism. It also helps workers seeking to go beyond the constraints and controls inherent in their job but which impede anti-racist action.

Traditional forms of training and allegiance to an allegedly neutral professionalism makes white social workers suspicious of collective working relations and prone to misconstruing the significance of collectivities within the black community. Yet, the collective support of black families and communities is vitally important in providing black individuals with the psychological and material resources necessary for surviving in a racist world. The protection that black collectivities offer black individuals is a powerful force which ties individuals and communities together in sets of mutual obligations (Lorde, 1984). Not grasping their centrality, white social workers do not appreciate black individuals' feelings of responsibility towards their collectivities and the support they derive from them. Within this framework, they label actions and behaviour affirming solidarity and collectivism amongst black people as 'undesirable', whilst those undermining them are deemed 'desirable'. For these reasons, white social workers consider allegiance to black life-styles pathological.

Such dynamics become especially relevant in white social workers' interventions with black youths in cases defined as 'problems of arranged marriages' or 'intergenerational conflicts'. White social workers who do not appreciate the impact that black collectivities have on black staff should not work with black people. Their interventions are likely to be inappropriate and cause them further hardship. Relating this matter back to their responses towards black youth, white social workers assume that, in questioning their collective framework, young black people are vilifying it. This is not usually the case. White social workers should not perceive conflict between black children and their parents as automatically implying either a rejection of their cultural values or a preference for British ones (Ahmed, 1978, 1984). These are areas to be explored and the wishes of the black person established openly, rather than interpreting whatever they say in terms acceptable to white social workers. Black youth seeking to establish their own parameters in life are just as likely to rebel against parental authority during adolescence as are white youth.

Black social workers have provided alternative models for working with black youths and have organised forms of intervention celebrating their achievements. These enable black youths to develop their individual potential and build their own specific sense of self-identity. White social workers should refer black youths to such provisions, for example the

Handsworth Alternative Scheme (Rhamdanie, 1978) and the Black Justice Project.

White social work intervention with older black people

Older people currently constitute a small proportion of the black population (Bhalla and Blakemore, 1981; Holland and Lewando-Hundt, 1986; Patel, 1990). However, they have been virtually neglected by statutory bodies and have seldom found provisions addressing their specific needs (Farrah, 1986; Holland and Lewando-Hundt, 1986; Patel, 1990). Part of the reason for their exclusion has been that social services departments have traditionally been concerned with the needs of children rather than older people. Choosing to spend their limited resources on statutory obligations, social services departments have colluded with the ageist nature of British society as well as its racism. Another reason has been the young age of the black population in this country (Holland and Lewando-Hundt, 1986). However, none of these reasons justifies the lack of provisions where it is needed. Myths about the support of the extended family in caring for its older members have also been used by white social workers and their institutions to deny the need for making appropriate services available.

This approach to the situation ignores the racist immigration laws which have engendered divisions in black extended families, spreading them across several continents. Also, resettlement patterns which separate extended family members entering Britain have hindered the recreation of extended family networks, for example the dispersal of Ugandan Asian refugees. Moreover, the lack of material resources, especially in income, to cover dependants outside the nuclear family, and housing, to cater for the needs of large families (Brown, 1984; Smith, 1976), does not facilitate the development of networks of this type. Consequently, substantial numbers of black elders have no family members in Britain. Bhalla and Blakemore (1981, p. 33) have found that 26 per cent of Asians and 9 per cent of Afro-Caribbean elders are in this position.

Unequal access to incomes is a particular problem for elders who have entered Britain as sponsored dependants, as they are not entitled to income support or supplementary benefit. This remains the case even in instances in which their sponsors, who may have been able to provide for them at the time of entry, can no longer do so, because they become unemployed, sick, or old themselves. The implications of this are quite disturbing, given disparities in state support for different ethnic groups. For example, Bhalla and Blakemore (1981, p. 17) have revealed that whilst 94 per cent of European and 83 per cent of Afro-Caribbean elders receive state pensions, only 46 per cent of Asian ones do. Moreover, 32 per cent of these do not get full pensions. Age Concern in Lewisham discovered that one quarter of black elders were not receiving full pension entitlements. Black people's low earning levels mean they are also denied the possibility of saving to purchase private pension plans, or acquiring sufficient contributions to augment low pension levels through state-inspired earnings-related or privately financed schemes. Moreover, publicly funded earnings-related state pensions are currently threatened with abolition. These factors may increase the vulnerability of black elders in old age.

Most local authorities do not have an accurate description of the numbers of elders from black communities living within their borders, let alone an analysis of their needs (Blakemore and Boneham, 1994; Farrah, 1986; Holland and Lewando-Hundt, 1986). Others, for example Coventry, have undertaken surveys to highlight ethnic elders and their needs. These have had limited practical outcomes (Holland and Lewando-Hundt, 1986). Local authorities' failure to take seriously their responsibilities towards older black people is reflected in inadequate service provisions. These include:

- few facilities available specifically for them;
- not informing them of the limited service provided;
- the low take-up of services which are on offer;
- offering inappropriate services; and
- expecting older black people to be assimilated into the white British way of life.

The failure of local authorities to inform black people of the limited services specifically provided for them means that few black people are aware of what is available, and they are therefore unlikely to demand these provisions (Patel, 1990). The Bhalla and Blakemore study reveals that whilst 64 per cent of Asian elders were not aware of the welfare provisions available to them, only 2 per cent of white elders shared their fate. Bhalla and Blakemore (1981, p. 29) also indicates that 19 per cent of European elders had home helps, but only 9 per cent of Afro-Caribbean and no Asian elders did so. Many Asian elders cannot use Meals-on-Wheels because they do not cater for their specific dietary requirements. Yet, Holland and Lewando-Hundt's work (1986, p. 28) suggests that

15 per cent of Asian elders want vegetarian Meals-On-Wheels, and 11 per cent would like Asian home helps. The lack of provisions which pick up on specific needs reflects assimilationist assumptions. The view that older black people are expected to adopt the white British life-style is reflected in the opinions expressed by practitioners. These were articulated as follows by a white care assistant when I interviewed her:

> We cannot provide for ethnic minorities here. It wouldn't be fair to the others. No, I treat them all the same. It's the only way.

Time has not substantially altered the inadequacy of services to black elders (see Blakemore and Boneham, 1994). Yet, if white social workers could actively seek and respond to consumers' assessments of their services, improvements could be fostered. For example, matching workers, including care assistants and home helps, with the elders into whose lives they enter could be pressed as a matter of priority. The attitude of indifferent neglect regarding the use of English as the only language of communication could be challenged. Bhalla and Blakemore's (1981, p. 14) study in Birmingham found that 88 per cent of older people from the Indian subcontinent did not speak English. The Farrah (1986, p. 9) research in Leicester revealed that only 11 per cent of the ethnic elders interviewed could speak English. Nonetheless, no interpreting service was available for black elders in either locality. Local authorities could provide translation facilities for black elders. Leaflets could be translated into other ethnic languages. Black workers could be employed to work specifically with them within mainstream provisions.

It is inappropriate for social services departments to pretend that developing the services needed by black elders is an 'immigrant problem that will go away'. Most black elders have settled permanently in Britain. Bhalla and Blakemore indicate that 85 per cent of the Asian and 67 per cent of the Afro-Caribbean elderly expect to remain here. However, the numbers may actually be much higher as only 8 per cent of the Asian group and 6 per cent of the Afro-Caribbean group have actively made plans to return to their country of origin (Bhalla and Blakemore, 1981, p. 33). This, combined with the relative youthfulness of black elders, suggests that their needs will become more pressing in future. Thus, social services departments should begin to plan now so that services can be there when needed. Unless they do so, they will continue to reproduce poor practices. These kinds of concern will become more important in the purchaser–provider environment of community care. Local authorities as purchasers of services will have to ensure that the facilities they buy meet the specific needs of black elders in their care and find ways of ensuring that the providers comply with their requirements. They also need to be aware that relying on contract compliance alone will not guarantee the delivery of an anti-racist service.

Black self-help groups have tried to compensate for the widespread dereliction of duty perpetrated by statutory agencies against black elders by providing services of their own (ASRA, 1981; Holland and Lewando-Hundt, 1986), for example day centres and sheltered accommodation. These provisions are locally based to ensure that independence, dignity and links between black communities and their elders can be maintained, and their religious, shopping and companionship needs met. Residential accommodation for black elders has wardens and workers who speak their mother tongues; there are the aids necessary for coping with the disabilities of old age; small units provide both private and communal facilities rather than there being large institutionalised accommodation; and a mix of people will include both able-bodied people and those with disabilities (ASRA 1981; Farrah, 1986). These provide a variety of ways in which services are tailored to respond to the 'whole' black elder. Consequently, the provisions that black people make available challenge the ageism, disablism and racism endemic in society.

This response by black self-help groups is essential in the short term to pick up on the pressing needs of individuals enduring hardship. However, it does not solve the problem of inadequate mainstream provision. Statutory institutions continue to neglect black elders' needs, thereby perpetuating racist and discriminatory practices. Black youths are beginning to question the diversion of black people's energies through self-help organisations. Claiming that black self-help projects have had negligible impact on institutionalised racism, they argue that these organisations have little clout in transforming broader social relations and raise questions about the length of time that short-term measures can or should be maintained (Gilroy, 1987). Moreover, these self-help initiatives do not provide the full range of services that black elders require because they are seriously under-resourced. Black people are also concerned that their self-help projects have become measures through which the state keeps militant black people occupied (Mullard, 1973).

Black people's growing unease over the state's use of black self-help initiatives to avoid making public provisions available is justified. An example of such evasion occurred in Royal Leamington Spa. Following a detailed examination of the needs of black elders, the local Community Relations Council asked Warwick District Council to provide 'special sheltered housing units for Asians'. Their extended families could not do so. Suggesting that this description of Asian elders 'special needs' was inaccurate, the Council's chief executive officer responded that a further study was necessary to assess the situation. However, a local councillor who rejected the necessity of funding public provisions for this purpose proclaimed, 'I am fundamentally opposed to any form of segregation' (*Coventry Evening Telegraph*, 1987). Besides revealing that white authorities prefer white scientific analyses to black ones, this suggests that special provisions are not segregation if provided by the Asian community through its own resources. Under-provision in the public sector is now even more likely given the New Right's commitment to cutting back the state and the chronic underfunding of community care.

Countering white social workers' racism

This chapter shows how important it is for white social workers to question the appropriateness of current interventions in black families. The accounts presented reveal that the imposition of racist value judgements on black families and their life-styles has been detrimental to their welfare and provide good reason for concluding that white social workers should not work with black families until they have demonstrated their ability to practise in anti-racist ways. The white social workers in the examples considered above require help in overcoming their racism. Doing so entails exposing the anglocentric nature of their thinking and providing materials for them to learn about black people and their life-styles. It also requires that they address white society's racism and their roles in perpetuating it. Racism cannot be countered simply by employing black social workers who are then charged with developing 'services for their communities' within mainstream agencies. Unless social services departments take active steps to prevent it, they may end up 'dumping' their responsibility for eliminating racism on black employees (Rooney, 1980).

Using black workers to work primarily with black clients can be no more than a temporary measure if their 'ghettoisation' is to be avoided. Whilst black professionals provide positive models for black youths, and enhance black people's sense of confidence and esteem over their status in white society, racism would be reinforced if they were held responsible for all or most of the social work undertaken with ethnic minority groups. The ensuing segregation would deny black social workers scope to practise their skills with other ethnic groupings and acquire competence across a wide range of fields, like their white counterparts. Furthermore, in a racist society, black people could perceive white powerholders' adherence to such allocation procedures as discriminatory for conveying the impression that black social workers are second rate employees capable of working only with second rate, i.e. black, clients (Kadushin, 1972; Mizio, 1972). 'Ghettoising' black social workers also allows white social workers to escape confronting their own racism. They could comfort themselves with the knowledge that, now that black people had black social workers, they would be getting the services they needed, and would end their concern with racism. Operating in these terms would challenge neither institutional racism nor the individual racism of white workers or clients.

White social workers should work in anti-racist ways so that black social workers can have real choices about the areas in which they would like to specialise and clients have access to the specific services they need. Thus, alongside the employment of black workers, agency policy and practice must encompass the retraining of all white staff members in anti-racist directions. Eliminating racism at the individual level is a complicated task requiring long-term work with white people in both one-to-one and group settings. White individuals' progress on this can be monitored and, only when they have demonstrated their commitment to working in anti-racist ways, should they be employed in social work. Those indicating a willingness to learn how to work with ethnic groups other than their own need to work as apprentices under black workers who can assess and monitor their work from a black perspective. This should not be seen as a daunting or unattainable a prospect. Black workers are constantly being monitored and assessed under the stewardship of white people. They have to demonstrate they can work across the 'race' divide to be judged competent practitioners. Asking white social workers to do likewise is simply asking them to meet the same levels of transferable competence.

The project of white social workers becoming anti-racists can be started by employers granting them paid leave to undertake anti-racism awareness training and plan a personalised programme for change. Such a proposal could be implemented more successfully if participants were not stigmatised as 'racists' when *all white people are involved in perpetuating racism in some form*, if not intentionally, then through their unintentional collusion with institutional and cultural racism. Simply labelling white people as racist is unhelpful. This sort of unproductive response can be avoided by incorporating anti-racism awareness training into normal office routines, with the expectation that every white member of the team should participate in it. This could be complemented through the introduction of the anti-racist apprenticeship model of social work along the lines described in Chapter 2. Moreover, paying attention to issues of process is important. Doing so should reflect open exchanges which promote learning and improvements in one's understandinig of racism and interaction with black people. White people working in anti-racist ways are likely to make mistakes as they proceed along their path. The crucial point here is that they *own* these and use the lessons derived from them to enhance their knowledge of and skills in relating to black people in an egalitarian manner. Acquiring the expertise required to become an anti-racist social worker should be treated as routinely as learning any new area of practice or piece of legislation necessary for working with clients in a competent professional matter.

White social workers committed to developing anti-racist social work practice and ultimately intending to work with black families need special training to make them:

- culturally aware from an anti-racist perspective, i.e. able to understand the significance of cultural factors without laying the responsibility for everything that goes wrong at culture's door;
- overcome the use of value judgements which presuppose the superiority of white British culture and norms;
- conscious of the impact of institutionalised racism on their work and to commit themselves to overcoming it;
- explore the impact of white power and privileges in their relationships with black people;
- draw connections between racism and the social control elements of social work; and
- draw connections between eliminating racism and getting rid of other forms of oppression.

In addition, it is not enough for white social workers developing anti-racist practice to rely on their personal commitment to see them through to successful anti-racist intervention in a black family. Institutional and organisational change has to accompany personal change. White social workers wishing to develop anti-racist social work practice have no option but to initiate the organisational process of changing the perceptions, priorities, commitments and behaviour of colleagues, managers, employers and clients in this direction if the complexity of society's racist infrastructure is to be dismantled. Moreover, employers would have to commit themselves to introducing anti-racist policies and practices in their agency to provide the climate and back-up support necessary for promoting racial equality and anti-racist social work. Getting this proposal incorporated into office policy and practice may entail a long and difficult struggle.

White clients should be encouraged, through anti-racist policies and practice, to choose black social workers. Simply offering clients a choice in the ethnic origins of the worker to whom they relate is not an appropriate way of embarking on this process. It carries the danger of increasing the hurtfulness directed at black social workers if they are rejected and legitimating white clients' racism. Changing the opinions of white racist clients needs sensitive handling. The *process* whereby their views are challenged is as important as confronting their inappropriateness. They must be encouraged actively to engage with the issue and understand the importance of addressing it for their own benefit as well as to reduce the damage they wreak in black people's lives.

Striking a balance between agency policy when it is publicly committed to eradicating racism, and the professed inclinations of individual workers and clients, may be tricky in instances in which racism remains endemic and the process of dismantling it is very drawn out. Initially, priority should be given to raising consciousness about racism as an issue to be tackled. People should subsequently be introduced to the procedures to be used in eliminating racist practices. To make offering black social workers to white clients a positive experience for black workers, agencies would first have to work on challenging white clients' racist stereotypes. White clients would need anti-racism awareness training and support in examining their reactions. The social workers working with them should belong to their particular racial grouping.

Black clients who have internalised white racism may also reject black social workers. They too need support in exploring how they feel about themselves and others. Anti-racist policies and practices can foster circumstances in which both black and white clients can relate positively to and interact effectively with black social workers. White social workers faced with black clients preferring white social workers should explore with them the reasons for their 'choice' and ascertain whether it stems from internalised racism. If this is the case, they should be referred to black social workers capable of working with them on this issue. Dealing with internalised racism may also involve black and white practitioners working together to complement each others' efforts in helping black clients through the process of valuing their own person and that of other black people.

Agencies should also support black workers dealing with rejection from white clients, white colleagues or other black people. Having a well-known and adhered to equal opportunities policy outlining the processes and procedures whereby it will be realised is an important element in this. Moreover, although an educational approach may be the initial point of engagement with the issue, the penalties which might be invoked if individuals refuse to treat black people with respect and dignity need to be in place and invoked if necessary. These might include fines for overt racist statements and comments from workers, or a refusal to provide clients with services if they harass black workers or clients. Such measures will also go some way towards backing black workers and enabling them to work in a more propitious environment.

White workers who persist in practising racial harassment should be disciplined and, if necessary, dismissed as incompetent in doing their job. To implement this action effectively and justly, employing authorities must develop well-publicised and understood grievance procedures covering racial harassment. These should secure justice for black people and initially allow white people the opportunity to alter their behaviour so that it complies with anti-racist norms.

There is also a strong case for white social workers to work alongside black groups challenging racism within the profession by identifying potential resources, organisational norms and decision-making processes for these groups to tap into. In reversing the power relationships between them, white social workers would become anti-racist community advocates working alongside black people in a common cause. Equalising power differentials between them and black people would free white social workers to develop new ways of responding to black service users.

Because challenging racism exposes bad practices all round, the development of anti-racist social work practice enlarges the spectrum of choice available to both black and white people. Thus, a strategy for tackling racism must be multi-faceted. From an anti-racist perspective, having one's welfare assured is a fundamental human right. All individuals are entitled to the welfare services they need – as of right, regardless of period of stay in their country of residence, conditions of admission for residence, skin colour, religious affiliation or linguistic capabilities.

5

Tackling Racism at the Organisational Level: Working on Agency Policies and Practices

Focusing on one's own practice and developing anti-racist struggles in relation to that is important. However, gains brought about through individual effort will be limited unless changes are also wrought in agency policy and practices. Organisational changes which shift agency policy and practices in egalitarian directions are necessary to provide the supportive foundation for consolidating, extending and further developing the anti-racist social work practice which is undertaken by individual practitioners. Moreover, initiatives in this arena must be buttressed by anti-racist policies and practices in both the local and central state apparatuses.

White social workers can begin to engage in the process of changing their own agency by:

- ending their involvement in the conspiracy of silence which denies and ignores the prevalence of institutionalised and cultural racism in their organisation;
- organising in their workplace for the implementation of an equal opportunities policy;
- initiating and continuing the debate which elaborates on the components of anti-racist social work practice; and
- establishing the machinery which will monitor progress on the realisation of anti-racist policies and practices in their agency.

This will require white anti-racist social workers to develop alliances with other workers, management, politicians, trade unionists and others sharing their anti-racist goals. Such work contains risks which can affect the whole of their careers and place their promotion prospects in jeopardy. Thus, white social workers committed to anti-racist social work must prepare themselves for a rough ride in pursuing their goals as well as having the satisfaction of knowing that, through their efforts, justice will prevail and service delivery promoting welfare will be enhanced. White social workers should develop support networks for their own survival in the crisis situations they will encounter as personal, interpersonal and institutional resistance to their anti-racist activities come to the fore. Securing changes at the level of a particular agency requires additional resources as well as a more equitable use of existing ones. Anti-racist social work cannot be obtained on the cheap.

Finally, changes wrought at agency level must be guaranteed continuity and stability through more generalised support, including that of the local and central state. White social workers working collectively through their unions, professional associations or organisations established specifically for this purpose must put sustained collective pressure on the political apparatuses of local and central government to ensure that they adopt and enforce anti-racist policies and practices through legislation, funding and the creation of a climate which fosters the further development of anti-racist social work. That this endorsement has to be struggled for rather than taken as given in democratic societies that subscribe to the liberal ideology of equality for all before the law, and advocate the observance of human rights and tolerance for all 'races', creeds, religions and ethnic groups, is a sad reflection on current reality. However, reality it is, as was highlighted by the backlash against anti-racist initiatives in British social work during the summer of 1993 (see Pinker, 1993; Phillips, 1993). Anti-racist social work seeks to intervene in bridging the gap between our realities and our ideals. This chapter explores the ramifications of organisational change aimed at introducing and maintaining anti-racist social work.

Ending the conspiracy of silence about racism in social work

Keeping quiet about the many manifestations of racism in social work is a major way in which white people render the distressing experience of black people invisible. Silence also facilitates white people's collusion with this state of affairs, rendering them powerless in tackling it. For these reasons, white social workers must end the conspiracy of silence regarding the racism lying at the very heart of social work. In speaking out against it, white people give the problem a name, thereby becoming free to do something about eradicating racism and empowering themselves to develop alliances based on equality with black people who are also pitting their energies against racism (Lorde, 1984).

When breaking this silence, white practitioners and educators will be compelled to:

- verify and demonstrate the existence of racism in social work practice in its varied forms;
- take a stand against these; and
- work both individually and collectively in bringing about anti-racist policies and practices.

The implementation of these three strategies requires both structural change at the organisational level and personal change. Organisational change with respect to anti-racist social work covers two levels: (a) employment policy and practice; and (b) service delivery. In terms of employment policy and practice, black people must be employed in substantial rather than token numbers throughout an organisation under terms and conditions which do not undervalue their qualifications, expertise and career prospects, or dump the elimination of racism on their backs. Otherwise, anti-racist intentions will be undermined. In undertaking organisational change, the white anti-racist social worker will be challenging political priorities, legislation, professional ethics, management and its decisions in the allocation of both resources and power, policies, practice, colleagues, professional associations, trade unions and clients.

Although white individuals committed to introducing anti-racist social work in their agency may feel powerless to do so, it is important that they do not feel discouraged from raising the issue with others. Regardless of the level at which support for their views can be found, the venture is worth pursuing. In many institutions, it has been the activities of individuals, often carried out over a number of years and at considerable personal cost to themselves, which have secured institutional commitment to equality of opportunity and anti-racist ways of working. Doing it on one's own is the most difficult way of achieving these goals. It is much easier to work on the matter if an individual can become part of a group with similar commitments.

Regardless of how individuals choose to work within their organisation, the task will be difficult for a number of reasons. One is that white people committed to anti-racist ways of working find translating their commitments to action to be problematic when their own emotional or material interests are at stake. Another reason is that some people will feel that it is not a problem in their particular setting, and will need convincing of the appropriateness of anti-racist action in their particular workplace. Having an equal opportunities policy can have a beneficial impact on introducing change and promote anti-racist behaviour if it is linked to assessing people's performance on the job. While such a policy is unlikely to alter the views of people whose racism is based on dogma, it promotes a climate delegitimating the public expression of such opinions. To carry people willing to engage in countering racism, such a policy must be adequately resourced, foster the development of support networks and pay attention to the processes whereby it is implemented. These must be fair, just and participative. Anti-racist social work may also be difficult to introduce because there is a widespread belief that working in anti-racist ways is optional for white people. These individuals fail to understand the damage they inflict on black people's welfare through inaction or inappropriate action. As one social worker recently remarked at an anti-racist social work conference:

> I have a choice about whether or not I take up the fight against racism. And, if I decide to do so, it is up to me to decide the ways in which I do it.

Besides highlighting the complexity of the problem and the difficulties that white social workers have in working collectively against racism, this white woman, who saw herself as a sensitive social worker, had a point. She does have a choice because as a white English person, racism is not directed at her. Neither she nor her close ones feel its barbs of injustice. Being out of racism's direct impact makes her blind to the damage her view perpetrates on black people who suffer the effects of racism as she speaks. And it is they who continue to be wounded by racism because millions of other white people share her view. Moreover, her comments reveal her failure to connect the ravages racism wreaks on black people with the damage it is causing her. She is denying her own humanity in so far as she denies black people theirs.

In taking this stance, this woman has become less of a person herself. For this reason, I would argue that white people do not have a choice about whether or not they struggle against racism. They only delude themselves *unless* they are willing openly to declare that the privileges that accrue to them because racism exists outweigh the value they place on their own humanity. If this were to be the case, they would be actively choosing to place their material interests to the fore and disregard any claims for justice. I cannot see this woman accepting this as the outcome of her stance. Hence, I remain convinced that if the casualties of her involved, but blasé, approach to racism could confront her in the shape of strong black people and herself being visibly crippled by her words as she spoke, this white woman would be amongst the first to recoil from her behaviour. And I continue to be equally sure that its impact on her would be profound enough to result in immediate behavioural change.

Moreover, once anti-racist change has been initiated in her behaviour, she would feel compelled to seek institutional change so that others occupying her previous position would be moved to do likewise. The invisibility of many of the processes whereby racism is perpetrated in the normal course of everyday life, and the difficulties white people have in making direct connections between their personal inaction, institution-alised oppression and its effect on black individuals and groups, make them tolerate morally reprehensible standpoints like that of having a 'choice' about tackling racism.

White anti-racist social workers will have to undertake a considerable amount of work with other white social workers who need convincing of the appropriateness of joining the campaign for anti-racist social work. Getting the agency to commit resources to retraining white people and sending them on anti-racism awareness training courses is an essential if initial component of an institution's commitment to equal opportunities. The resources for promoting this must not be diverted from those being required by black people to enter the institution in the first place or those needed for them to receive the training they require as black people, whether they are employed there or receive its services. Implementing a policy of equal opportunities, therefore, requires some additional resourcing on both personal and institutional levels. Seeking alliances and organising alongside management, other workers, relevant trade unions and professional organisations to bring about an end to the conspiracy of silence and the declaration of an equal opportunities policy does not preclude additional individual action. Individuals can continue their efforts in other aspects of the work, for example in their relationships with black clients, by raising the issue in team meetings, or tackling racist comments.

Racisim must be resisted regardless of the employing agency involved. Probation officers, social services departments, community work agencies, hospital settings and voluntary agencies each have specific forms of racism which must be overcome as well as forms which they hold in common with other organisations. Eliminating racism requires agencies and individuals to acknowledge black people, their needs and their contributions to society; become familiar with the work black people have already done in countering racism; challenge prevailing (racist) definitions of social work; and develop anti-racist policies and practice. At the forefront of the struggle against racism are a series of questions which white anti-racist social workers need to address. These are:

- What needs doing?
- By whom should it be done?
- How is it to be done?
- What targets need to be set?
- What blockages will be encountered?
- How can these be overcome?

Ending the conspiracy of silence also requires denouncing the invidious position in which organisations place black people allegedly employed as part of their strategy in combating racism. This means exposing the dumping of anti-racist work entirely on the shoulders of black staff, and challenging authorities which hinder the development of links between black staff and their communities for fear that black staff's accountability would be community based rather than employer based (see Rooney, 1980). Black people have become concerned that black professionals are being incorporated by the 'race relations' side of an organisation's work through their terms and conditions of employment. Others feel quite strongly that the whole 'race relations' apparatus has become another mechanism of social control for black people and their aspirations (ALTARF, 1984; Mullard, 1973).

The 'new' black professional middle class has been created by the 'race relations' apparatus which includes the Commission for Racial Equality (CRE)/Communications Relations Commission (CRC), local authorities, social services departments and the educational system. The racism endemic in these institutions means that black workers occupy a contradictory position within them – as representatives of oppressed communities and as state employees forming part of an oppressive state apparatus (Mullard, 1973). Pressures emanating from institutional constraints, for example workload allocations, the decision-making processes and departmental priorities, incorporate black staff into its social control functions and prevent them from effectively promoting the interests of black people (Gilroy, 1987; Rooney, 1980). Resisting these is extremely difficult for black people to do on their own. Yet, they are frequently expected to do so in an unrealistic appraisal of their commitment to 'black perspectives'. These expectations form an integral part of black people's hopes for a better future and the 'dumping' approach that white people have to eradicating racism.

Moreover, dealing with this contradiction becomes particularly difficult in a situation of scarce resources engendered by public expenditure cuts. These compel black and white social workers to ration provisions across the largest number of clients. The need to implement such policies, whatever the justice of the cases being handled, often puts black social workers at odds with both their employer and their communities who expect them to resolve their problems. Budgetary limits introduced through the purchaser–provider split in service delivery can exacerbate these difficulties. Since race relations structures are multiracial in the sense that teams include both black and white members, the potential of these to incorporate and deradicalise black people and their aspirations, and the mechanisms whereby the diffusion of their critique is achieved, must be understood. Otherwise, subsequent anti-racist changes in organisational structures and, in Britain, the reformulation of the 1976 Race Relations Act, will be unable to stem institutionalised racism, redefine black people's social status, or reallocate their share of society's power and resources to them.

In addition, the tendency of local authorities and the central state to employ people with attitudes coinciding with their own predisposes them to appoint small 'c' conservatives from within black communities (Rooney, 1980). The entry of such appointees into jobs with reasonable salaries and some form of long-term security may distance them from parts of their communities, particularly their working class elements who have been excluded from white people's privileges. White social workers have commented on how black 'middle class' people they have brought in to work with black families have put black 'working class' clients down. For example, one white social worker recalled how shocked she was when a 'middle class' Brahmin woman called in to translate in a case involving a Muslim woman from the Gujerat said of her, 'She is really an ignorant peasant who doesn't understand very much'. There is an assumption amongst white social workers that black people should respect one another simply because they are black. They also believe that 'the black community' is homogeneous, when this is far from the case. Black people may have racism in common, but they are culturally, linguistically, socially, religiously, economically and politically diverse – just as Europeans are.

White social workers should acknowledge the heterogeneity of black communities in their work, instead of perpetuating the racist stereotype that 'they are all the same'. In addition, they must not be lulled into mistakenly thinking that racism does not affect black professionals because they are 'middle class'. The experience of 'middle class' black professionals is not the same as that of 'middle class' white professionals. The former's experience of racism will inevitably mediate their experience of class (Dominelli *et al.*, 1995; Gilroy, 1987). Understanding these dynamics is a task that white social workers have to undertake if they are actively to participate in ending the conspiracy of silence.

White anti-racist social workers can pursue measures seeking to convince employing authorities to foster the creation and maintenance of effective links between black professionals and their communities. This can be facilitated by employers actively encouraging black workers to form black support groups and networks for themselves and other black people. Ending the conspiracy of silence in this respect requires white people to take responsibility for drawing black professionals into power structures which isolate them from their communities, i.e. recognising that this distancing has been of white people's making. White people can avoid placing black people in this position by not employing them as isolated individuals and providing them with the time, space and other resources necessary for developing black support groups and maintaining their community networks.

Opportunities of this nature are seldom made available to black social workers. Barney Rooney (1980), in a well-documented account of Liverpool's employment of black social workers as part of its attempt at increasing rapport between the social services department and the 'alienated' black community, mounts a scathing attack on an authority paying scant attention to the needs of its black staff. Rooney goes beyond this in her criticism and criticises Liverpool on a number of counts. These are:

- employing black social workers having little connection with the communities they are to serve other than the colour of their skin;

- employing black social workers outside mainstream career grades through the Urban Aid Programme and dispersing them throughout the city;
- dumping the responsibility for handling all of the 'race' issues on their shoulders;
- obliging them to work with black people within established priorities and methods of working, i.e. heavy workloads emphasising one-to-one work;
- destroying black social workers' credibility with their communities.

Condemning Liverpool's actions as merely token, Rooney explains that the situation was one in which 'black people are recruited into an organisation to give the impression of change and then using them to consolidate resistance to change' (Rooney, 1980, p. 48). She argues that Liverpool devised its strategy of employing black workers to ensure that mainly black workers who would not challenge the organisation and its ways of working were appointed. Such a strategy, she claims, enables the local authority to use black workers to control black people. Because these workers did not come from Liverpool, they lacked a shared experience of being at the receiving end of the department's services and close links with the black communities there. Consequently, Rooney maintains, these black social workers were unable to develop forms of collective organisation which could effectively challenge the local authority's ways of working with black people, transform its definition of social work, develop appropriate forms of service delivery to black clients, and empower black people.

Rooney also declares that white people are hostile to black social workers because they fear their strengths, particularly their contacts with black communities and their ability to identify with black clients. These ways of communicating are deemed 'unprofessional' by white social workers and white managers. Such labelling is aimed at getting black workers to work with black clients as if they were white workers, thereby decontextualising black staff and denying the racism that black workers and clients experience. Her comments have been backed in an interview I had with a district team manager who said:

They [black social workers] demonstrate a capacity to get over-involved. We don't hold with social workers – any social worker black or white – not being able to stand back and make a professional assessment of a situation.

But in Rooney's terms, the real problem for white employers is that black social workers with close links with their community will identify with black clients rather than their employers and might make demands for improving services which they may feel unable to meet. These differences are clearly manifest, for example, in the handling of confidentiality. A black social worker might extend the circle of confidentiality to include the client, and members of their extended family, thus enlarging the circle encompassed by the confidentially requirements which the white organisation expects its staff to uphold (Rooney, 1980). Additionally, white social workers and institutions subject black social workers to racial harassment by presuming them to be clients rather than workers during initial encounters, and asking for their credentials, rather than taking their word for it as they do for white people. This description reveals that black social workers experience anything but equal opportunities when they are appointed as social workers. Rectifying the situation requires agencies to take positive steps in ending the conspiracy of silence about such practices. Countering these also demands the implementation of an equal opportunities policy in its broadest sense.

Establishing an equal opportunities policy: setting the climate for anti-racist social work

Under the Race Relations Act 1976, all institutions providing services to the public are responsible for ensuring that these do not, either directly or indirectly, discriminate against people for racial and ethnic reasons. Although government departments can plead immunity from its provisions, there is scope for using this legislation in getting employers to formulate, adopt and implement an equal opportunities policy essential for creating a climate conducive to anti-racist social work. The policy is not, in itself, anti-racist social work. However, having such a policy enables practitioners to achieve two things: it gets people who would not normally think about anti-racist social work to do so, and it provides institutional back-up for individuals struggling to get anti-racist social work established in the workplace. Discussions around the adoption of an equal opportunities policy are particularly important in offices which are exclusively or largely white, where the following dicta prevail:

'We have no racism operating here.'

'There are no black workers applying to come to us.'

'We have no black clients demanding our services.'

Addressing the issue in these offices is vital because the debate about whether racism exists in their office or district is independent of the physical presence of black people (Dominelli, 1991a). Equal opportunities policies are necessary in such situations because the discussion around their formulation and implementation enables white people to start thinking about how racism can affect them as white people who perpetrate it, exist regardless of the absence or presence of black people, be reflected in their personal work and agency policies, and be eradicated by using their commitment to do so. Obtaining the willing and informed consent of white workers at all levels of an organisation to address racism is indispensable in ensuring that anti-racist social work becomes the norm in the workplace.

Blockages to equal opportunities

There are a number of dangers bedevilling the efforts of white social workers trying to implement equal opportunities in policy and practice in their agency. One worry is that overt racism will go underground. People will become more subtle and covert in their resistance to racial equality and undermine efforts aimed at securing it. Or, it may foster a white backlash, as has happened in the USA against affirmative action generally during the 1990s, and in Britain against anti-racist initiatives in local authorities during the 1980s and in social work during the 1990s (see Dunant, 1994; Livingstone, 1987). Another is to mistake the implementation of an equal opportunities policy for the establishment of anti-racist social work. This produces situations in which black people are led up the road of false promises where a small part (equal opportunities policies) is taken for the whole (anti-racist social work). So, employing large numbers of black people in the lower echelons of the labour hierarchy or having a few token black people sitting on committees are mistakenly deemed to fulfil equal opportunities policy requirements. I quote one equal opportunities employer who said to me, 'We have our specialist ethnic minorities unit. What more do you want?'

An equal opportunities policy is no more than a tool for endorsing and sustaining other initiatives aimed at implementing anti-racist ways of working and egalitarian relations between black people and white. The outcomes of such efforts need to be monitored and evaluated regularly and effectively. The most appropriate people to monitor and evaluate the progress that white people make in realising an agency's anti-racist aims and objectives are black workers and black users of its services organised collectively as a monitoring group. To allay white people's fears of vulnerability when the racism in their work becomes visible and prevent these from blocking progress on the anti-racist front, white anti-racist social workers and their managers should ensure that:

- careful preparatory work is done with these individuals;
- networks are established to support them in developing their contribution to anti-racist social work; and
- due process is followed in helping them improve their performance.

One-to-one counselling which will help them talk through their anxieties and supportive groupwork, coupled with the knowledge that the institution will provide them with the back-up and retraining they need to ensure they work effectively in an anti-racist environment, is essential in ensuring that white resistance does not thwart either personal ambitions in becoming anti-racist or institutional aims and objectives in this direction. White anti-racist social workers need their own support networks to help them collectively to cope with their fears, release their creativity, share experiences with others and make demands which are impossible for individuals to take on alone.

Endorsing an equal opportunities policy requires additional resources

Organisations have been declaring themselves equal opportunities employers without releasing the resources necessary for this policy to become a reality. Their initiatives have been restricted to stating that the institution is an 'equal opportunities employer' in advertisements, advertising in the 'ethnic press' and collecting statistics on the ethnic background of applicants for specified jobs. Advertising in the ethnic press makes the statement that, as an employing authority, the institution is interested in considering applications from groups normally excluded by its usual recruitment procedures. Whilst an important advance on previous practice, this move is only an initial step in changing racialised social relations. Employment practices throughout the organisation have to be transformed from the selection process to the employment of black people at all levels of an organisation in sufficient numbers not to be token, and under terms and conditions of employment which do not 'dump' the responsibility of dealing with racism in the authority on them. Unless all these things happen, the policy is worthless.

Employers have to consider recruitment and selection procedures, examining the ways in which vacancies are notified to applicants, how employees are selected or not for particular jobs, and employment practices once candidates are in post. Recent history is littered with examples of organisations declaring themselves equal opportunities employers, but where black people are found in small numbers, at the lowest rungs of the employment hierarchy and overworked through the interminable demands made on them (Dominelli *et al.*, 1995; Drew, 1995; Rooney, 1980). Institutions run primarily by white people must find ways of demonstrating that they accept that tackling institutional, cultural and individual racism is their responsibility and not that of their black employees. Their employment practices must treat black workers on a par with white ones. This does not mean 'ghettoising' black workers as 'race experts', forcing them to assume duties which are not contained in their job descriptions, not paying for all the work they do, and not promoting them for achieving substantially more than what is required of them (Ohri and Manning, 1982; Rooney, 1980).

White organisations and individuals are continually exploiting the knowledge and goodwill of black people who have a vested interest in eradicating racism by asking them to act as teachers whilst keeping them in the role of pupils. White people have devised elaborate structures whereby black people become 'race' experts compelled to work with other black people according to white definitions of the problem. These pathologise black people and seek to strangle their resistance against racist practices (Gilroy, 1987; Mullard, 1973). Such approaches have created black 'race relations' experts in the lower levels of the enterprise working to promote black people's interest. These black workers are then helped to develop 'good' relationships with their employing agency and elevated to the status of 'community' leaders acceptable to white people for undertaking the task of directly controlling black communities (Mullard, 1973).

Fortunately for the future of society, enough black people have resisted this process of incorporation and co-option, highlighting instead the widespread subversion of the aspired-to egalitarian relations between black and white people. What white anti-racist social workers need to do now is endorse their exposure of the disservice being done to black communities throughout the country and demand changes in existing government policy and practice. Central government must actively foster anti-racist activities for widespread change to occur. The importance of securing central state commitment to anti-racist ways of working is evident in its abolition of the Greater London Council (GLC). Moreover, its hostility ensured that many of the GLC's anti-racist initiatives have been discredited through central government action and subsequently denied funding either to get off the ground or to consolidate their activities; one example is the Police Monitoring Committee. The demise of the GLC resulted in other activities being completely dropped. Resistance from the central state can be anticipated because racism is a useful tool for rationing resources. White anti-racist social workers can guard against government opposition by ensuring that their actions are deeply rooted in and strongly supported by the community at large.

Demanding that both the local and central state desist from incorporating black activists can lead to the release of resources which have been 'misused' by the 'race relations' industry. These can be reclaimed and put under the control of people with a black perspective who can use them to develop the services that black people need and want. This process can be commenced by altering current policies in relation to the employment of black workers, their recruitment and selection, and the terms and conditions under which they are employed, and by restructuring the CRE and its attendant organisations so that it becomes a pressure group under the control of the black population rather than a government-controlled quango. Forming a lobby, it can define its terms of reference, propose new legislation and offer a programme of action for getting rid of racism in every aspect of public life.

The exploitation of black workers through Section 11 posts

Whilst the commitment to employ more black social workers is being adopted by more local authorities and probation services as they become 'equal opportunities employers', many are temporary appointments made through Section 11 monies. Black social workers need to be employed in greater numbers in mainstream services to overcome the effects of previous racist policies which have undervalued their practice experience and educational qualifications, and exacerbated the disadvantages that racism has brought into their lives.

Employing black workers primarily through Section 11 contracts reinforces racism in another guise because these are outside mainstream provisions. Posts created under Section 11 of the 1966 Local Government Act are attractive to local authorities because the Home Office guarantees 75 per cent funding for measures reducing discrimination in 'immigrant communities'. Whilst this Act provides one of the few sources of funding specifically targeting racial discrimination, the criticisms against it from an anti-racist perspective are legion.

To begin with, the framing of this provision, directed at a section of the population defined as 'the problem', endorses institutionalised racism. It focuses on 'immigrant' communities from the New Commonwealth (later amended to include Pakistan when it left the Commonwealth) which need help in adjusting to the white British way of life. Black people are defined in transient terms rather than allowing for their becoming a settled population. The aims of the legislation are assimilationist and rooted in notions of white supremacy – asking black people to become like white people. Their specific needs and experiences can subsequently be ignored because, except for their skin colour, they will have become 'just like us'. Secondly, it assumes that as 'immigrants' black people would not want to retain their culture and own way of life. Desires to the contrary are deemed temporary. Moreover, the funding provided under these provisions is vulnerable. There have been several attempts to eliminate it from the statute books. Whilst these have not come to fruition, public expenditure cuts at the local level have meant that local authorities have reduced funds allocated to these provisions.

The legislation also contributes to defining black people as 'permanent immigrants' rather than settlers making their own unique contribution to the British way of life. Because black people have not been accepted as settlers, the children and grandchildren of black people who have emigrated from Third World countries continue to be called 'immigrants' despite their being born in Britain. This perpetuates the idea that black people are temporary residents. White practitioners reinforce these definitions when they talk about British-born blacks as 'children of immigrants' – a comment often found in social enquiry reports. For example, they do not feel compelled to state 'Jack was the son of Scottish Presbyterian parents who moved to England in 1981' in their reports to the courts. Thus, when they declare that 'Muhammed was the son of Muslim parents who came from Pakistan in 1969', there is an implicit message which they expect white readers of the report to grasp. The message is a racist one which negates black people's contribution to this country and denies their right to be here on the same terms as white people. This theme has been furthered in immigration legislation and the 1981 Nationality Act which now prohibits children born in Britain from automatically acquiring British citizenship unless they already have one British parent. Similar legislation exists in other European countries and is aimed at reducing the number of black people becoming European nationals (Gordon, 1992).

The use of Section 11 to provide additional funding for social work posts has been problematic. There have been allegations of the widespread misuse of the monies derived from this particular source of funding (Duffield, 1985; Ely and Denney, 1987). This has resulted in funds intended for specific use in black communities being diverted to support activities that departments with dwindling resources have been unable to finance from general revenues. These have subsequently cushioned deficits caused by cash limits, block grants and other cuts in public expenditure. This has depoliticised the impact of these cuts because services which would have otherwise been abolished or withdrawn have continued in some fashion. Seeing local authorities struggling to keep services going, white people have kept quiet about declining standards and provisions arising from the cuts.

Using Section 11 funding for general purposes has endangered black organisations by starving them of resources vital to the well-being of black claimants. For example, black self-help groups such as the Asian Resources Centre in Birmingham have for a long time been crying out for funds to finance many of their activities, for example welfare rights and immigration advice, Asian women's refuges, day care facilities for black elders (Sondhi in Cheetham, 1982b; Guru, 1987). Meantime, their local authority has been using Section 11 monies inappropriately (Sharron, 1985). Consequently, black people have been deprived of resources specifically earmarked for them, whilst white people have gained additional resources at their expense. The use of Section 11 funding in these ways is racist. Additionally, as many Section 11 posts have gone to white people, another layer of 'white experts' has been added to those already preventing black people from attending to the needs of black communities in a paid capacity. As one black social worker I interviewed commented:

> I get really upset over the way Section 11 money has been used in this borough. I know that Section 11 money stinks to begin with because it's full of racist ideas. But it was one of the few sources of public money that was to go straight through to black people. But the way it's been used here means that black people were the last ones to see the benefit of it.

White people employed through Section 11 funding can go unnoticed because they can easily be incorporated into the general system. Black people are in a different position. Besides being more noticeable, their jobs are often specifically highlighted as Section 11 posts and attached to part of the organisation dealing with 'ethnic minority issues'. Thus, black people employed through Section 11 funding are locked onto career ladders with virtually no rungs on them. Jobs secured under this funding are temporary, thereby increasing black people's vulnerability to unemployment. Arrangements for automatically transferring Section 11 funded black employees to mainstream career grades are rare. Black workers are excluded from a natural progression through to the upper echelons of the labour hierarchy and denied the promotion opportunities open to their white colleagues who are fully employed by local authorities. Section 11 can be useful in securing a breakthrough for the employment of black workers, but it is not good anti-racist practice to stop at this point.

Black social workers should be brought into mainstream career structures by immediately being fully employed on the social services payroll. The unions, particularly UNISON (made up through a merger of NALGO, NUPE and COHSE), should become involved in securing this piece of organisational change by incorporating its realisation into the collective bargaining process. In addition, black social workers who are locked into specialist units are required to undertake highly specialised tasks at low rates of pay unless they are employed in a department which is competing for their skills with nearby authorities. Again, I quote a black social worker who told me:

> I was paid next to nothing until a neighbouring borough offered me a job. Then, all of a sudden I was popular. They were falling over themselves trying to keep me with them. The pay rise which had been a thorn in their flesh for months, suddenly became an open coffer.

Section 11 posts have provided employers with a means for 'ghettoising' black workers. White anti-racist social workers need to ensure that their organisation's employment policies do not lock black people into Section 11 posts but move them into mainstream grades with proper opportunities for advancing their careers.

Collective strategies and methods in implementing organisational change

Initiating organisational change in an employing agency is a complex task involving the orchestration of action seeking to remove individual racism, institutional racism and cultural racism in both policy and practice, whilst sustaining the morale of individuals and groups involved in it. Individuals can contribute towards organisational change by breaking the conspiracy of silence and speaking out against those instances of racism they detect. It means becoming personally aware of the issues at stake, taking steps to raise consciousness of issues to be confronted, promoting anti-racist norms and facilitating action that endorses them.

White individuals challenging their organisations also continually have to subject their actions to scrutiny, seek support to maintain their own morale, sharpen their analysis, work effectively collectively with peers and ensure that their actions do not transgress anti-racist objectives. Beginning to work along these lines requires two forms of organisational change. The first is that they subject their work to being monitored and evaluated by black people. The second is that they form anti-racist collectives with white people sharing their anti-racist objectives and develop ways of working together and supporting each other. White people are also more used to competing with other white people than working collaboratively to benefit one another, even when allegedly working in teams. Nonetheless, white people will have to work together if they are successfully to promote anti-racist policies and practices in the face of opposition from some white people. Working together across the racial divide can also be problematic because white people have difficulty in accepting an inversion of the normal power relationships between black and white people, including black colleagues.

White anti-racist social workers will have to introduce organisational change at all levels of their institutions, including management, other departments in their authority, professional associations and the relevant trade unions. By creating alliances to underpin campaigns, engaging in direct action and demanding change among these echelons of their organisation, white anti-racist social workers will strengthen their positions. Without support at these levels, it will be easy for those resisting anti-racist social work to block its implementation. One reason for developing alliances both horizontally and vertically within an organisation is that all aspects of an organisation's policies and practices will be touched by anti-racist changes in one area. People throughout the organisation will be affected. Priorities will have to be re-ordered to reflect anti-racist objectives; competition for scarce resources will be exacerbated; well-known routines will be overturned. Uncertainty and fear of what is being asked of white people will become consonant with strife. In the face of such widespread changes, white people will demand a say in what happens. Without careful preparatory work being undertaken with the individuals concerned, they may well block attempts at altering a racist *status quo*.

White people may fear losing the privileges they enjoy and not appreciate the gains that can accrue from working in an anti-racist organisation. For example, implementing an anti-racist curriculum in social work education requires that sociologists, social policy teachers and psychologists change their teaching content and methods. Whilst white social work educators may see the need for introducing new practices, it may be difficult for them to convince colleagues in other departments of this. Departmental sovereignty, interdepartmental rivalry, professional autonomy and notions of personal liberty and academic freedom will be used to hinder anti-racist action. The controversy which erupted at Birmingham Polytechnic during the 1986–87 academic year between the social work department and the polytechnic management following the dismissal of a black lecturer is indicative of the difficulties facing a single department embarking on the process of implementing anti-racist social work education (*Social Work Today*, April 1987; Willis, 1987). The 'moral panic' created around anti-racist social work education in the summer of 1993 (see Phillips, 1993; Appleyard, 1993; Pinker, 1993) indicates the obstacles and complexities which need to be resolved in addressing the issue. It also reveals how the media caricatures both the progress made and the problems which need to be sensitively handled.

Another reason for developing alliances at all levels of an organisation is that it enhances the chances of being successful in introducing changes. Carrying people with one enables them to engage in convincing others who are sceptical about any proposals. Also, the burden of transforming the workplace is spread across a number of shoulders, making it easier for each individual to maintain energy and enthusiasm for the work. A further reason is that if organisational change is instituted throughout an agency, it becomes more difficult for white people to fob off black colleagues or clients with token gestures. A collective commitment to anti-racist social work makes it more likely to happen in practice. Demonstrating the reality of anti-racist social work through their practice allows white people to make a real statement about their commitment to fighting racism. This in turn facilitates the possibility of white people being able to support initiatives developed by black people in ways that do not undermine them, and form alliances based on equality with them.

6

Campaigning for the Transformation of Social Work: the White Social Worker as an Anti-Racist Advocate and Change Agent

The major task of white anti-racist social work advocates and change agents is the transformation of existing social work practice and the social relations expressed through and within it. Working in this direction requires white anti-racist social work advocates and change agents to break their silence about the destruction that racism wreaks on black people's lives. It also demands that they cease acting as 'experts' who can speak for and on behalf of black people. In implementing strategies predicated on challenging racism in both the personal and structural dimensions, white anti-racist social work advocates and change agents will have to work simultaneously along all three levels: the individual (or personal), the institutional and the cultural. This will require white anti-racist social work advocates and change agents both to work on their own and collectively to deal with individual distress and overcome the structural constraints through which racist practices are perpetuated. The following case studies examine how this work can be done in different contexts – divided families, situations combining sexism with racism, protecting civil liberties and endorsing various forms of kinship.

The continued critique of their work by black activists has made white social workers become increasingly aware of the deprivation endured by black people. Much of it has been reinforced through social work intervention which perpetuates racism. White social workers can speak out against this state of affairs and bring about change by assuming the role of anti-racist social work advocates and change agents. White anti-racist social workers adopting this role would highlight the interconnectedness between the more generalised aspects of institutionalised racism prevalent in society and that occurring within social work, and devote their energies to tackling these simultaneously. However, each individual would not necessarily work on both tasks at the same time. Each one would be involved with others doing different aspects of this work by being supportive and informed, lending others whatever assistance was possible.

White anti-racist social work advocates and change agents can engage in organisational change as well as initiate changes in individual practices. Handling this task requires white social workers to adopt an overtly political stance eschewing the 'neutrality' of their position as professionals. For in so far as neutrality endorses the *status quo*, the neutral approach individualises and vacuum-packs social problems, thus making it easy for professionals to pathologise those they are endeavouring to help and hold them solely responsible for their predicament. Through this approach, they collude in maintaining the white supremacy inherent in the way in which social relations are currently organised.

In challenging white professionalism, white anti-racist social work advocates and change agents begin by redefining the social work task and the relations between themselves as employees and their employers; themselves as professionals alongside their professional peers; and themselves as workers relating to service users. Their job is one of constantly highlighting and countering racist policies and practices. Assuming such a position can place white anti-racist social work advocates and change agents in an oppositional stance *vis-à-vis* white employers, colleagues and service users who are indifferent or hostile to anti-racist social work. In this process, working in anti-racist ways exposes the contradictory relationship between social work's controlling function and its caring one, as their actions reveal how social work is used as a tool of oppression, to reinforce social control and keep oppressed people in their place by containing their demands and aspirations instead of providing for their welfare. These also highlight the ways in which traditional social work demands that oppressed people change themselves by adopting more acceptable attitudes; improve their behaviour so that it is in line with the dominant social norms; cope more effectively with their oppression by accepting their predicament as their fault; and ensure that they do not challenge existing social relations. The discussion below focuses on how the complex interplay between institutionalised racism and personal suffering can be countered through anti-racist collective action which draws on the energies of white anti-racist social work advocates and change agents.

Campaigns against institutionalised racism and the denial of black people's rights

Countering the enforced division of black families

White social work advocates and change agents have a role in campaigning for black people to have a guaranteed right to family life and enjoy family forms they themselves define as appropriate. The following account illustrates how easily black people's aspirations can be thwarted by institutional racism:

> A Punjabi Sikh man lost his job in a foundry when he became seriously ill. Although his oldest son, aged 15, lived with him in England, his wife and three other children aged 12, 10 and 5 resided in India. He had begun seeking entry certificates for them 15 months earlier, when his health first started deteriorating. His attempts to get compensation from his employers for his illness failed. He was also unsuccessful in getting the DHSS to register him as disabled. His claim for supplementary benefits was allowed only for him and his 15 year old son, leaving his wife and children in India without any means of support. He went to an Advice Centre for help, but was politely informed by the white workers that none could be provided. The law did not allow him to claim either child benefit or income support in respect of family members not resident in Britain.

What could white anti-racist social work advocates do in this case? The situation is a difficult one in which to intervene because the social security law currently excludes black people from claiming for dependants not resident in Britain. Intervention is possible, but it would have to encompass several levels. On the personal level, a white anti-racist social worker would offer the Punjabi Sikh man support in dealing with individual distress, putting him in touch with black organisations with experience in these matters. Moreover, the social worker would ensure that the claimant was receiving all the benefits to which he and his dependants were entitled, including examining the possibility of lodging appeals against the decisions taken by his former employer and the DHSS. They would also check out whether or not financial support could be provided from other public sources and charities.

The white anti-racist social worker would then address the structural level, i.e. institutionalised racism, by linking up with existing campaigns to eliminate the racist basis of social security and immigration legislation, and eliciting the support of relevant MPs and other organisations such as the United Kingdom Immigrants Advisory Service (UKIAS) and the Joint Council for the Welfare of Immigrants (JCWI) to pursue the matter further. This element would also need to address cultural racism which says that black people need different boundaries drawn around their eligibility for entitlement from white people because they will otherwise 'abuse the system' through fraudulent claims. A mass campaign in educational establishments and the media would need to underpin action aimed at countering such rigid views. But, as many other black people suffer like this claimant, changing the law could alleviate considerable personal suffering amongst a larger group of black people. In trying to secure just and humane legislation, both black and white people would learn how to work together. Moreover, in challenging the existing definitions of eligibility prescribed by the law, the process of beginning to transform the nature of social work and of questioning the injustice of regulations that require people to contribute to welfare benefits whilst being denied full access to claiming them would be set in train. It would also change social work from what it is – a source of 'help' which colludes with excluding people from receiving justice – to one that gives primacy of place to just treatment for all people.

Challenging the distortion of family relationships

White anti-racist social work advocates and change agents would also become involved in campaigns endorsing the right of black people to bring their families into Britain by challenging the reinforcement of biological racism through immigration controls emphasising nuclear family relationships and by struggling for the recognition of extended family and other sociological family units. This would lead to questioning the use of blood tests to prove paternity for black people when paper documentation suffices for others. Asking for proof of biological kinship denies that there are other forms of parenting which society can and does recognise, for example fostering and adoption. Long-term fostering and adoption of children by others, particularly those who are closely connected with the children's original families, is a common pattern of child care amongst people from West Africa (Ellis, 1972), the Asian sub-continent and the Caribbean. In the context of only blood ties being accepted as legitimate proof of kinship by immigration control, many children fostered and adopted by others are deprived of the chance to join their rightful parents. The following case study reveals the complexity which can be found in black family life:

Farah was a black Muslim woman who married Ali, a black Muslim man. Together they had three children – two girls aged 5 and 3 and a 1 year old boy. After six years of marriage, Ali started physically abusing his wife. Farah sought assistance from her in-laws, but they sided with Ali, saying he was not a violent fellow, so she must have done something dreadful to deserve such punishment. Farah did not seek help from the social services department because she was afraid they would bring in the police.

One day she went into a local greengrocer's where she met Joanne, one of her white neighbours with whom she exchanged greetings on the rare occasions that they met. She tried to avoid Joanne because her face was bruised on one side. However, other customers blocked her path and she came face to face with her. The look of shock on Joanne's face was too much for Farah and having said 'hello', she burst into tears. Joanne put her arm around her and took her into her house where Farah told her what had happened. Joanne told her that she should move out, taking the children with her. She would willingly let her stay at her house but felt Farah would be safer further away from Ali and his family. Farah told her moving out was impossible. She would lose her children, everything. Joanne tried to talk her into calling social services as she felt they would be sure to help her keep the children away from Ali. Farah said, 'No'. Besides Ali had never hit the children. Then she said she had to go home.

Farah saw more of Joanne after this and welcomed the opportunity she provided to talk about her troubles freely and without fear. Eventually their friendship deepened and the two women fell in love. Ali had noticed that Farah was spending more time with Joanne, but as she was a single woman living on her own, he was not unduly perturbed at first. However, he became jealous of the time she was spending with Joanne and started picking fights with her over it. About a year after their affair had started, Ali had taunted Farah with "you love her, don't you" during one of their rows. Farah's spontaneous 'Yes' was followed by revengeful wrath. Farah was beaten so badly she became unconscious and Ali rushed her to the hospital, telling the doctors she had fallen downstairs.

Fortunately, the children had been at Ali's mother's house and had not witnessed the horrendous scene. Farah had concussion and broken ribs as well as extensive bruising. She was in hospital for a long time. Ali rarely came to see her; Joanne came regularly. Farah refused to talk to her about the assault. Eventually, Ali wrote to say he was divorcing her under Muslim law. When she finally came out of hospital, Ali had gone to Pakistan with the children to stay with his grandmother and aunt. He had left Farah a note saying she was not to try to trace him. Under Muslim law, the children were his and he had told the children she was dead and would never see them again. As a lesbian she was not fit to be either mother or wife, he had added. He also informed her he was selling the house which was in his name and that she had to find somewhere else to live.

Farah was devastated. Fortunately Joanne had been with her, otherwise she thought she would have committed suicide. Although she still didn't want to go to the police and charge Ali with assault, she wanted the children back. She went to see her in-laws to ask them to intercede on her behalf to bring the children back. They refused to open the door to her. She went to see a (white) lawyer who told her she could apply to the courts for a 'residence order' to get the children to live with her, but even if she were successful, it would be difficult to enforce given that the children were in Pakistan. He also said that whatever happened, under the 1989 Children Act, Ali would retain his parental rights over the children. Farah did not tell him about Ali's assault on her. Feeling extremely depressed and upset, she went home to find that the locks had been changed and a 'For Sale' sign posted in the lawn. She sat on the front steps and wept. Joanne found her there in a distraught state four hours later when she returned from work and took her to her house.

This case study depicts the complexity of issues that anti-racist social workers should be able to address. However, their doing so requires them to undertake sensitive work simultaneously on a number of levels. They need the knowledge base and skills to deal with racism on a number of levels, to intervene in complicated interpersonal dynamics that impinge upon family relationships when old ones are in the process of breaking down and being replaced with new ones with a degree of cultural awareness and confidence that ensures that the physical well-being of women and children is safeguarded and the law upheld as appropriate. Moreover, this case needs to take on board the issues of sexism and homophobia as the same time as racism. The intricacy of the work that needs to be done would require more than one social worker to be involved if the moral, ethical and legal dilemmas that arise are to be handled appropriately. Both black and white workers would need to work closely as a team if a solution which acknowledges Farah's rights is to be arrived at. Yet, having a 'team' working on one case and providing advocates for each of the parties involved in the conflict require a level of resourcing which is beyond the ability of cash-starved authorities to provide. Nonetheless, this is another issue that anti-racist social workers need to pursue through their networks and alliances which lay the issue before government. This situation also raises the question of intervention beyond national borders. Most departments are poorly equipped to respond to the demands doing so imposes. They may have to develop a regional facility to support clients like Farah. In identifying gaps of this nature in existing provisions, anti-racist social workers would also be embarking on a series of changes that would benefit others.

Fighting the combination of sexism and racism

Sexism combines with racism to exacerbate the distress endured by black women. The following cases depict instances in which the social security legislation and its implementation in practice operates to the detriment of black women's welfare:

> After living in England for several years, Shama's marriage broke down because her husband physically abused her and her daughter aged 3. She sought safety in a white women's refuge because there were no facilities nearby specifically earmarked for Asian women. Her claim for supplementary benefit was rejected because she could not produce her passport. It was being held by her husband who said he would give it to her when she returned home.

Besides exposing the racism evident in the demand that Shama produce her passport to establish her residence in Britain rather than taking her word for it in a crisis, as happens for white people, this case reveals the sexism underpinning the social security system. Shama cannot prove her claim to social security because she is dependent on her husband and does not have her own passport. White anti-racist social work advocates and change agents can become involved in campaigns abolishing the requirement that black people produce passports in order to have access to resources when in need and demanding women's right to an independent income.

White anti-racist social work advocates and change agents would address both the personal and structural levels simultaneously. They would respond to Shama's personal distress by helping her find a place in an Asian women's refuge, driving her to one and supporting her claim for supplementary benefit, passing the case on to a black organisation if the issues to be addressed were more complicated than just advice giving. (See Mama, 1989 for a clear exposition of the specific problems including the risk of deportation and racial harassment that black women surviving domestic violence encounter when they seek support from white agencies.) Having done this, white anti-racist social work advocates and change agents would focus on the institutionalised racism. Becoming involved in campaigns directed at securing resources for autonomous refuges for black women, and the employment of black workers in centres allegedly catering for the needs of all women who come through their doors, would constitute part of the struggle against that. Compiling a dossier of the inequities that black women have to overcome in securing assistance would provide details which could substantiate their claims. These would have to be suitably anonymised so as not to put individuals in the media spotlight and impose upon victim-survivors the burden of personally countering institutional racism. Finally, they would back campaigns insisting on women's right to resources responding to their specific needs, for example housing and employment. They would also pass information on to others for further action if necessary.

Campaigning for an anti-racist social security system

The British income maintenance system caters primarily for the needs of white British people. Its provisions are based on norms that are consistent with reinforcing class rule by maintaining the work ethic (Ginsburg, 1979); reproducing gender oppression by treating women as dependent on men and having similar working patterns to men (Dominelli, 1991b; Pascall, 1986); and perpetuating racial oppression (Gordon, 1985; Williams, 1987, 1989). Those elements within the social security system which comprise institutionalised racism include disallowing child benefit for people living in Britain if their children reside overseas, even though this may be the result of immigration laws preventing their entry (Gordon, 1985); denying supplementary benefit to sponsored dependants (Chapeltown Citizens' Advice Bureau, 1983); and refusing to pay family income supplement and unemployment benefit for dependants living overseas when the person providing their main source of income resides in Britain (Gordon, 1985). Yet, regardless of their immigration status all black workers pay national insurance contributions and taxes on their earnings. The changes introduced in the income maintenance system following the Fowler Review and deepened under subsequent Social Security Acts have intensified institutionalised racism through the 'residence test' and demands for passports to establish eligibility for those who 'appear foreign' (LSSC, 1986). Social workers will become more extensively involved in the implementation of this requirement when supporting applications for money from the Social Fund and public housing.

Other changes in black people's position have resulted from linking immigration status with income maintenance entitlements. The 1980

Social Security Act has made the obligation of sponsors to maintain their dependants legally enforceable. Failure to do so now constitutes a criminal offence. Consequently, people who become unemployed and register as such after sponsored dependents arrive are unable to claim income support for them. This puts black families under enormous financial pressure during times of hardship because the sponsoring family's money will have to be stretched to cover also the needs of the sponsored dependents. The net effect of this will be further to impoverish and divide black families.

Other aspects of the social security legislation which need changing cover a range of additional categories denied access to the system despite demonstrable hardship and suffering. These are 'overstayers', even if the delay has been caused by the Home Office's failure to respond quickly to an application for a visa extension or exemption, 'overseas' students' and 'illegal immigrants'. This latter term has become an increasingly elastic one which can be expanded arbitrarily. Black people, particularly refugees, can be classified as 'overstayers' or 'illegal immigrants' simply if they are in Britain whilst the Home Office processes their application (Gordon and Newnham, 1985). Regulations concerning deportation orders prohibit black people from applying for supplementary benefit if they are appealing such an order (D'Orey, 1984). Overseas students cannot claim either housing or supplementary benefits (now Income Support), although they may receive urgent needs payments for limited periods, for example if their funds have been delayed by postal failure, or coups in their countries of origin. 'Illegal immigrants' are excluded from access to public income maintenance provisions. Asylum seekers have recently been excluded from drawing income support by specific legislation excluding their entitlement.

The term 'illegal immigrant' is especially contentious. It has become very broadly defined to include people who have withheld information from immigration officers, unintentionally as in the case of Zamir heard in the House of Lords in 1980, although this possibility was rejected when the House of Lords adjudicated on the case of Khawaja in 1982; and those whose information, including documentary evidence such as birth and marriage certificates, immigration officers do not believe (CRE, 1985). These expanded definitions of illegality have undermined the position of legally settled black people. Police 'fishing raids', justified under the banner of seeking 'illegal immigrants' (Gordon, 1985), jeopardise the civil liberties of black people whose home is Britain and amplify the racist view that they do not 'really belong here'. White anti-racist social work advocates can be involved in campaigns affirming the rights of black people to be in Britain as full citizens, regardless of their length of stay. An anti-racist social security system would grant rights to all people living and working here by virtue of this fact alone. Simply living and working in Britain and being in need should constitute the eligibility requirement. The 'overseas' dependants of people living and working in Britain would automatically be covered under its provisions.

Protecting civil liberties through campaigns

Parveen Khan's situation reflects the position that black people face when, thinking they are legally settled in Britain, they find their status officially undermined (Gordon and Newnham, 1985). The continuous expansion of the definition of 'illegal immigrant' in the hands of the Home Office, the police and the courts makes the outcome of struggles aimed at ensuring justice in particular circumstances difficult to predict.

> Parveen Khan was declared an illegal immigrant when her husband, who had come to Britain when 13, was found to have done so as the son of a sociological rather than biological parent. When threatened with deportation, her husband went into hiding, and Parveen Khan went to claim supplementary benefit. However, despite the Khawaja ruling, Parveen was considered an 'illegal immigrant' and her claim was refused. Her child benefit for her British-born child was also withdrawn. A campaign was launched to prevent her removal from Britain and to raise money for her support. As a result of this campaign, Parveen Khan was able to remain. (Gordon and Newnham, 1985)

> A further example of a campaign safeguarding a black person's right to work in this country and provide a service to black people was that of Mohamed Idris. Mohamed Idris was a social worker threatened with deportation when asking for an extension to his visa. A lengthy campaign mounted in his defence rallied NALGO as well as black and white social workers to his cause. Mohamed Idris was ultimately allowed to stay.

White anti-racist social work advocates can join campaigns resisting encroachment on the civil liberties of black people and participate actively in campaigning organisations such as the Action Group on Immigration and Nationality (AGIN) or the Campaign against Double Jeopardy (CADJ) of the Campaign Against Double Punishment (CADP). They can support individuals experiencing immigration difficulties by putting black clients in touch with others in a similar predicament and with black people and organisations having specific expertise on these issues. On the organisational front, white anti-racist social workers can join campaigns aimed at changing the law in directions which secure the civil liberties of black people, for example prohibiting 'fishing raids'.

White anti-racist social work advocates concerned with ensuring justice in the situations described above can become involved in campaigns which demand that:

1. the arrest without warrant of those suspected of being 'illegal immigrants' cease;
2. allegations of 'illegal immigration' status be proved by the Home Office and the police;
3. immigration laws assume that people are innocent until proved guilty rather than the reverse;
4. immigration detainees receive humane treatment;
5. the racism inherent in the immigration laws, the nationality laws and the remainder of the legal system be eliminated;
6. the racism inherent in the prison system, police service, probation service and personal social services be dismantled;
7. the description of black people as 'immigrants' on the basis of the colour of their skin be abolished;
8. the gamut of black family forms be acknowledged; and
9. black women's rights both within the family and outside it be safeguarded.

Joining campaigns outside mainstream social work will enable white anti-racist social work advocates and change agents to make connections between enhancing black people's welfare and making demands for better personal social services for other client groups.

Anti-racist social work practice is good practice

The cases considered above demonstrate that white anti-racist social work advocates and change agents have a role in highlighting gaps in provisions and the failure of services to meet black people's needs. They can argue that black people are damaged by inappropriate intervention on the part of white social workers, for example the destruction of black children's identity through their being inappropriately placed for transracial adoption (Maximé, 1986); the unjust penalising of black youth in the juvenile justice system (Hood, 1992); the exclusion of black people from the benefits of the income maintenance system (Gordon and Newnham, 1985); and the lack of facilities to meet the specific needs of black women (Guru, 1987; Mama, 1989). Highlighting effective work with black people can also enable social workers to draw parallels between anti-racist social work and good practice generally, thereby also improving services for white people. White anti-racist social work advocates and change agents would also devote their energies towards bringing black and white people together on the basis of equality, using their commitment to anti-racist ways of working in building a bridge leading white people to the creation of a non-racist social work. Thus, they can add to the celebration of a common struggle through the recognition of equality in diversity described by black women as 'Many Voices, One Chant' (*Feminist Review*, 1984). Differences can be acknowledged, valued and celebrated as a source of growth and richness in interpersonal interactions between people rather than as manifestations of inferiority.

White anti-racist social work advocates can challenge bad practice on a more general level, for example the absence of interpretation facilities for all peoples not familiar with English as their main tool of communication. Currently, the lack of either sufficient bilingual social workers or appropriate translation services has led to bad practice on a wide scale regardless of setting. For example, social services use children to translate for their elders, and probation services use volunteer interpreters without adequate training, pay or understanding of the work they are undertaking. White anti-racist social work advocates can also work to attract resources for oppressed groups and support black people's demands for resources, power and autonomy. Their work reveals the necessity of introducing different techniques and methodologies such as consciousness-raising and community-based interventions, into mainstream social work.

Their relationships with service users would be characterised by equality and an expertise geared towards servicing individuals and groups who define for themselves the provisions they need. The major aim of a professional–client relationship based on providing user-centered services would be to provide individuals and groups with the information and back-up support required for them to achieve their goals. White anti-racist social work advocates would also constantly ask the question, '*What are the implications of what I am doing for black people?*', so as not to decontextualise 'race' or ignore the significance of racism in their behaviour, thoughts and actions. In becoming

anti-racist social work advocates and change agents, white social workers would have to lose their stereotypes of black individuals and communities and acquire detailed knowledge about the existence of resources which could be marshalled in favour of deprived communities, both black and white.

Focusing on putting *justice* back into their work, white anti-racist social work advocates and change agents would seek to empower powerless groups acting for themselves. The business of acting as facilitators in the self-empowerment of others puts them in the position of listeners responding to the voices of service users. Oppressed people have their own voices and can and do speak for themselves, but their voices are seldom heard in a bureaucracy which takes its own goals and objectives as the definitive ones when making decisions about people's lives. White anti-racist social work advocates and change agents would be listening to voices which are already there to be heard. Their activities reveal the necessity of introducing non-pathologising techniques and methodologies into mainstream social work. Community action approaches, with their campaigning, networking and collective ways of working, become essential tools for white anti-racist social work advocates and change agents.

Bringing community action approaches, with their emphasis on collective ways of working, into mainstream social work facilitates the recognition of the connection between individuals' positions, their personal suffering and the structural factors which impinge on their lives. Looking at the situation in these terms enables white anti-racist social work advocates to put meaning into the statement that the 'personal is political' and acknowledge that individual woes reflect a person's social status. In using community action tools and tactics, white anti-racist social work advocates would contribute towards exposing the real nature of the problems to be tackled and redefining these by focusing on the impact wrought by the racist nature of society; organising with others collectively to introduce structural change; and using political analyses and action in responding to personal needs. By giving them real control and choice over what to do with their lives, structural change becomes essential in liberating individuals. Structural change aimed at furthering equality also promotes the welfare of all people – black and white.

The links between anti-racist struggles and poverty more generally have to be highlighted and incorporated in the action plans of white anti-racist social work advocates and change agents. This means dealing with white working class clients' racism, particularly in inner-city areas, so that they can build bridges between black and white communities, acknowledge their different but unequal starting points, and focus on identifying commonalities in their struggle. These bridges cannot be constructed on the assumption that class oppression has precedence over 'race', but on recognising the multiple aspects of oppression that black people have to endure. Nor can these bridges be built on pious hopes and abstract words. They have to have a concrete reality which demystifies relationships between black and white communities.

Equalising action, not 'positive discrimination'

Tackling racism means getting the discussion going on the right tracks. As long as 'positive discrimination' is popularly construed as giving oppressed groups 'something they do not deserve', talking about 'positive discrimination' for black people will not induce many deprived white people to fight against racism. Such terminology confirms white racist stereotypes of the inferiority of black people and prepares the ground for the white backlash, as the American experience is demonstrating. 'Positive discrimination' defined in these terms makes the relationship between black and white people one of recipient and donor respectively and reproduces paternalism. Moreover, it mystifies the real problem that needs to be addressed, i.e. that black people as a group are not receiving their entitlements, and that their existing experience and qualifications are being ignored (Brown, 1984; Smith, 1976).

The 'positive discrimination' approach disguises the fact that a real redistribution of resources from one group to another requires the transferral of resources on three levels simultaneously – from the wealthy to the poor, i.e. between classes, from men to women, and from white to black. 'Positive discrimination' also negates the position of black people as they experience it. In not acknowledging black people's view of being denied access to power and resources and being deprived of common justice, *'positive discrimination' is denying black people their voice and making invisible their experience of racism as a particular form of social exclusion.* It also denies the substantial contribution that black people make to society, including its economic growth.

Equalising action

Thus, white anti-racist social work advocates and change agents need to talk about *equalising action in securing justice for black people.* **Equalising action** is aimed at redistributing social power and resources towards black people so that they receive their share of society's power and wealth and gain full recognition of the qualities they already possess. In demystifying the nature of the social relations inherent in policies of 'positive discrimination', white anti-racist social work advocates and change agents will complement the work of others similarly involved in exposing the real nature of the social relations underpinning racist situations. Doing so will enable both black and white people to see the specific points at which their struggles converge, thereby enabling the commonalities in their struggle against racism to become invisible.

White anti-racist social work advocates and change agents would highlight the purpose of their struggle as righting past and present injustices meted out to black people and increasing resources to everyone in deprived communities. This goal would be achieved through immediate action aimed at an egalitarian transformation of the system whereby wealth and power are distributed. Such an approach offers white anti-racist social work advocates and change agents a stronger basis for united action between black people and white people for it to overcome the divisiveness which is a central feature in the dynamics of racism. Their activities against racism in social work must also link up with anti-racist struggles being carried out more generally in society and with black people's demands for the righting of past wrongs, for example through compensation. The claim to compensation for racist discriminatory treatment has already been recognised, for example by Canada in the case of Japanese Canadians wrongly interned or forcibly removed from their homes during World War II. Compensation here took the form of a financial sum awarded to individuals and a public apology issued by the federal government.

Engaging in anti-racist ways of working enables white anti-racist social work advocates and change agents to examine the specific ways in which class, 'race' and gender oppress different groups of people and how these interact with each other. White anti-racist social work advocates and change agents have to struggle against inequalities evident in all social divisions, for example 'race', class, gender, disability, sexual orientation and age, because these are used to both control people and ration resources between them. Oppression can occur along any number of dimensions. Oppression on the basis of class, 'race', gender, disability, age and sexual orientation is central to our present society which is permeated by relations of domination and subordination. Individuals experiencing oppression on a number of these dimensions experience them at the same time, not separately one by one. Thus, oppression operates on the principle of simultaneous multiplicity rather than accumulation.

The anti-racist struggle is a struggle for the equality of all people regardless of their status in society. But to foster a common struggle between black and white people against class or any other form of oppression, alliances must be constructed on foundations which explicitly acknowledge the different starting points between people. This would mean recognising the significance that such differences have in their life chances and in the opportunity to develop their particular strengths. It also involves eliminating differences in the power relations between them and uncovering through careful study the more general similarities in their experience of oppression (Lorde, 1984). White anti-racist social work advocates must not prioritise one form of oppression over another, thereby creating a new hierarchy of oppression in the organisations they create to eliminate it. Moreover, in making connections between one dimension of oppression, for example 'race', and another, such as gender or class, white anti-racist social work advocates and change agents must ensure that they do not use these as diversions taking attention away from the business of tackling racial oppression. At the same time, they must take care not to conclude that the specificity of one form of oppression can be subsumed by another, or that all forms of oppression are the same.

White anti-racist social work advocates and change agents should become involved in a number of campaigns, challenging the racist bases of social work and its provisions. Approaches will include campaigning against racist immigration rules which divide black families and cause untold sorrow and hardship (CRE, 1985; Gordon, 1986); arguing for the proper funding of social services for black people instead of their relegation to Section 11 provisions; demanding resources especially earmarked for black women (Guru, 1987) and black elders (ASRA, 1981; Patel, 1990); reversing racist stereotypes and images of black individuals, families and communities; and demanding the elimination of racist conditions in social security provisions, housing, education, health and employment.

Campaigning in these areas is important for enhancing the conditions underpinning the quality of life and welfare of black people. Provisions coming through the personal social services can augment the quality of black people's lives, but they cannot substitute for it. However, provisions in the personal social services can confirm, condone and continue inequality unless social work deliberately fosters goals alternative to those reinforcing social exclusion through resource rationing and control. Thus, white anti-racist social work advocates have a role in exposing those elements of social work which control people and their aspirations. They need to make connections between activities and campaigns aimed at transforming social relations in society generally with those specifically occurring within the social work arena, thereby initiating and supporting all forms of anti-racist action in social work policy and practice.

7

Conclusions: Developing Anti-Racist/Non-Racist Social Work

Racist social work education and practices have been inadequately challenged for far too long. The glaring injustice these perpetuate and the damage they cause to black and white people can no longer be tolerated. White people have no choice but to become anti-racist if they wish to reclaim their humanity and live in a society which accords each person their dignity. To be worth living in, such a society must be non-racist. In it, justice, caring, individual fulfilment and collective concern would reign. Anti-racist social work has a role to play in creating a non-racist society. Fulfilling this role calls for the transformation of social work and demands that its own practice espouses equality for all; fosters consumer involvement; develops provisions geared to meet people's needs rather than ration resources; and endorses a professionalism based on caring for people instead of excluding them.

The implementation of these demands requires the employment of workers who have demonstrated an ability to work with anyone, across racial divides, client groups and sexes, and who have an empathy based on knowledge of the significance of differences between black and white people, rather than on the pretence that people are all the same. This requires a change in the fundamental basis of social work and the redefinition of its task. It means asserting the values of being human in a context lacking notions of racial superiority, but in which respect, dignity and value are accorded to all. It is also not about one set of individuals or groups gaining at the expense of others. Competition between people would give way to collaboration. Egalitarian working relations would replace hierarchical ones.

Anti-racist social work guidelines

Anti-racist social work has to tackle personal, institutional and cultural racism by introducing change at both individual and structural levels. Individual conduct in interpersonal relations and the allocation of power and resources in society have to be transformed if racism is to be eliminated. To get anti-racist social work firmly embedded in the social fabric, white people must engage in a number of activities which will promote it. The following guidelines are aimed at providing pointers for people seeking to become anti-racist practitioners and educators:

1. Change the current definition of the social work task to one which does not render oppression invisible.
2. Negate the 'objectivity' currently embedded in a professionalism underpinning a *status quo* which has been found seriously wanting.
3. Alter the existing power relationship between the users of services and workers. The voice of 'the expert' should not substitute for that of oppressed people.
4. Do not deny consumers their right to determine the types of welfare provision provided.
5. Stop treating people's welfare at both individual and group level as a commodity that can be rationed for the purposes of excluding people and their aspirations. Instead, it should enhance personal fulfilment and social well-being.
6. Change the basis of training from one which assumes a false neutrality on the major social and ethical issues of the day to one making explicit its value base and taking a moral and political stance against oppression in any of its forms.
7. Terminate an allocation of power and resources which perpetuates injustice and misery and replace it with one committed to implementing justice and equality for all.
8. End the theoretical separation between social work and (a) other key elements of the state, especially its welfare sectors, for example housing, education, health and social security; and (b) the 'law and order' apparatus including the police and the courts, the Home Office and the Immigration Service. Instead, the connections between each of these parts must be made visible.
9. Expose the connections between policy and practice by challenging their being dealt with as unrelated entities.

10. Replace the lack of political commitment to ending racial inequality, with one which operates in the opposite direction.

From the variety of changes that are envisaged, it is clear that anti-racist social work will not only confront racism in social work, but also expose and tackle other forms of oppression which are reproduced by and perpetuated through social work. For example, changes eradicating class and gender inequality will be included in the transformation resulting from struggles against racism. Through its impact on other forms of oppression, anti-racist social work will signal the implementation of good social work practice all round. In addition, tackling racism aimed at black people undermines the racist practices perpetrated against other non-Anglo-Saxon ethnic minorities.

Having adopted and developed an anti-racist position in social work, white social workers will have to move on to developing non-racist social work. This will have to be done in conjunction with black social workers, on the basis of equality in the relationships that are established between them. This means equal power, equal access to resources, equal opportunities and prospects, and acknowledging work that is equal in value. Ultimately, the development of non-racist social work will mean that both black and white social workers will work across the whole range of client groups.

However, the nature of their work will have been transformed. Their main emphasis will not be on rationing resources unfairly, but on using them effectively, collectively, in providing people with the services they require when they need them. Their efforts will in turn have to be underpinned by egalitarianism and involve consumers fully in determining the nature of service provision and delivery. To be available to all at the point of need, these services will have to be funded through the public purse. Thus, to secure non-racist social work, black and white social workers will have to make changes in the political, juridical and social bases of current practice. When this has taken place, anti-racist social work will provide the foundation for achieving equality and transforming welfare provisions for both black and white people. Social work, redefined according to anti-racist criteria, is not about social control as exclusion, but about realising significant improvements in the life chances and well-being of individuals, regardless of their gender, 'race', class, age, physical or intellectual abilities, sexual orientation, religious affiliation or linguistic capabilities. Anti-racist social work, therefore, is a bridge between social work in a racist society and social work in a non-racist one.

Useful Addresses

All Faiths for One Race (AFFOR)
1 Finch Road
Lozells
Birmingham B19 1HS
Tel: 0121 523 8076

Manchester Law Centre
584 Stockport Road
Longsight
Manchester M13 0RQ
Tel: 0161 225 5111

Commission for Racial Equality (CRE)
Elliot House
10–12 Allington Street
London SW1E 5EH
Tel: 0171 828 7022

Joint Council for the Welfare of Immigrants (JCWI)
115 Old Street
London EC1V 9JR
Tel: 0171 251 8706

The Runnymede Trust
11 Princelet Street
London E1 6QH
Tel: 0171 375 1496

United Kingdom Immigrants Advisory Service (UKIAS)
2nd Floor
190 Gt Dover Street
London SE1 4YB
Tel: 0171 357 6917

Action Group on Immigration and Nationality (AGIN)
400 Cheetham Street
Manchester M80 7DL
Tel: 0161 740 7722

Black and In Care Steering Group
c/o Children's Legal Centre
20 Compton Terrace
London N1 2UN
Tel: 0171 359 6251

The White Collective for Anti-Racist Social Work
c/o The Department of
Applied Social Studies
The University of Warwick
Coventry CV4 7AL
Tel: 01203 523523

The New Black Families Unit
Lewisham Social Services
392–4 Brixton Road
London SW9 7AW

Southall Black Sisters
52 Norwood Road
Southall UB2 4DW
Tel: 0181 574 3412

Black Resource Centre
The Old Library
Cheetham Hill Road
Manchester M8 7JN
Tel: 0161 740 7575

Bibliography

ABAFA (Association of British Adoption and Fostering Agencies) (1977) *Soul Kids Campaign Report*, London: ABAFA.

ABSWAP (Association of Black Social Workers and Allied Professionals) (1981) *Black Children in Care: Evidence Submitted to the Select Committee on Child Care*, London: ABSWAP.

ACW/Mainframe (Association of Community Workers/Mainframe) (1994) *Community Work Competences*, London: ACW.

Adamson, M. and Borgos, S. (1985) *The Mighty Dream: Protest Movements in the United States*, London: Routledge.

ADSS/CRE (Association of Directors of Social Services/Commission for Racial Equality) (1978) *Multi-Racial Britain: The Social Services Response*, London: ADSS/CRE.

AFFOR (All Faiths for One Race) (1978) *Talking Blues*, Birmingham: AFFOR.

Age Concern (1984) *Housing for Ethnic Elders*, London: Age Concern.

Ahmad, B. (1990) *Black Perspectives in Social Work*, Birmingham: Venture Press.

Ahmed, S. (1978) 'Asian Girls and Cultural Conflicts' in *Social Work Today*, 8 August, 14–15.

Ahmed, S. (1982) 'Social Work with Minority Children and Families', Unit 16 in *Ethnic Minorities and Community Relations*, Open University Course No. E354, Milton Keynes: Open University.

Ahmed, S. (1984) 'Social Work with Ethnic Minorities', paper given at the BASW Annual Conference at Nene College, April.

Ahmed, S., Cheetham, J. and Small, J. (1987) *Social Work with Black Children and Their Families*, London: Batsford.

ALTARF (All London Teachers Against Racism and Fascism) (1984) *Challenging Racism*, London: ALTARF.

Amos, V. and Parmar, P. (1984) 'Challenging Imperial Feminism' in *Feminist Review*, Autumn, **17**:3–19.

Appleyard, B. (1993) 'Why Paint so Black a Picture?' in *The Independent*, 4 August.

Arnold, E. (1982) 'Finding Black Families for Black Children' in J. Cheetham (ed.) *Social Work and Ethnicity*, London: Allen & Unwin.

ASRA (Asian Sheltered Residential Accommodation) (1981) *Asians' Sheltered Residential Accommodation*, London: ASRA.

BCSG (Black and In Care Steering Group) (1984) *Black and in Care: Conference Report*, London: Blackrose Press.

Bagley, C. and Young, L. (1982) 'Policy Dilemmas and the Adoption of Black Children' in J. Cheetham (ed.) *Social Work and Ethnicity*, London: Allen & Unwin.

Bailey, R. and Brake, M. (1975) *Radical Social Work*, London: Edward Arnold.

Banks, G. (1971)'The Effects of Race on One-to-One Helping Interviews' in *Social Service Review*, June, **45**:137–46.

Barker, M. (1981) *The New Racism. Conservatives and the Ideology of the Tribe*, London: Junction Books.

Begum, N. (1993) 'Black Disabled Women Speak' in *Community Care*, July, **23**.

Ben-Tovim, G. and Gabriel, J. (1982) 'The Society of Race: Time to Change Course?' in A. Ohri *et al.* (eds) *Community Work and Racism*, London: Routledge.

Beresford, P. and Croft, S. (1986) *Whose Welfare: Private Care or Public Services*, Brighton: Lewis Cohen Urban Studies Centre.

Bhalla, A. and Blakemore, K. (1981) *Elders of the Ethnic Minority Groups*, Birmingham: All Faiths for One Race (AFFOR).

Bhavani, K.K. (1993) 'Talking Racism and the Editing of Women's Studies' in D. Richardson and V. Robinson (eds) *Introducing Women's Studies*, London: Macmillan.

Billingsley, A. and Giovannoni, J. (1972) *Children of the Dream*, New York: Harcourt Brace Jovanovich.

Bjorgo, T. and Witte, R. (1993) *Racist Violence in Europe*, London: Macmillan.

Black Assessors (1994) 'DipSW Consultation a Sham' in *Community Care*, October, **20**:13–18.

Blakemore, K. and Boneham, M. (1994) *Age, Race and Ethnicity: A Comparative Approach*, Buckingham: Open University Press.

Blom-Cooper, L. (1986) *A Child in Trust: The Report of the Panel of Inquiry Into the Circumstances Surrounding the Death of Jasmine Beckford*, London Borough of Brent: Kingswood Press.

Bolger, S., Corrigan, R., Docking, J. and Frost, N. (1981) *Towards Socialist Welfare Work*, London: Macmillan.

Braham, P., Rattansi, A. and Skellington, R. (1992) *Racism and Anti-Racism: Inequalities, Opportunities and Policies*, Buckingham: Open University/Sage.

Brent Community Health Council (1981) *Black People and the Health Service*, Brent: Brent CHC.

Brinton, L. and Welch, M. (1983) 'White Agency, Black Community' in *Adoption and Fostering*, **7**(2):16–18.

Brittan, A. and Maynard, M. (1984) *Sexism, Racism and Oppression*, Oxford: Blackwell.

Bromley, D. and Longino, C. F. Jr (1972) *White Racism and Black Americans*, Cambridge, Mass.: Schenkman.

Brook, E. and Davis, A. (1985) *Women, the Family and Social Work*, London: Tavistock.

Brown, B. (1986) 'Adding the "Cream" Weakens' in *Social Work Today*, 7 July, p. 7.

Brown, C. (1984) *Black and White Britain: The Third PSI Survey*, London: Heinemann.

Brummer, N. (1988) 'White Social Workers/Black Children: Issues of Identity' in J. Aldgate and J. Simmonds (ed.) *Direct Work with Children: A Guide for Social Work Practitioners*, London: Batsford.

Bryan, B., Dadzie, S. and Scafe, S. (1985) *The Heart of the Race: Black Women's Lives in Britain*, London: Virago.

Burden, D. and Gottlieb, N. (eds) (1987) *The Woman Client: Providing Human Services in a Changing World*, London: Tavistock.

Butrym, Z. (1968) *Medical Social Work in Action*, London: Bell.

Carby, H. (1982) 'White Woman Listen! Black Feminism and the Boundaries of Sisterhood' in Centre for Contemporary and Cultural Studies, *The Empire Strikes Back*, London: Hutchinson.

Cashmore, E. (1979) *Rastaman*, London: Allen & Unwin.

Cashmore, E. and Troyna, B. (eds) (1982) *Black Youth in Crisis*, London: Allen & Unwin.

Castles, S. and Kosack, G. (1972) 'The Function of Labour Immigration in Western European Capitalism' in *New Left Review*, May/June **73**:8–21.

CCCS (Centre for Contemporary and Cultural Studies) (1982) *The Empire Strikes Back: Race and Racism in 1970s Britain*, London: Hutchinson.

CCETSW (Central Council for Education and Training in Social Work) (1978) *Social Work Training and Ethnic Minorities*, London: CCETSW.

CCETSW (Central Council for Education and Training in Social Work (1985) Ethnic Minorities and Social Work Training, Paper 21.1, London: CCETSW.

Chapeltown Citizens' Advice Bureau (1983) *Immigrants and the Welfare State*, London: Blackrose Press.

Cheetham, J. (1972) *Social Work with Immigrants*, London: Routledge.

Cheetham, J. (1981) *Social and Community Work*, London: Routledge.

Cheetham, J. (1982a) *Social Work Services for Ethnic Minorities in Britain and the USA*, London: DHSS.

Cheetham, J. (ed.) (1982b) *Social Work and Ethnicity*, London: Allen & Unwin.

Cheles, L., Ferguson, R. and Vaughan, M. (1991) *Neo-Fascism in Europe*, Harlow: Longman.

Chestang, L. (1972) 'The Dilemma of Bi-Racial Adoption' in *Social Work*, May, 102–18.

CIS (Counter Information Services) (1978) *Racism*, London: CIS.

Cleaver, E. (1971) *Soul on Ice*, New York: Pan Books.

Coard, B. (1971) *How West Indian Children are made Educationally Subnormal*, London: New Beacon.

Cohen, P. (1986) The Perversions of Inheritance, unpublished paper from the Institute of Education, London.

Cohen, P. and Bains, H. (eds) (1988) *Multi-Racist Britain*, London: Macmillan.

Cohen, S. (1980) *Folk Devils and Moral Panics*, 2nd edn, Oxford: Martin Robinson.

Cohen, S. (1981) *The Thin End of the White Wedge: The New Nationality Laws – Second Class Citizenship and the Welfare State*, Manchester: Manchester Law Centre.

Collins, P. H. (1991) *Black Feminist Thought: Knowledge, Consciousness and the Politics of Empowerment*, London: Routledge.

Comer, J. P. and Poussaint, A. P. (1975) *Black Child Care*, New York: Pocket Books.

Cook, D. and Hudson, B. (1993) *Racism and Criminology*, London: Sage.

Coombe, V. and Little, A. (1986) *Race and Social Work: A Guide to Training*, London: Tavistock.

Compton, B. and Galaway B. (1975) *Social Work Processes*, Homewood, Ill.: The Dorsey Press.

Corrigan, P. (1977) 'The Welfare State and Class Struggle' in *Marxism Today*, March, 20–5.

Corrigan P. and Leonard, P. (1979) *Social Work Under Capitalism*, London: Macmillan.

Coventry Evening Telegraph (1987) 'Homes Call Needs More Study', 4 June, p. 2.

Cox, O. (1970) *Caste, Class and Race*, New York: Monthly Review Press.

Cowell, T., Jones, T. and Young, J. (1982) *Policing the Riots*, London: Junction Books.

CRC (Community Relations Commission) (1976a) *Between Two Cultures: A Study of Relationships Between Generations in the Asian Community in Britain*, London: CRC.

CRC (Community Relations Commission) (1976b) *Working in Multi-Racial Areas: A Training Handbook for Social Services Departments*, London: CRC.

CRE (Commission for Racial Equality) (1977) *A Home from Home? Some Policy Considerations on Black Children in Residential Care*, London: CRE.

CRE (Commission for Racial Equality) (1979) *Barlavington Manor Children's Home: Report of a Formal Investigation*, London: CRE.

CRE (Commission for Racial Equality) (1984) *Hackney Housing Investigated: Summary of a Formal Investigation Report*, London: CRE.

CRE (Commission for Racial Equality) (1985) *Immigration Control Procedures: Report of a Formal Investigation*, London: CRE.

Curno, P. (ed.) (1978) *Political Issues in Community Work*, London: Routledge .

Dalrymple, J. and Burke, B. (1995) *Anti-Oppressive Practice: Social Care and the Law*, Buckingham: Open University Press.

Davis, A. (1981) *Women, Race and Class*, London: The Women's Press.

Davis, A. (1987) A Class Approach to the Struggle Against Racism, Lecture given in Hackney Race Relations Unit Celebrations for International Women's Week, 8 March.

Denney, D. (1983) 'Some Dominant Perspectives in the Literature Relating to Multi-Racial Social Work' in *British Journal of Social Work*, **13**(2):149–74.

Denney, D. (1992) *Racism and Anti-Racism in Probation*, London: Routledge.

DeSouza, P. (1991) 'Black Students' in *One Step Towards Racial Justice*, London: CCETSW.

Devine, D. (1983) 'Defective, Hypocritical and Patronising Research' in *Caribbean Times*, 4 March, p. 4.

Devine, D. (1985) *Submission to the Beckford Inquiry*, June.

Devine, D. (1986) 'Fostering Getting' in *West Indian Digest*, October, **134**:10–15.

Dominelli, L. (1978a) 'Racism' in *Bulletin of Social Policy*, Summer, 2.

Dominelli, L. (1978b) 'The Welfare State and the Public Expenditure Cuts' in *Bulletin of Social Policy*, Spring, 1.

Dominelli, L. (1979) 'The Challenge for Social Work Education' in *Social Work Today*, **10**(25):27–9.

Dominelli, L. (1982) *Community Action: Organising Marginalised Groups*, Reykjavik: Kwenna Frambothid.

Dominelli, L. (1983) *Women in Focus: Community Service Orders and Female Offenders*, Warwick University, Nuffield Foundation Research Report.

Dominelli, L. (1984) 'Working with Families: A Feminist Perspective paper delivered at BASW Annual Conference', Nene College, April.

Dominelli, L. (1986) 'Father–Daughter Incest: Patriarchy's Shameful Secret' in *Critical Social Policy*, Spring, **16**:8–22.

Dominelli, L. (1987) Speech at Anti-Racist Social Work Conference at Sheffield University, 6–9 April.

Dominelli, L. (1991a) "Race' and Gender of Social Work' in Davies, H. (ed.) *The Sociology of Social Work*, London: Routledge.

Dominelli, L. (1991b) *Women Across Continents: Feminist Comparative Social Policy*, London: Harvester Wheatsheaf.

Dominelli, L. and McLeod, E. (1982) 'The Personal and the A-Political: Feminism and Moving Beyond the Integrated Methods Approach' in R. Bailey and P. Lee (eds) *Theory and Practice in Social Work*, Oxford: Blackwell, pp. 112–27.

Dominelli, L. and McLeod, E. (1989) *Feminist Social Work*, London: Macmillan.

Dominelli, L., Jeffers, L., Jones, G., Sibanda, S. and Williams, B. (1995) *Anti-Racist Probation Practice*, Aldershot: Arena.

D'Orey, S. (1984) *Immigration Prisoners: A Forgotten Minority*, London: Runnymede Trust.

Drew, D. (1995) *'Race', Education and Work: The Statistics of Inequality*, Aldershot: Avebury.

Duffield, M. (1985) Discretionary Grants and Student Funding, *Social Work Today*, 15 April, **18**.

Dunant, S. (1994) *The War of the Words: The Political Correctness Debate*, London: Virago.

Ebony, (1986) Special Edition on Black Families, August.

Eichler, M. (1984) *Families In Canada Today. Recent Changes and Policy Consequences*, Toronto: Gage.

Ellis, J. (1972) 'The Fostering of West African Children in England' in J.Triseliotis (ed.) *Social Work with Coloured Immigrants and their Families*, London: Institute of Race Relations/Oxford University Press.

Ely, P. and Denney, D. (1987) *Social Work in a Multi-Racial Society*, Aldershot: Gower.

Emecheta, B. (1983) *Adah's Story*, London: Allison and Busby.

Essed, P. (1991) *Understanding Everyday Racism: An Interdisciplinary Theory*, London: Sage.

Eysenck, A. R. (1971) *Race, Intelligence and Education*, Aldershot: Temple Smith.

Fanon, F. (1968) *Black Skins, White Masks*, London: MacGibbon & Kee.

Farrah, M. (1986) *Black Elders in Leicester*, Leicester: Leicester Social Services Department Report.

Federation of Community Work Training Groups and Mainframe (1995) *Community Work S/NVQ Project*, London: FCWTG/Mainframe.

Feminist Review, (1984) Special edition on Race.

Fernando, S. (1988) *Mental Health, Race and Culture*, London: Macmilan.
Fitzherbert, J. (1967) *West Indian Children in London*, London: Bell.
Fletchman-Smith, B. (1984) 'Effects of Race on Adoption and Fostering' in *International Journal of Social Psychiatry*, **30**:121–8.
Foner, N. (1979) *Jamaica Farewell*, London: Routledge.
Foot, P. (1965) *Immigration and Race in British Politics*, Harmondsworth: Penguin.
Foren, R. and Batta, I. (1970) 'Colour as a Variable in the Use Made of a Local Authority Child Care Department' in *Social Work Today*, **27**(3):10–15.
Fox, L. (1982) 'The Value Position in Recent Child Care Law and Practice' in *British Journal of Social Work*, **12**(3):265–90.
Freeman, M. D. A. (1992) *Children, their Families and the Law: Working with the Children Act*, London: BASW/Macmillan.
Freire, P. (1970) *The Pedagogy of the Oppressed*, Harmondsworth: Penguin.
Fryer, P. (1984) *Staying Power: The History of Black People in Britain*, London: Pluto.
Genovese, E. (1974) *Roll Jordon Roll: The World the Slaves Made*, New York: Pantheon.
Gifford, Lord (1986) *The Broadwater Farm Inquiry*, London Borough of Haringey.
Gilder, G. (1982) *Wealth and Poverty*, London: Buchan and Enright.
Gill, O. and Jackson, B. (1982) *Black Children in White Families: Transracial Adoption in Britain*, London: Batsford.
Gilroy, P. (1980) 'Managing the Underclass: A Further Note on the Sociology of Race Relations in Britain' in *Race and Class*, **22**(1):47–62.
Gilroy, P. (1982a) 'Police and Thieves' in Centre for Contemporary and Cultural Studies, *The Empire Strikes Back*, London: Hutchinson.
Gilroy, P. (1982b) 'You Can't Fool the Youths: Race and Class Formation in the 1980s' in *Race and Class*, **23**(213):207–22.
Gilroy, P. (1987) *There Ain't No Black in the Union Jack*, London: Hutchinson.
Ginsburg, N. (1979) *Class, Capital and Social Policy*, London: Macmillan.
Gitterman, A. and Schaeffer, A. (1972) 'The White Professional and the Black Client' in *Social Casework*, May, 280–91.
Glazer, N. (1988) *The Limits of Social Policy*, London: Harvard University Press.
GLC (Greater London Council) (1984) Anti-Racist Trade Union Working Group Report, London.
Gobineau, J. A. (1953, reprinted 1963) *Essai sur L'Inégalité des Races Humaines*, 4th edn, Paris: Firmin and Didot.
Gordon, P. (1981) *Passport Raids and Checks: Britain's Internal Immigration Controls*, London: Runnymede Trust.
Gordon, P. (1984) *White Law: Racism in the Police, Courts and Prisons*, London: Pluto.
Gordon, P. (1985) *Policing Immigration: Britain's Internal Controls*, London: Pluto.
Gordon, P. (1986) 'Racism and Social Security' in *Critical Social Policy*, Autumn, **17**:10–32.
Gordon, P. (1992) *Fortress Europe? The Meaning of 1992*, London: The Runnymede Trust.

Gordon, P. and Newnham, A. (1985) *Passport to Benefits: Racism in Social Security*, London: Child Poverty Action Group/The Runnymede Trust.

Gulbenkian Community Work Group (1973) *Current Issues in Community Work*, London: Gulbenkian (Calouste) Foundation.

Gurnah, A. (1984) 'The Politics of Racism Awareness Training' in *Critical Social Policy*, Winter, **11**:6–20.

Guru, S. (1987) 'An Asian Women's Refuge' in S. Ahmed *et al.* (eds) *Social Work with Black Children and Their Families*, London: Batsford.

Gutman, H. (1976) *The Black Family in Slavery and Freedom: 1925–1970*, New York: Vintage.

Haig-Brown, C. (1988) *Resistance and Renewal: Surviving the Indian Residential School*, Vancouver: Tillacum Library, Arsenal Pulp Press.

Hall, S. (1980a) 'Race, Articulation and Societies Structured in Dominance' in UNESCO (ed.) *Sociological Theories: Race and Colonialism*, pp. 305–45.

Hall, S. (1980b) 'Popular Democratic Versus Authoritarian Populist: Two Ways of Taking Democracy Seriously' in P. Hunt (ed.) *Marxism and Democracy*, pp. 157–87.

Hall, S. *et al.* (1978) *Policing the Crisis: Mugging, the State and Law and Order*, London: Macmillan.

Hanmer, J. and Statham, D. (1988) *Women and Social Work: Towards Woman Centred Practice*, London: Macmillan.

Hartmann, L. and Husband, C. (1974) *Racism and the Media*, London: Davis-Poynter.

Hearn, J. (1982) 'Radical Social Work: Contradictions, Limitations and Political Possibilities' in *Critical Social Policy*. **2**(1):19–34.

Hill, R. (1972) 'The Strengths of Black Families' in D. Bromley *et al.* (ed.) *White Racism and Black Americans*, Cambridge, Mass.: Schenkman.

Hiro, D. (1971) *Black British, White British*, New York: Monthly Review Press.

Holland, B. and Lewando-Hundt, G. (1986) *The Ethnic Minority Elderly Survey: Method, Data and Applied Action*, Coventry Social Services Department, Ethnic Minorities Development Unit.

Home Office (1986) *Ethnic Minorities, Crime and Policing*, London: HMSO.

Hood, R. (1992) *A Question of Judgement: Race and Sentencing*, London: HMSO.

hooks, b. (1981) *Ain't I A Woman: Black Women and Feminism*, London: Pluto.

hooks, b. (1989) *Talking Back: Thinking Feminist, Thinking Black*, Boston, Mass.: South End Press.

Husband, C. (1980a) 'Culture, Context and Practice: Racism in Social Work' in R. Bailey and M. Brake. (eds) *Radical Social Work*, pp. 6–85.

Husband, C. (1980b) Notes on Racism in Social Work Practice' in *Multi-Racial Social Work*, **1**:5–15.

Husband, C. (1982) *Race, Identity and British Society*, Open University course E354 Units 5 and 6, Milton Keynes: Open University.

Husband, C. (1986) 'Racism, Prejudice and Social Policy' in V. Coombe and A. Little (eds) *Race and Social Work*, London: Tavistock, pp. 3–13.

Hutchinson-Reis, M. (1986) 'After the Uprising – Social work on the Broadwater Estate' in *Critical Social Policy*, Autumn, **17**:70–80.

Jacobs, S. (1985) 'Race, Empire and the Welfare State: Council Housing and Racism' in *Critical Social Policy*, Summer, 13.

Jansari, A. (1980) 'Social Work with Ethnic Minorities: A Review of the Literature' in *Multi-Racial Social Work*, **1**:17–34.

Jensen, A. R. (1972) *Genetics and Education*, London: Methuen.

John, G. (1978) *Black People*, Milton Keynes, Open University, Unit 23.

Jones, C. (1977) *Immigration and Social Policy in Britain*, London: Tavistock.

Jones, C. (1983) *State Social Work and the Working Class*, London: Macmillan.

Kadushin, L. (1972) 'The Racial Factor in the Interview' in *Social Work*, May, 173–89.

Katz, J. (1978) *White Awareness*, Norman, Oklahoma: University of Oklahoma Press.

Kent, B (1972) 'The Social Worker's Cultural Pattern as it affects Casework with Immigrants' in J. Triseliotis (ed.) *Social Work With Coloured Immigrants and Their Families*, London: Institute for Race Relations/ Oxford University Press, pp. 38–54.

Khan, V. (ed.) (1979) *Support and Stress: Minority Families in Britain*, London: Macmillan.

King, M. and May, C. (1985) *Black Magistrates*, London: The Cobden Trust.

Langan, M. and Day, L. (1989) *Women, Oppression and Social Work*, London: Tavistock.

Langan, M. and Lee, P. (1989) *Radical Social Work Today*, London: Unwin Hyman.

Lambeth Social Services Committee (1981) *Black Children in Care Report*, London: Lambeth SSD.

Lawrence, E. (1981) 'You Can't Take a Fool to Water' in *The Empire Strikes Back*, Birmingham, CCCS.

Lawrence, E. (1982a) 'Just Plain Common Sense: The Roots of Racism' in Centre for Contemporary and Cultural Studies, *The Empire Strikes Back*, London: Hutchinson, pp. 47–94.

Lawrence, E. (1982b) 'In the Abundance of Water the Fool is Thirsty' in Centre for Contemporary and Cultural Studies, *The Empire Strikes Back*, London: Hutchinson, pp. 95–142.

Lawrence, J. (1983) 'Should White Families Adopt Black Children?' in *New Society*, 30 June, 499–501.

Layton-Henry, Z. (1985) *The Politics of Race in Britain*, London: Allen and Unwin.

Lea, J. (1980) The Contradictions of the Sixties Race Relations Legislation' in *Permissiveness and Control*, National Deviancy Conference, London: Macmillan, pp. 127–48.

Lees, R. and McGrath, M. (1975) 'Community Work with Immigrants' in *British Journal of Social Work*, **4**(2):175–86.

Littlewood, R. and Lipsedge, M. (1982) *The Aliens and the Alienists: Ethnic Minorities and Psychiatry*, Harmondsworth: Penguin.

Livingstone, K. (1987) *If Voting Changed Anything, They'd Abolish It*, London: Collins.

Loney, M. (1986a) *The Politics of Greed: The New Right and the Welfare State*, London: Pluto.

Loney, M. (1986b) 'Imagery and Reality in the Broadwater Farm Riot' in *Critical Social Policy*, Autumn, **17**:81–6.

Loney, M. (1987) *The State or the Market: Politics and Welfare in Contemporary Britain*, London: Sage.

Lorde, A. (1984) *Sister Outsider*, New York: The Crossing Press.

Lorenz, W. (1994) *Social Work in a Changing Europe*, London: Routledge.

Lowe, R. (1993) *The Welfare State in Britain since 1945*, London: Macmillan.

LSSC (Leeds Social Security Campaign) (1986) *The Response to the Fowler Review and the 1986 Social Security Act*, Leeds: LSSC.

McCulloch, J. and Kornreich, R. (1974) 'Black People and the Social Services Departments: Problems and Perspectives' in M. Brown (ed.) *Social Issues and the Social Services*, London: Charles Knight, pp. 145–76.

Malek, F. (1985) *Asian Women and Mental Health or Mental Ill Health: The Myth of Mental Illness*, Southwark: Asian Women's Aid.

Mama, A. (1984) 'Black Women, the Economic Crisis and the British State' in *Feminist Review*, Autumn, **17**:19–36.

Mama, A. (1989) *The Hidden Struggle: Statutory and Voluntary Responses to Violence Against Black Women in the Home*, London: London Race and Housing Unit.

Manning, B. and Ohri, A. (1982) 'Racism: the Response of Community Work', in A. Ohri *et al.* (eds) *Community Work and Racism*, London: Routledge, pp. 3–23.

Marchant, H. and Wearing, B. (1986) *Gender Reclaimed*, Sydney: Hale and Iremonger.

Maximé, J.E. (1986) 'Some Psychological Models of Black Self Concept' in S. Ahmed, J. Cheetham and S. Small (eds) *Social Work with Black Children and their Families*, London: Batsford.

Miles, R. (1982) *Capitalism, Racism and Migrant Labour,* London: Routledge.

Miles, R. (1987) 'Recent Marxist Theories of Nationalism and the Issue of Racism' in *British Journal of Sociology*, **38**(1):24–43.

Milner, D. (1975) *Children and Race*, Harmondsworth: Penguin.

Milner, D. (1983) *Children and Race – Ten Years On*, Harmondsworth: Penguin.

Minford, P. (1984) 'State Expenditure: A Study in Waste' in *Economic Affairs*, April–June, 79–90.

Mizio, E. (1972) 'White Worker – Minority Client' in *Social Work*, May, 183–9.

Moore, R. (1975) *Racism and Black Resistance in Britain*, London: Pluto.

Moore, R. (1978) *Racism and Resistance*, London: Routledge.

Morris, L. (1994) *Dangerous Classes: The Underclass and Social Citizenship*, London: Routledge.

Morrison, T. (1986) *The Bluest Eye*, London: Triad/Grafton Books.

Moynihan, D. P. (1965) *The Negro Family: The Case for National Action*, Washington DC: US Department of Labour.

Mullard, C. (1973) *Black Britain*, London: Allen & Unwin.

Mullender, A. and Miller, D. (1985) 'The Ebony Group: Black Children in White Foster Homes' in *Adoption and Fostering*, **9**(1):33–49.

Murray, C. (1990) *The Emerging British Underclass: Choice in Welfare Series No. 2*, London: Institute of Economic Affairs.

Murray, C. (1994) *Underclass: The Crisis Deepens*, London: Institute of Economic Affairs.

178   *Anti-Racist Social Work*

Network 21: *A Newsletter to Promote an Anti-Racist Perspective in Social Work Education and Training* (1986) Edinburgh, Moray House College of Education, October.
NISW (National Institute for Social Work) (1994) *The Black Students' Handbook*, London: NISW.
Oakley, A. (1972) *Sex, Gender and Society*, London: Temple Smith.
Ohri, A., Manning, B. and Curno, P. (1982) *Community Work and Racism*, London: Routledge.
Orphanides, K. (1986) 'The Cypriot Community in Britain' in V. Coombe and A. Little (eds) *Race and Social Work*, London: Tavistock, pp. 80–87.
Ousley, H. (1981) *The System*, London: The Runnymede Trust.
Ousley, H. (1983) *Ethnic Minorities and Social Services – Children in Care*, London: GLC.
Panton, D. (1986) 'Educating the Whites' in *Social Work Today*, 21 July, 6.
Parmar, P (1982) 'Gender, Race and Class: Asian Women in Resistance' in Centre for Contemporary Culture Studies, *The Empire Strikes Back*, London: Hutchinson, pp. 23–75.
Pascall, G. (1986) *Social Policy: A Feminist Analysis*, London: Tavistock.
Patch, N. (1990) *Race Against Time: Ethnic Elders*, London: Runnymede Trust.
Patel, N. (1990) *Race Against Time: Ethnic Elders*, London: Runnymede Press.
Pennie, P. and Williams, W. (1987) 'Black Children Need the Richness of Black Family Life' in *Social Work Today*, 2 February, 12.
Phillips, M. (1982) 'Separatism or Black Control' in A. Ohri and B. Manning (eds) *Community Work and Racism*, London: Routledge, pp. 103–20.
Phillips, M. (1993) 'Oppressive Urge to End Oppression' in the *Observer*, 1 August.
Philp, M. (1979) 'Notes on the Form of Knowledge in Social Work' in *The Sociological Review*, 27(1):83–111.
Pincus, A. and Minahan, A. (1973) *Social Work Practice: Model and Method*, Itasca, Ill.: F.E. Peacock Publishers.
Pinder, R. (1984) Probation Work in a Multi-Racial Society, unpublished paper, University of Leeds.
Pinker, R. (1993) 'A Lethal Kind of Looniness' in *The Times Higher Educational Supplement*, 10 September.
Plummer, J. (1978) *Divide and Deprive*, London: Joint Council for the Welfare of Immigrants.
Pollert, A. (1985) *Unequal Opportunities: Racial Discrimination and the Youth Training Scheme*, Birmingham: TUC Publishing.
Powell, D. and Edmonds, J. (1985) 'Are You Racist Too?' in *Community Care*, 14 September, 18–20.
Prescod-Roberts, M. and Steele, N. (1980) *Black Women: Bringing it All Back Home*, Bristol: Falling Wall Press.
Pryce, K. (1979) *Endless Pressure: A Study of West Indian Life-Styles in Bristol*, Harmondsworth: Penguin.
Rainwater, L. (1966) *A Response to the Moynihan Report*, New York: Black Scholar Press.
Rainwater, L. (1972) 'Crucible of Identity: The Negro Lower Class Family' in D. Bromley and C.F. Longino Jr (eds) *White Racism and Black Americans*, Cambridge, Mass.: Schenkman.

Raynor, L. (1970) *Adoption of Non-White Children: The Experience of a British Adoption Project*, London: Allen & Unwin.

Read, M. and Simpson, A. (1991) *Against a Rising Tide*, Nottingham: Spokesman Books.

Reeve, A. and Stubbs, P. (1981) 'Racism and the Mass Media: Revising Old Perspectives' in *Multi-Racial Education*, **9**(2):41–55.

Reeves, J. F. (1983) *British Racial Discourse*, Cambridge: Cambridge University Press.

Rex, J. (1981) 'Errol Lawrence and the Sociology of Race Relations: An Open Letter' in *Multi-Racial Education*, **10**(1):49–51.

Rex, J. (1982) *Race Relations in Sociological Theory*, London: Routledge.

Rex, J. and Moore, R. (1967) *Race, Community and Conflict: A Study of Sparkbrook*, London: Institute of Race Relations/Oxford University Press.

Rex, J. and Tomlinson, S. (1979) *Colonial Immigrants in a British City: A Class Analysis*, London: Routledge.

Rhamdanie, B. (1978) Handsworth Alternative Scheme, A Project Undertaken under the Auspices of the West Midlands Birmingham Probation Service.

Riley, J. (1985) *The Unbelonging*, London: The Women's Press.

Rooney, B. (1980) 'Active Mistakes – A Grass Roots Report' in *Multi-Racial Social Work*, **1**:43–54.

Rooney, B. (1982) Black Social Workers in White Departments' in J. Cheetham (ed.) *Social Work and Ethnicity*, pp. 184–96.

Rose, E. (1968) *Colour and Citizenship*, London: Oxford University Press/Institute of Race Relations.

Rowe, J. and Lambert, I. (1973) *Children Who Wait*, London: Association of British Adoption Agencies.

Ruben, G. (1975) 'The Traffic in Women' in R. Reiter (ed.) *Toward an Anthropology of Women*, New York: Monthly Review Press, pp. 165–9.

Ryan, W. (1972) 'Savage Discovery: The Moynihan Report' in D. Bromley and C. F. Longino Jr (eds) *White Racism and Black Americans*, Cambridge, Mass.: Schenkman.

Satymurti, C. (1981) *Occupational Survival*, Oxford: Blackwell.

Scarman, L. (1982) *The Brixton Report 10–12 April 1981: The Report of an Enquiry*, London: HMSO.

Seebohm, Lord (1968) *Report of the Committee on Local Authority and Allied Personal Social Services*, London: HMSO.

Segal, L. (ed.) (1983) *What's To Be Done About The Family?*, Harmondsworth: Penguin.

Sewell, T. (1985) 'The Black Child in Danger' in *The Voice*, 7 September, 14.

Sharron, H. (1985) 'Rob the Poor – Give to the Rich' in *Social Work Today*, **16**(27):6–7.

Simpkins, M. (1980) *Trapped Within Welfare. Surviving Social Work*, London: Macmillan.

Sivanandan, A. (1976) 'Race, Class and the State: the Black Experience in Britain' in *Race and Class*, **17**(4):437–8.

Sivanandan, A. (1983) 'Challenging Racism' Strategies for the 80s' in *Race and Class*, **25**(2):1–11.

Sivanandan, A. (1985) 'RAT and the Degradation of Black Struggle' in *Race and Class*, **26**(4):1–33.

Sklair, L. (1991) *Sociology of the Global System*, London: Harvester Wheatsheaf.

Small, J. (1984) 'The Crisis in Adoption' in *International Journal of Psychiatry*, Spring, **30**:129–41.

Small, J. (1987) 'Transracial Placements: Conflicts and Contradictions' in S. Ahmed *et al.* (eds) *Social Work with Black Children and Their Families*, London: Batsford.

Small, S. (1993) *Racialised Barriers: The Black Experience in the United States and England*, London: Routledge.

Small, S. (1994) *Radicalised Barriers: the Black Experience in the U.S. and England in the 1980s*. London: Routledge.

Smith, D. (1976) *The Facts of Racial Disadvantage: PEP Report*, Harmondsworth: Penguin.

Social Work Today, (1987) Special Edition on Race, April.

Solomos, J. *et al.* (1982) 'The Organic Crisis of British Capitalism and Race: The Experience of the Seventies' in Centre for Contemporary and Cultural Studies, *The Empire Strikes Back*, London: Hutchinson, pp. 9–46.

Solomos, J. (1986) 'Varieties of Marxist Conceptions of "Race", Class and the State, A Critical Analysis' in J. Rex and D. Mason (eds) *Theories of Race and Ethnic Relations*, Cambridge: Cambridge University Press, pp. 49–78.

Sondhi, R. (1982) 'The Asian Resources Centre' in J. Cheetham (ed.) *Ethnicity and Social Work*, London: Oxford University Press, pp. 165–74.

Spender, D. (1980) *Man Made Language*, London: Routledge.

Staples, R. (1988) *Black Masculinity: The Black Man's Role in American Society*, San Francisco: Black Scholar Press.

Statham, D. (1978) *Radicals in Social Work*, London: Routledge.

Stone, M. (1981) *The Education of the Black Child in Britain: The Myth of Multiracial Education*, London: Fontana.

Stubbs, P. (1985) 'The Employment of Black Social Workers: From "Ethnic Sensitivity" to Anti-Racism' in *Critical Social Policy*, Spring, **12**:6–27.

Stubbs, P. (1987) 'Racism and the Left' in *Critical Social Policy*, Autumn, **20**:91–7.

Stubbs, P. (1987) 'Professionalism and the Adoption of Black Children' in *British Journal of Social Work*, **17**(5):473–92.

Taylor, W. (1981) *Probation and After-Care in a Multi-Racial Society*, London: CRE.

Thoburn, J. (1986) *Permanence in Child Care*, Oxford: Blackwell.

Thompson, N. (1993) *Anti-Discriminatory Practice*, London: Macmillan.

THTA (Tower Hamlets Tenants Federation) (1986) *Tenants Tackling Racism*, Stepney, Dame Colet House.

Tipler, J. (1986) *Is Justice Colour Blind? A Study of the Impact of Race in the Juvenile Justice System in Hackney*, Hackney Social Services Department Research Paper, No. 6.

Tizard, B. (1977) *Adoption, A Second Chance*, London: Open Books.

Tizard, B. and Phoenix, A. (1993) *Black, White or Mixed Race? Race and Racism in the Lives of Young People of Mixed Parentage*, London: Routledge.

Triseliotis, J. (ed.) (1972a) *Social Work with Coloured Immigrants and their Families*, London: Institute of Race Relations/Oxford University Press.

Triseliotis, J. (1972b) 'The Implications of Cultural Factors in Social Work With Immigrants' in J. Triseliotis (ed.) *Social Work with Coloured Immigrants and their Families*, London: Institute of Race Relations/Oxford University Press.

Weare, P. (1986) 'Why Dan and Oliver Can Deal with Racism' in *Social Work Today*, 28 July, 9.

White, E. (1984) 'Listening to the Voices of Black Feminism' in *Radical America*, **18**(2/3):7–12.

Whitehouse, P. (1986) 'Race and the Criminal Justice System' in V. Coombe and A. Little (eds) *Race and Social Work*, London: Tavistock, pp. 113–25.

Williams, F. (1987) 'Racism and the Discipline of Social Policy: A Critique of Welfare Theory' in *Critical Social Policy*, September, 19–36.

Williams, F. (1989) *An Introduction to Social Policy*, London: Routledge.

Willis, M. (1987) *Ethnic Minority Students on Social Work Courses*, Birmingham: Birmingham Polytechnic.

Willis, P. (1977) *Learning to Labour: How Working Class Kids Get Working Class Jobs*, Aldershot: Gower.

Wilson, A. (1978) *Finding a Voice*, London: Virago.

Wilson, E. (1977) *Women and the Welfare State*, London: Tavistock.

Wilson, M. (1995) *Crossing the Boundary: Black Women Survive Incest*, London: Virago.

Wood, C. (1974) 'Life Styles Among West Indians and Social Work Problems' in *New Community*, **3**(3):249–54.

Wright, R. (1968) *Native Son*, Harmondsworth: Penguin.

Index